"Men shun the thought of death as sad, but death will only be sad to those who have no thought of it," wrote the great Archbishop Francois Fenelon. He is one of over 130 authors whose profound words make this the most complete collection of Catholic writings on death.

This is, chiefly, a book of consolation and preparation — "the best thoughts of the best minds" — thoughts which can console us in the death of loved ones and help us to prepare for our own.

When this book first appeared in 1959, columnist Joe Breig took the unusual step of devoting an entire page to it in the respected review, *Ave Maria*. An excerpt:

"This is a volume of great riches, one to cherish because it can be read and re-read.... and every time we take it up, it will help us not alone to face manfully the fact of death as life's climax, but also *to see life in the light of death*. And this is the light that illuminates life's true meaning and ends our groping. Ulanov shows us how our finest fellow men through the ages have bravely looked at this central significance of existence and drawn wisdom from it....

"The greatest value of the book, it seems to me ... is that although it is a book about death, it is not something to shrink from. Rather it eases the way for us to an indispensable achievement in life: the honest facing of the fact of death as a thing for which to prepare in order to accomplish triumphantly. It is good to commune with hundreds of sensitive and perceptive souls who have done that."

Comments Fr. William Ashley about the present edition:

"In an age when the reality of death is glossed over even at funerals, where beatification seems to be the order of the day, Roman Catholic Books has done us all a service in reprinting this compilation of the wisdom of the ages. *Death: A Book of Preparation and Consolation* legitimizes the human reality of tears, just as the God-Man wept at the death of his friend Lazarus, and leads us ineluctably to the joy of resurrection. A wonderful compendium, indeed!"

$21.95

DEATH
a book of
preparation and
consolation

DEATH

a book of preparation and consolation

compiled by

BARRY ULANOV

ROMAN CATHOLIC BOOKS
P.O. Box 2286
Ft. Collins, CO 80522-2286

First published in 1959

ISBN 0-912141-36-0

Publisher's Note to the 1996 edition

Some selections by non-Catholic authors may not be in conformity with Catholic teaching. Where questions arise, we urge readers to consult a reliable priest or other authority.

Acknowledgments

I wish to thank the following authors and publishers for their kind permission to reprint prose and poetry in this anthology:

Catholic Book Publishing Co. for excerpts from St. Alphonsus de Liguori's *The Way of Salvation;* P. J. Kenedy & Sons for excerpts from St. Augustine's *Nine Sermons on the Psalms,* translated by Edmund Hill, O.P.; Henry Regnery Company for an excerpt from *The Mystery of Being,* by Gabriel Marcel (copyright 1950 by Henry Regnery Company); Oxford University Press, Inc., for "Overtures to Death" in *Short Is the Time,* by C. Day Lewis (copyright 1940, 1943 by Oxford University Press, Inc.) and "Spring and Fall: To a Young Girl," "That Nature Is a Heraclitean Fire," and "Adoro Te ac Devote" (S. Thomae Aquinatis) from *Poems of Gerard Manley Hopkins* (Third Edition; copyright 1948 by Oxford University Press, Inc.); Vanguard Press, Inc., for an excerpt from *My Heart Laid Bare,* by Charles Baudelaire, translated by Norman Cameron; Faber & Faber Ltd. for "A Similitude of the Ant" in Ruysbroek's *The Spiritual Espousals,* translated by Eric Colledge; The Newman Press for excerpts from *The Living Flame of Love,* by St. John of the Cross, translated by E. Allison Peers, and St. Cyprian's *The Unity of the Catholic Church,* translated by Maurice Bevénot, S.J., in Ancient Christian Writers; Random House, Inc., for "The Trolls" from *Springboard: Poems 1941–1944,* by Louis MacNeice (copyright 1944 by Random House, Inc.; reprinted by permission); "Musée des Beaux Arts" from *The Collected Poetry of W. H. Auden* (copyright 1940 by W. H. Auden; reprinted by permission of Random House, Inc.); "Depravity: A Sermon" from *The Collected Poetry of W. H. Auden* (copyright 1945 by W. H. Auden; reprinted by permission of Random House, Inc.); Pantheon Books, Inc., for excerpts from *Journal in the Night,* by Theodor Haecker, translated by Alick Dru, *The Last Things,* by Romano Guardini, translated by C. E. Forsyth and G. B. Branham, and from "Unedited Notes" of St. Thérèse de Lisieux in *The Hidden Face,* by Ida Friederike Goerres; Beacon Press, Inc., for excerpts from *Tragedy Is Not Enough,* by Karl Jaspers, translated by H. A. T. Reiche, H. T. Moore, and K. W. Deutsch, and "The Immortality of Man," by Jacques Maritain, in *Man's*

Destiny in Eternity (Garvin Lectures); Templegate for excerpts from St. Thérèse de Lisieux's *Just for Today;* Herder, Saint Louis, for excerpts from St. Thomas Aquinas's *Compendium of Theology,* translated by Cyril Vollert, S.J., and St. Bonaventure's *Breviloquium,* translated by Erwin E. Nemmers (Saint Louis: B. Herder Book Co., 1946); Herder, Saint Louis, and Routledge & Kegan Paul Ltd. for an excerpt from "The Eight Beatitudes: The Mourners" in Bossuet's *Panegyrics of the Saints,* translated by D. O. O'Mahony; Meridian Books, Inc., for an excerpt from *Understanding the Sick and the Healthy,* by Franz Rosenzweig (first published by Noonday Press, 1954); Eugen Rosenstock-Huessy for an excerpt from *The Christian Future,* published by Charles Scribner's Sons; Barrie and Rockliff for excerpts from *Be Not Afraid,* by Emmanuel Mounier, and *The Experience of Death,* by Paul-Louis Landsberg, both from the English translations of Cynthia Rowland; The Free Press of Glencoe, Illinois, for an excerpt from *The Elementary Forms of the Religious Life, by* Emile Durkheim, translated by Joseph Ward Swain; Rinehart & Company, Inc., and André Deutsch Limited for "For a Child Born Dead" in *A Way of Looking,* by Elizabeth Jennings (copyright 1955 by Elizabeth Jennings); Arthur Probsthain, Publisher, for an excerpt from Hsuntze's *On the Rules of Proper Conduct,* translated by Homer H. Dubs; Librairie Gallimard for an excerpt from "Clio I" in *Temporal and Eternal,* by Charles Péguy, translated by Alexander Dru; J. M. Dent & Sons Ltd. for an excerpt from Prudentius' *Hymns,* translated by R. M. Pope and R. F. Davis; Grove Press, Inc., for "The Killing" in *One Foot in Heaven,* by Edwin Muir, published by Grove Press in 1956; University Press Cambridge for an excerpt from *The Nature of the Physical World,* by Sir Arthur Eddington; Cambridge University Press, American Branch, for selections from *Mind and Matter,* by Erwin Schrödinger, and from *On Education,* by Juan Luis Vives, translated by Foster Watson; The Cresset Press for "The Paradox" in *Urania,* by Ruth Pitter; The John Day Company, Inc., for excerpts from Lao-tse's *The Way of Life,* translated by Witter Bynner; S. P. C. K. for excerpts from "Churchyards" in *Poems in the Porch,* by John Betjeman and Tertullian's *Concerning the Resurrection of the Flesh,* translated by A. Souter; Harcourt, Brace and Company, Inc., for an excerpt from "East Coker" in *Four Quartets* (copyright 1943 by T. S. Eliot); New Directions for "And Death Shall Have No Dominion" in *The Collected Poems of Dylan Thomas* (copyright 1939, 1942, 1946 by New Directions; copyright 1952, 1953 by Dylan Thomas; reprinted by permission of New Directions); also J. M. Dent & Sons Ltd. for "And Death Shall Have No Dominion" in *The Collected Poems of Dylan Thomas;* Princeton University Press for excerpts from *Concluding Unscientific Postscript* and *The Unchangeableness of God*, by Soren Kierkegaard; E. P. Dutton & Co., Inc., and J. M. Dent & Sons Ltd. for an excerpt from *The Mystical Element in Religion*, by Friedrich von Hügel; The Macmillan Company for an excerpt from De Estella's "Devout Meditations on the Love of God" in *Mystics of Spain*, translated by E. Allison Peers, and for excerpts from Dostoyevsky's *The Brothers Karamazov* and Turgenev's *Poems in Prose*, both translated by Constance Garnett; Morehouse-Gorham Co., Inc., for a selection from St. Bernard's *On the Song of Songs*, translated by A Religious of C. S. M. V.; Cassell and Company Ltd. for an extract from *My Life in Christ*, by John Sergieff, translated by E. E. Goulaeff; John M. Watkins, Publisher, and Alec R. Allenson, Inc., for an excerpt from *The Cloud of Unknowing*, edited by Evelyn Underhill.

Dame Edith Sitwell for an excerpt from "The Canticle of the Rose," reprinted with the permission of the publisher, The Vanguard Press, from *The Collected Poems of Edith Sitwell* (copyright 1949, 1954, by Edith Sitwell).

Thanks are also due for excerpts from the following books published by Sheed & Ward, Inc.: *Spiritual Letters*, by Dom John Chapman; *The Works of St. Teresa of Avila*, translated by E. Allison Peers; *Catholicism*, by Henri de Lubac, translated by Lancelot C. Sheppard; *Holy Week*, by Bede Jarrett; *Within That City*, by Arnold Lunn; *Before the Dawn*, by Eugenio Zolli, and *The Missal in Latin and English*.

I am indebted to Miss Patricia I. Clark for her many services in the preparation of the manuscript, services graciously offered and handsomely performed, and to those whose efforts supplemented hers, Miss Lorraine Shea, Miss Mona Gharzouzi, and Miss Joan Nelson.

No acknowledgment can adequately indicate the contributions of my wife, Joan Geddes Ulanov, her good taste, her wise counsel, her endless encouragement.

B. U.

Contents

Preface

Much of the weight and wisdom of a society may be discerned from its attitudes toward death. If it trembles and quakes, stutters and starts at the mention of death, indeed makes every effort to avoid thinking, talking or reading about the subject, then, to the extent that any generalization about a society may be made with confidence, it may be said of this hypothetical one that it is immature, weak at the foundation, and by definition of poor spirits. If it moves toward the inevitable—its death and the death of its individual members—with something approaching confidence, ease, and acceptance, then it may be said of this enviable civility that it has made its peace with God and found that balance of the here and now with the hereafter without which any maturity is quite impossible.

How do we learn about any given society's attitudes toward death? One way, I suppose, is to examine the stories in which death figures in the daily newspapers, the weekly and monthly magazines, and at the same time to look at the advertisements of the funeral parlors and cemeteries in the streets and trains and alongside the great highways. Another is to engage people at every level of that society in discussions about death. Still another is to watch, with some special awareness, the treatment of death in the popular arts, the mass media: the motion pictures, television, the comic books, if we are to speak of our civilization; the theatre, the street fairs, if we are concerned with an earlier one; the jousts of the gladiators, the religious festivals, if we are looking into one much earlier still.

All these methods make sense; much is to be learned about

death from each of them. In our time, for example, we should quickly glean from the ads that death, like refrigerators and television sets, can be paid for on the installment plan; from conversation and from the newspapers and magazines, that death bloody and violent and effected by means more or less novel is of much greater interest than death natural or achieved through illness more or less familiar; from the popular arts, as from talk and the periodicals, that death, dull, unimaginative, in bed (hospital or home), is only rivalled for lack of public interest by birth, dull, unimaginative, in bed (hospital or home). These insights, real as they may be, lack finality however. They offer little more than a quasi-statistical approach toward the death attitudes of twentieth-century America; they fail to reveal the thought processes of Americans about death. For the fuller, the more profound penetration into these attitudes, one must turn today as in the past to the poets, the philosophers, and the theologians. With the priest in the confessional or dispensing the viaticum and the psychiatrist probing the various imbalances, neurotic and psychotic, in which death may figure, the meditative man shares the knowledge of a society's innermost feelings and convictions about death. But unlike the priest or the psychiatrist the artist is not bound by any seal that encloses his confidences and makes his very substantial knowledge secret.

It is to the artists of meditation and contemplation, then, that I suggest we should turn to discover man's thinking about death. It is to their arts that we should go, not necessarily to learn how to think and behave in the face of death, but at least to observe how others have thought and behaved and from that observation to take courage or at the very least to be protected, as some knowledge can protect one, from the fears which have beset so many at the approach of death. In a poem, in a novel, in a philosophical dialogue, in a theological soliloquy; in a phrase here, an image there, a cadence somewhere else may be found just that extension of revelation which has so often made art the valuable ancillary of theology. Indeed, it is my own conviction that in this kind of musing may be found a truth about death by no means unknown to scientific theology, but one perhaps too frequently neglected, and that it is to the meditative arts that we must turn to be reminded of this truth about death and through it of a very basic truth about our lives.

Beyond everything else, what one learns from these men and their arts is that there is no one way to accept or reject death. While it is hardly true that there are as many ways to think about death, or to deal with it, as there have been poems or dramas or mystical compositions in which death plays a leading role, it is—one learns from a Shakespeare, a Dante, a Donne, a T. S. Eliot, a Gabriel Marcel; an Augustine, a Gregory the Great, a John Chrysostom, a Gregory of Nyssa, a Bernard, a Thomas Aquinas; a Fénelon, a Pascal, a Dostoyevsky, a Newman—an incontrovertible fact that death has occupied much of the thinking of the pre-eminent artists of Western civilization. In their thinking about death these artists have again and again revealed what it is that makes them significant in their societies. It is one of the special—and not at all unhappy—ironies of our lives that in the vast levelling process which is death many men assert their individualities most vigorously. In this assertion, in this irony, lies eternal truth. We are, we remain, individuals from here to eternity. In each man's going, as in each one's coming, no matter how many may perish with him, is recorded one single and unique life, precious for itself and to itself and so marked by its Creator. The corollary of this great truth is that each of us must think very seriously about death; whether we question it or answer it or stand aside from it in bewilderment, thought must precede action.

The enormous size a man's meditation about death may assume is best exemplified by the work of Dante Alighieri called his *Commedia*, a comedy because of its supremely happy ending in Paradise. It is, of course, entirely around the subject of death that this astonishing allegory of divine judgment and eternal transfiguration is constructed. To some extent it is the conversion into a poet's multifaceted metaphor of the revelations of the Church concerning the rewards of heaven and the punishments of hell, and the purgation that must ultimately yield one the first and spare one the second. At least as much as that, however, it is the translation into epic terms of a poet's very personal faith in the love of human beings, the love of one for another which is charity, which is motivated by love of God and directed entirely toward Him. It is, essentially, Dante's unassailable faith in the power to intercede for him in heaven of his blessed beloved after her death that gives his work its narrative strength, not simply because it is she interceding for him, but because in so doing she acts out for the reader the poet's conviction that we find our beatitude in a demonstrated love of neighbor for the sake of God. All through the *Comedy* properly called *Divine* by an enthusiastic critic years after Dante's own death, it is this relationship of men that is configured by the personages—saints and sinners, angels and devils, men of good will and men of malice—who populate heaven, hell, and purgatory. It is this offering, at once dedicated and disinterested, which Dante acknowledges in those touching words with which he bids Beatrice farewell after she has left him in the hands of St. Bernard, two cantos before the end of the *Commedia:*

> O Lady in whom my hope has its force and who didst suffer for my salvation to leave thy footprints in hell, of all the things that I have seen I acknowledge the grace and virtue to be from thy power and goodness. Thou didst draw me from bondage into liberty by all those ways, by all those means that were in thy power. Preserve in me thy great bounty, so that my spirit, which thou hast made whole, may be released from the body still pleasing to thee.

And thus does Dante pass on to confront the Queen of Heaven— she for whom "her faithful Bernard" is "all on fire with love," even as Dante is enflamed with devotion to Beatrice, and by analogy to Bernard's great lady and the Lord both serve—and the assemblage of the saints gathered together in the mystic Rose of Paradise. Through the mediation of Beatrice, the clearest possible "type" or "figure" of Mary, Dante finally sees the Eternal Light of God Himself. In His love—"the love that moves the sun and the other stars"—life and death both achieve meaning, purposeful order, a place in the design of eternity in which death is served by life and both serve God.

At its best, then, death brings the happiness of heaven with some immediacy, and, the Christian poet reminds us, offers much consolation. It can bring surcease to a life lived too much in the world, not enough apart from it, and such surcease will be reward enough for the moment, as it is for tortured old King Lear. "O, let him pass!" the Earl of Kent says in one of the very last speeches of Shakespeare's great meditative drama about life and death: "He hates him / That would upon the rack of this tough world / Stretch him out longer."

Death can also bring unspeakable punishment. That is the terror that haunts Hamlet as he plots revenge. That is the point of that much misinterpreted soliloquy—the most famous of Shakespeare's speeches—in which Hamlet names "the rub": "For in that sleep of death what dreams may come . . . must give us pause." And because he fears hell it is more than a passing irony which prompts him to conclude his musing and begin his exchange with Ophelia with the request that she remember "all my sins" in her prayers.

The theme of intercessory prayer is the central one; the illustrations, necessarily, are many. One can find, with very little investigation, the parallel passages to Dante's on Beatrice: Petrarch's on his lady Laura (it is worth remembering that in Italian one salutes such a lady as "madonna"); John Donne's lengthy lamentations in the two "Anniversary" poems for Elizabeth Drury, the child of his patron, who died at the age of fifteen ("She, shee is dead; shee's dead; when thou knowst this, Thou knowest how lame a cripple this world is."); Geoffrey Chaucer's *Boke of the Duchesse*, in which his Beatrice is Blanche of Lancaster, the dead first wife of John of Gaunt. Eternal punishment, the dreadful judgment of a just God, has its poetry too, from Dante's *Inferno,* through Hamlet's cautioning vision, to the hell of the London underground and overground of the first of T. S. Eliot's *Four Quartets,* "Burnt Norton," the subway hell, literally on earth, which belches its victims forth across "the gloomy hills of London," an "Eructation of unhealthy souls into the faded air. . . ."

That is the Christian tradition. If one turns away from it, one finds little enough. Among the pre-Christian pagans, the sketchiest notion of a Hades, of Elysian Fields, of Islands of the Blest, must suffice, yielding the reader perhaps a certain fantasy of peace and hope, but nothing of much consolation for the mind dissatisfied by illusion and uncertainty. Among the moderns who would be pagans again if only their environment, their education, their vocabularies permitted, there is something worse than fantasy. They offer the paradigms of futility, the conjugations and declensions of which make up many of Yeats's poems ("Man," he says with painful emptiness, "has created death.") and those of others too numerous and too hollow to mention.

And as with poetry, so too with philosophy and theology. The insights of the giants are those of a revealed religion, but not necessarily arrived at through the customary channels of revelation. But they come, "these infiltrations of the invisible," as Gabriel Marcel calls them, to those craftsmen of contemplation who persist, going on and on, wherever their love takes them. Thus the Spanish mystics compose their requiems and paint their pietàs in words, permitting their similitudes and analogies to become as extravagant as any rhetoric the world has ever known, but somehow, in the midst of their impassioned writing, learning and passing on something more of the meaning of the redeeming Passion than they or we knew before. Thus the French philosophers of death, in letters of consolation like Fénelon's or Bossuet's, in long lyrical essays like Montaigne's, or in three-sentence treatises like Pascal's, start with conventional phrases of comfort and end by reconciling us to death and to life and to almost all the torments that daily afflict the suffering souls on earth. Thus Dostoyevsky's Alyosha Karamazov, keeping vigil beside the body of the saintly monk Father Zossima, is given a vision of eternity that leads him to kiss the unpaved soil of the monk's cell: "The mystery of earth was one with the mystery of the stars. . . . "

Wisdom has its own eloquence. It does not need the trappings of rhetoric to persuade. And yet wise words are more often than not beautiful ones. This, to some extent, the selections in this volume have been chosen to show. It was not a design difficult to pick out. The eloquence of John of the Cross and Thomas More, of Jonathan Swift and Jeremy Taylor, or Thomas Browne and Thomas Traherne and Lancelot Andrewes, of Juliana of Norwich and Francis de Sales and Catherine of Siena, of Saint Teresa and Dr. Johnson and Soren Kierkegaard is obvious. I did not have to hunt far to find passages of marked beauty in their works or in those of most of the other men and women with whom they share these pages. A closer and a more labored look was required to avoid the commonplace and to secure the wisdom with which we are here concerned. In almost every case wisdom turned out to be the companion of personality. Father of the Church, romantic poet, Anglican divine, modern physicist—each in his own way asserts his identity, firmly and felicitously, as he offers his apperception.

There is, it seems to me, a plea implicit in these various works of meditative art, a plea for understanding, a plea for appreciation, a plea for wisdom and strength and comfort. The understanding they ask for is the understanding of the human personality in all its confounding, confusing, and compelling variety, nowhere more various or more sympathetic than in death. The appreciation they demand is of the particular approach they have made to death, the special revelation upon which they have concentrated. The wisdom and strength and comfort they seek are, altogether, the substance of the words of that beatitude which is most directly concerned with death: "Blessed are they that mourn, for they shall be comforted." What these artists have written is a biblical commentary which, like all other commentaries of size or value, returns again and again, with an all-consuming ardor and most marvelous richness of communication, to the biblical text itself.

—BARRY ULANOV

DEATH

a book of
preparation and
consolation

1 · All Things Have Their Season

All things have their season, and in their times all things pass under heaven. A time to be born and a time to die. A time to plant, and a time to pluck up that which is planted. A time to kill, and a time to heal. A time to destroy, and a time to build. A time to weep, and a time to laugh. A time to mourn, and a time to dance. A time to scatter stones, and a time to gather. A time to embrace, and a time to be far from embraces. A time to get, and a time to lose. A time to keep, and a time to cast away.

—Ecclesiastes 3:1–6

. . . As a father hath compassion on his children, so hath the Lord compassion on them that fear him: for he knoweth our frame. He remembereth that we are dust: man's days are as grass, as the flower of the field so shall he flourish. For the spirit shall pass in him, and he shall not be: and he shall know his place no more. But the mercy of the Lord is from eternity and unto eternity upon them that fear him. . . . The Lord hath prepared his throne in heaven: and his kingdom shall rule over all. . . . Bless the Lord, all his works: in every place of his dominion, O my soul, bless thou the Lord.

—Psalm 102:13–16, 19, 22

Charity never falleth away: whether prophecies shall be made void, or tongues shall cease, or knowledge shall be destroyed. For

we know in part, and we prophesy in part. But when that which
is perfect is come, that which is in part shall be done away. When
I was a child, I spoke as a child, I understood as a child, I thought
as a child. But, when I became a man, I put away the things of a
child. We see now through a glass in a dark manner; but then
face to face. Now I know in part; but then I shall know even as
I am known.

—St. Paul I Corinthians 13:8–12

What else is our life but a light vapor, which is driven away and
disappears with the wind—a blade of grass which is dried up in
the heat of the sun?

—St. Alphonsus de Liguori, *The Way of Salvation*

Canst thou feel the wind beat on thy face, and canst thou forget
that thou holdest thy tenement by a puff of wind? Canst thou sit
by the river side, and not remember that as the river runneth, and
doth not return, so is the life of man? Canst thou shoot in the
fields, and not call to mind that as the arrow flieth in the air, so
swiftly do thy days pass?

—Elizabeth Grymeston, *Miscelanea*

VIRTUE

Sweet day, so cool, so calm, so bright!
The bridal of the earth and sky;
The dew shall weep thy fall to-night:
For thou must die.

Sweet rose, whose hue angry and brave
Bids the rash gazer wipe his eye,
Thy root is ever in its grave,
    And thou must die.

Sweet spring, full of sweet days and roses,
A box where sweets compacted lie;
My music shows ye have your closes,
    And all must die.

Only a sweet and virtuous soul,
Like season'd timber, never gives;
But though the whole world turn to coal,
    Then chiefly lives.

—GEORGE HERBERT

THE DEATH OF KINGS

Let 's talk of graves, of worms and epitaphs;
Make dust our paper and with rainy eyes
Write sorrow on the bosom of the earth.
Let 's choose executors and talk of wills:
And yet not so, for what can we bequeath
Save our deposed bodies to the ground?
Our lands, our lives and all are Bolingbroke's,
And nothing can we call our own but death,
And that small model of the barren earth
Which serves as paste and cover to our bones.
For God's sake, let us sit upon the ground
And tell sad stories of the death of kings:
How some have been deposed; some slain in war;
Some haunted by the ghosts they have deposed;

Some poison'd by their wives; some sleeping kill'd;
All murder'd: for within the hollow crown
That rounds the mortal temples of a king
Keeps Death his court, and there the antic sits,
Scoffing his state and grinning at his pomp,
Allowing him a breath, a little scene,
To monarchize, be fear'd and kill with looks,
Infusing him with self and vain conceit,
As if this flesh which walls about our life
Were brass impregnable, and humour'd thus
Comes at the last and with a little pin
Bores through his castle wall, and farewell king!
　　　　—King Richard in SHAKESPEARE's *Richard II*, III, ii

It's necessary to die, but nobody wants to; you don't want to, but you are going to, willy-nilly. A hard necessity that is, not to want something which cannot be avoided. If it could be managed, we would much rather not die; we would like to become like the angels by some other means than death. "We have a building from God," says St. Paul, "a home not made with hands, everlasting in heaven. For indeed in this we groan, longing to be clothed over with our dwelling from heaven; provided, though, we be found clothed, and not naked. For indeed we who are in this dwelling-place groan, being burdened; in that we do not wish to be stripped, but to be covered over, so that what is mortal may be swallowed up by life" (2 Cor. 5:1). We want to reach the kingdom of God, but we don't want to travel by way of death. And yet there stands Necessity saying "This way, please." Do you hesitate, man, to go this way, when this is the way that God came to you?
　　　　—ST. AUGUSTINE, *Sermon I on Psalm 30 (31)*
　　　　(EDMUND HILL, O.P.)

SPRING AND FALL
To a young child

Margaret, are you grieving
Over Goldengrove unleaving?
Leaves, like the things of man, you
With your fresh thoughts care for, can you?
Ah! as the heart grows older
It will come to such sights colder
By and by, nor spare a sigh
Though worlds of wanwood leafmeal lie;
And yet you will weep and know why.
Now no matter, child, the name:
Sorrow's springs are the same.
Nor mouth had, no nor mind, expressed
What heart heard of, ghost guessed:
It is the blight man was born for,
It is Margaret you mourn for.

—GERARD MANLEY HOPKINS

Now lift up thy eyes and see where thou dost belong. Thou dost belong to the Fatherland of the celestial paradise. Thou art here as a stranger guest, a miserable pilgrim; therefore, as a pilgrim hastens back to his home where his dear friends expect him, and wait for him with great longing, so shouldst thou desire to hasten back to thy fatherland, where all will be glad to see thee, where all long so ardently for thy joyous presence, that they may greet thee tenderly, and unite thee to their blessed society for ever. And didst thou but know how they thirst after thee, how they desire that thou shouldst combat devoutly in suffering, and behave chivalrously in all adversity, even such as they have overcome, and how they now with great sweetness remember the cruel years through which they once passed, truly, all suffering would only be the easier to thee, for, the more bitterly thou shalt have suffered, the more honourably wilt thou be received.

—Blessed Henry Suso, *Eternal Wisdom*

Blessed is he who lives in faith, trusts to none save God, and uses this world as though he were already beyond it.

—Archbishop Fénelon, *Letters to Men* (H. L. S. Lear)

. . . in so far as we allow ourselves to give ear to the solicitations —countless in number even if slight in substance—which come to us from the invisible world, then the whole outlook undergoes a change: and by that I mean that the transformation takes place *here below*, for earthly life itself is at the same time transfigured, it clothes itself in a dignity which cannot be allowed to it if it is looked at as some sort of excrescence which has budded erratically on a world which is in itself foreign to the spirit and to all its demands . . . from the moment when we open ourselves to these infiltrations of the invisible, we cease to be the unskilled and yet pretentious soloists we perhaps were at the start, and gradually become members, wide-eyed and brotherly, of an orchestra in which those whom we so inaptly call the dead are quite certainly much closer to Him of whom we should not perhaps say that He conducts the symphony, but that He *is* the symphony in its profound and intelligible unity; a unity in which we can hope to be included only by degrees, through individual trials, the sum total of which, though it cannot be foreseen by each of us, is inseparable from his own vocation.

I agree that all I have said does not reach as far as revelation, properly so called, and dogma. But it is at least a way of approaching it; it is a difficult road and strewn with obstacles, but it is by following this pilgrim road that we can hope one day to see the radiance of that eternal Light of which a reflection has continually shone on us all the time we have been in this world—that Light without whose guidance we may be sure that we should never have started our journey.

—GABRIEL MARCEL, *The Mystery of Being* (G. S. FRASER)

We are pilgrims in this world, for so the Holy Scriptures call us, and we journey toward Thee, O Lord, as toward our own country, and to our soul's true native land, wherein, as the Apostle says, we live and move and have our being. And, whenever we sin, we are hindered and halt on the way; the great marvel, and the great wonder, is that such trivial things can hinder us. My love is the force that moves me. By love I am borne whithersoever I go. Wheresoever my love rests, thither goes my soul; and even as Thou, O Lord, hast given a stone such force that, as it falls, it will go toward its centre and natural place, even so hast Thou given the same force to our souls—namely, a desire for the highest Good, to the end that it may the more readily be drawn to Thee by this attraction. If this be so, then, O my good God, how can it be that every soul that Thou hast created doth not go toward Thee with great speed? And yet we see souls hanging and suspended from a breath of wind, bereft of all good thereby, yet laughing and content and at rest.

How is it possible that any creature capable of union with Thee should not go toward Thee with all its strength, O infinite Centre infinitely good, and hence of infinite attraction? What can detain a creature capable of reaching so great a Good? O great weight of sin which, laid upon the neck of mankind, weighs it down and causes it to sink to the ground, that it may not rise to its rightful sphere, for which it was created!

Of a truth, it is a greater miracle that souls should not mount
up to their God by love, than that rocks should be raised up and
suspended by a breath of wind that they may not fall to their
centre; or than that a mere slip of paper should impede the course
of a rapid torrent rushing toward the sea. Who, indeed, could
endure his life patiently if he knew clearly and distinctly of what
great good he is being deprived and how much good he is losing?
O most ungrateful veil of my flesh, of how much joy dost thou
deprive me! Who can hinder me from tearing and rending thee
with my own hands, so that I may go and behold my God, and
enjoy Him, and find my rest in Him? Oh, of how many pleasures
and of what great happiness am I bereft because of thee! And,
what is worse, how do I suffer thee, how do I laugh and remain at
ease, well knowing, and seeing, and perceiving all this, and do not
rather weep and groan, for days and nights, as would be just, over
this my exile and blindness and pitiable plight?

How can I practise so evil and ungrateful a form of patience but
that the veil is set between me and God, and that a fleshly cloud
obstructs the sun's brightness from shining in my soul? Remove
this veil which hinders me, and thou shalt see with what force my
soul will travel toward its centre. Consider the souls of the saints,
that are already loosed from this veil and are free: with what
swiftness and lightness do they journey toward their God! Who
can hinder them? Who can keep them back? Who can exile them
from their rightful place? For therein is full and perfect rest;
therein is eternal satisfaction for all the soul's restless desires.

—Diego De Estella, *Devout Meditations on
the Love of God* (E. Allison Peers)

Death is the lot of cities and of States;
Pomp, luxury, 'neath sand and grass do lie,
Yet man, it seems, is wroth that he must die.
—Torquato Tasso, *Gerusalemme Liberata, XV*, 20

If we were to live here always, with no other care than how to feed, clothe, and house ourselves, life would be a very sorry business. It is immeasurably heightened by the solemnity of death. The brutes die even as we; but it is our knowledge that we have to die which makes us human. If nature cunningly hides death, and so permits us to play out our little games, it is easily seen that our knowing it to be inevitable, that to every one of us it will come one day or another, is a wonderful spur to action. We really do work while it is called today, because the night cometh when no man can work. . . . And knowing that his existence here is limited, a man's workings have reference to others rather than to himself, and thereby into his nature comes a new influx of nobility. If a man plants a tree, he knows that other hands than his will gather the fruit; and when he plants it, he thinks quite as much of those other hands as of his own. Thus to the poet there is the dearer life after life; and posterity's single laurel leaf is valued more than a multitude of contemporary bays. Even the man immersed in money-making does not make money so much for himself as for those who may come after him.

—ALEXANDER SMITH, *Dreamthorp*

. . . Man cometh forth like a flower from concealment, and of a sudden shews himself in open day, and in a moment is by death withdrawn from open view into concealment again. The greenness of the flesh exhibits us to view, but the dryness of dust withdraws us from men's eyes. . . . For whereas infancy is going on to childhood, childhood to youth, youth to manhood, and manhood to old age, and old age to death, in the course of the present life he is forced by the very steps of his increase upon those of decrease, and is ever wasting from the very cause whence he thinks himself to be gaining ground in the space of his life. For we cannot have a fixed stay here, whither we are come only to pass on. . . .

—ST. GREGORY THE GREAT, *Morals on the Book of Job*

Mark this well, for of this thing we be very sure, that old and young, man and woman, rich and poor, prince and page, all the while we live in this world we be but prisoners, and be within a sure prison, out of which there can no man escape. And in worse case be we than those that be taken and imprisoned for theft. For they, albeit their hearts heavily harkeneth after the sessions, yet have they some hope either to break prison the while, or to escape there by favour, or after condemnation some hope of pardon.

But we stand all in other plight: we be very sure that we be already condemned to death, some one, some other, none of us can tell what death we be doomed to, but surely can we all tell that die we shall. And clearly know we that of this death we get no manner pardon. For the King by Whose high sentence we be condemned to die, would not of this death pardon His own Son.

—St. Thomas More, *The Four Last Things*

A MEDITATION UPON A BROOMSTICK

This single stick, which you now behold ingloriously lying in that neglected corner, I once knew in a flourishing state in a forest: it was full of sap, full of leaves, and full of boughs: but now, in vain does the busy art of man pretend to vie with nature, by tying that withered bundle of twigs to its sapless trunk: it is now at best but the reverse of what it was, a tree turned upside down, the branches on the earth, and the root in the air; it is now handled by every dirty wench, condemned to do her drudgery, and, by a capricious kind of fate, destined to make her things clean, and be nasty itself: at length, worn out to the stumps in the service of the maids, it is either thrown out of doors, or condemned to the last use of kindling a fire. When I beheld this, I sighed, and said within myself, SURELY MAN IS A BROOMSTICK! Nature sent him into the world strong and lusty, in a thriving condition, wearing his own hair on his head, the proper branches of this reasoning vegetable, until the axe of intemperance has lopped off his green boughs, and left him a withered trunk: he then flies to art, and puts on a periwig, valuing himself upon an unnatural bundle of hairs (all covered with powder), that never grew on his head; but now, should this our broomstick pretend to enter the scene, proud of those birchen spoils it never bore, and all covered with dust, though the sweepings of the finest lady's chamber, we should be apt to ridicule and despise its vanity. Partial judges that we are of our own excellences and other men's defaults!

But a broomstick, perhaps you will say, is an emblem of a tree standing on its head; and pray what is man but a topsy-turvy creature, his animal faculties perpetually mounted on his rational, his head where his heels should be grovelling on the earth? And yet, with all his faults, he sets up to be a universal reformer and corrector of abuses, a remover of grievances, rakes into every slut's corner of nature, bringing hidden corruption to the light, and raises a mighty dust where there was none before; sharing deeply all the while in the very pollutions he pretends to sweep away: his last days are spent in slavery to women, and generally the least deserving; till, worn out to the stumps, like his brother besom, he is either kicked out of doors, or made use of to kindle flames for others to warm themselves by.

—Jonathan Swift

SUMMER'S LAST WILL
AND TESTAMENT

Adieu! farewell earth's bliss!
This world uncertain is:
Fond are life's lustful joys,
Death proves them all but toys.

None from his darts can fly:
I am sick, I must die.
            Lord, have mercy on us!

Rich men, trust not in wealth!
Gold cannot buy you health;
Physic himself must fade;
All things to end are made;
The plague full swift goes by:
I am sick, I must die.
            Lord, have mercy on us!

Beauty is but a flower
Which wrinkles will devour;
Brightness falls from the air;
Queens have died young and fair;
Dust hath closed Helen's eye;
I am sick, I must die.
            Lord, have mercy on us!

Strength stoops unto the grave:
Worms feed on Hector brave;
Swords may not fight with fate;
Earth still hold ope her gate;
Come! come! the bells do cry.
I am sick, I must die.
            Lord, have mercy on us!

Wit with his wantonness
Tasteth death's bitterness;
Hell's executioner
Hath no ears for to hear
What vain art can reply:
I am sick, I must die.
            Lord, have mercy on us!

Haste, therefore, each degree
To welcome destiny:
Heaven is our heritage,
Earth but a player's stage:
Mount we unto the sky.
I am sick, I must die.
            Lord, have mercy on us!
                 —THOMAS NASHE

THE PULLEY

When God at first made man,
Having a glass of blessings standing by;
Let us (said He) pour on him all we can:
Let the world's riches, which dispersed lie,
     Contract into a span.

So strength first made a way,
Then beauty flow'd, then wisdom, honour, pleasure;
When almost all was out, God made a stay,
Perceiving that alone of all His treasure
     Rest in the bottom lay.

For if I should (said He)
Bestow this jewel also on My creature,
He would adore My gifts instead of Me,
And rest in Nature, not the God of Nature:
     So both should losers be.

Yet let him keep the rest,
But keep them with repining restlessness:
Let him be rich and weary, that at least,
If goodness lead him not, yet weariness
     May toss him to My breast.
                 —GEORGE HERBERT

. . . Thou sayest to me, Behold, He smiteth the more innocent, and passeth over the more guilty. Wonder not; death, whencesoever it come, is good to the good man. And whence dost thou know what punishment is reserved in secret for that more guilty man, if he be unwilling to be converted? Would not they rather be scorched by lightning, to whom it shall be said in the end, "Depart into everlasting fire"? The needful thing is, that thou be guiltless. Why so? Is it an evil thing to die by shipwreck, and a good thing to die by fever? Whether he die in this way or in that, ask what sort of man he is who dieth; ask whither he will go after death, not how he is to depart from life. We shall depart from hence by whatever may befall us. By what deaths were the martyrs worthy to die? Was it by fevers? How is it that many wish to be set free by fever? Some perished by a single blow of the sword, some by fire, some by wild beasts. Wild beasts devoured the bodies of the martyrs, yet feared they not that their bodies would perish. For God will bring back from all quarters the bodies of the saints, God by Whom "the very hairs of our head are numbered." When He willed to, He delivered the Three Children from the fire. Did He therefore desert the Maccabees in the fire? The former He openly set free, the latter He secretly crowned. God then knoweth what He doeth. Do thou fear, and be good. For whatsoever way He will that thou depart hence, let Him find thee ready. For here thou art a sojourner, not a possessor of the house. For the house is let to thee, this house is let to thee, not given: loth though thou be, thou must depart from it: neither hast thou received it on such terms, as that thou hast any fixed time. What said thy Lord? "Whensoever I will, whensoever I shall say, Depart, be thou ready. I drive thee from thy lodging, but I will give thee a home: thou art a sojourner on earth, thou shalt be possessor in heaven."

—St. Augustine, *Exposition of Psalm 148*

2. Let Not Your Heart Be Troubled

Fear not, for I am with thee: turn not aside, for I am thy God: I have strengthened thee, and have helped thee, and the right hand of my just one hath upheld thee.

—Isaias 41:10

Are not five sparrows sold for two farthings, and not one of them is forgotten before God? Yea, the very hairs of your head are all numbered. Fear not therefore: you are of more value than many sparrows.

—St. Luke 12:5

Jesus said to them: I am the bread of life: he that cometh to me shall not hunger: and he that believeth in me shall never thirst. . . . All that the Father giveth to me shall come to me; and him that cometh to me, I will not cast out. Because I came down from heaven, not to do my own will, but the will of him that sent me. Now this is the will of the Father who sent me: that of all that he hath given me, I should lose nothing; but should raise it up again in the last day. And this is the will of my Father that sent me: that every one who seeth the Son, and believeth in him, may have life everlasting, and I will raise him up in the last day.

—St. John 6:35–40

Peace I leave with you, my peace I give unto you: not as the world giveth, do I give unto you. Let not your heart be troubled, nor let it be afraid.

—St. John 14:27

>Be absolute for death; either death or life
>Shall thereby be the sweeter. Reason thus with life:
>If I do lose thee, I do lose a thing
>That none but fools would keep: a breath thou art,
>Servile to all the skyey influences,
>That dost this habitation, where thou keep'st,
>Hourly afflict. Merely, thou art death's fool;
>For him thou labour'st by thy flight to shun,
>And yet run'st toward him still. Thou art not noble:
>For all th' accommodations that thou bear'st
>Are nurs'd by baseness. Thou art by no means valiant;
>For thou dost fear the soft and tender fork
>Of a poor worm. Thy best of rest is sleep,
>And that thou oft provok'st; yet grossly fear'st
>Thy death, which is no more. Thou art not thyself;
>For thou exist'st on many a thousand grains
>That issue out of dust. Happy thou art not;
>For what thou hast not, still thou striv'st to get,
>And what thou hast, forget'st. Thou art not certain;
>For thy complexion shifts to strange effects,
>After the moon. If thou art rich, thou'rt poor;
>For, like an ass whose back with ingots bows,
>Thou bear'st thy heavy riches but a journey,
>And death unloads thee. Friend hast thou none;
>For thine own bowels, which do call thee sire,
>The mere effusion of thy proper loins,
>Do curse the gout, serpigo, and the rheum,
>For ending thee no sooner. Thou hast nor youth nor age;

But, as it were, an after-dinner's sleep,
Dreaming on both; for all thy blessed youth
Becomes as aged, and doth beg the alms
Of palsied eld; and when thou art old and rich,
Thou hast neither heat, affection, limb, nor beauty,
To make thy riches pleasant. What 's yet in this
That bears the name of life? Yet in this life
Lie hid moe thousand deaths: yet death we fear,
That makes these odds all even.
　　　—WILLIAM SHAKESPEARE, *Measure for Measure*, III, i

If *eternal* life were not free from "dread," I should not desire it.
But supposing for a moment there was a man in this life who was
entirely without "dread" (and at the present time there are many
in high places who pride themselves upon the fact), then I should
not want to be that man. I should indeed "dread" him.
　　　—THEODOR HAECKER, *Journal in the*
　　　　　　　　Night (ALICK DRU)

. . . every man is afraid of the death of the flesh; few, of the death
of the soul. In regard to the death of the flesh, which must certainly come some time, all are on their guard against its approach:
this is the source of all their labor. Man, destined to die, labors to
avert his dying; and yet man, destined to live for ever, labors not
to cease from sinning. And when he labors to avoid dying, he
labors to no purpose, for its only result will be to put off death for
a while, not to escape it; but if he refrain from sinning, his toil
will cease, and he shall live for ever. Oh that we could arouse men,
and be ourselves aroused along with them, to be as great lovers of
the life that abideth, as men are of that which passeth away! What
will a man not do who is placed under the peril of death? When

the sword was overhanging their heads, men have given up every means of living they had in reserve. Who is there that has not made an immediate surrender of all, to escape being slain? And, after all, he has perhaps been slain. Who is there that, to save his life, has not been willing at once to lose his means of living, and prefer a life of beggary to a speedy death? Who has had it said to him, Be off to sea if you would escape with your life, and has delayed to do so? Who has had it said to him, Set to work if you would preserve your life, and has continued a sluggard? It is but little that God requires of us, that we may live for ever: and we neglect to obey Him. God says not to thee, Lose all you have, that you may live a little time oppressed with toil; but, Give to the poor of what you have, that you may live always exempt from labor. The lovers of this temporal life, which is theirs, neither when, nor as long as they wish, are our accusers; and we accuse not ourselves in turn, so sluggish are we, so lukewarm about obtaining eternal life, which will be ours if we wish it, and will be imperishable when we have it; but this death which we fear, notwithstanding all our reluctance, will yet be ours in possession.

—St. Augustine, *Tractate XLIX, On the Gospel of St. John*

Men who have to fight for their living
And are not afraid to die for it
Are higher men than those who, stationed high,
Are too fat to dare to die.

—Lao-tse (Witter Bynner)

Marcolphus. It was never my lot to be by where any one was dying. *Phaedrus.* But it has been mine too often, if I might have had my wish. *Ma.* Well, but is death so terrible a thing as they make it? *Ph.* The way to it is worse than the thing itself, so that if a man could free his mind from the terror and apprehension of it, he would take away the worst part of it. And, in short, whatsoever is tormenting either in sickness or in death itself is rendered much more easy by resignation to the will of God; for as to the sense of death, when the soul is departing from the body, I am of opinion they are either wholly insensible or the faculty is become very dull and stupid, because nature, before it comes to that point, lays asleep and stupefies all the sensible faculties.

Ma. We are born without sense of pain as to ourselves. *Ph.* But we are not born without pain to our mother. *Ma.* Why might we not die so? Why would God make death so full of pain? *Ph.* He was pleased to make birth painful and dangerous to the mother to make the child the dearer to her, and death formidable to mankind, to deter them from laying violent hands upon themselves; for when we see so many make away themselves as the case stands, what do you think they would do if death had no terror in it? As often as a servant or a son is corrected, or a woman is angry at her husband, anything is lost, or anything goes cross, men would presently repair to halters, swords, rivers, precipices, or poisons. Now the bitterness of death makes us put a greater value upon life, especially since the dead are out of the reach of the doctor. Although, as we are not all born alike, so we do not all die alike— some die suddenly, others pine away with a languishing illness; those that are seized with a lethargy and such as are stung by an asp are, as it were, cast into a sound sleep, and die without any sense of pain. I have made this observation that there is no death so painful but a man may bear it by resolution.

—Erasmus, *The Funeral* (Nathan Bailey)

Remember that you have only one soul; that you have only one death to die; that you have only one life, which is short and has to be lived by you alone; and that there is only one glory, which is eternal. If you do this, there will be many things about which you care nothing.

—St. Teresa of Avila, *Maxims of the Mother
Teresa of Jesus Written for Her Nuns*
(E. Allison Peers)

"So death will come to fetch you?" "No, not death, but God Himself. Death is not the horrible spectre we see represented in pictures. The catechism teaches that death is the separation of the soul from the body; that is all. I am not afraid of a separation which will unite me for ever with God."

—St. Thérèse of Lisieux, *Counsels and Memories*

It is impossible that anything so natural, so necessary, and so universal as death, should ever have been designed by providence as an evil to mankind.

—Jonathan Swift, *Thoughts on Religion*

Death has a look of finality;
We think we lose something but if it were not for
Death we should have nothing to lose, existence
Because unlimited would merely be existence
Without incarnate value. The trolls can occasion
Our death but they are not able
To use it as we can use it.
Fumbling and mumbling they try to
Spell out Death correctly; they are not able.

    . . . Time
Swings on the poles of death
And the latitude and the longitude of life
Are fixed by death, and the value
Of every organism, act and moment
Is, thanks to death, unique.
                    —LOUIS MACNEICE, *The Trolls*
                    (Written after an air-raid, April 1941)

Ought the mind of the Christian to be troubled even at the prospect of death? . . . let us for our part confine our attention to the Sacred Scriptures, and with the Lord's help seek rather such a solution of this question as will in harmony with them; and then, seeing it is written, "When He had thus said, He was troubled in spirit," we will not say that it was joy that disturbed Him; lest His own words should convince us of the contrary when He says, "My soul is sorrowful, even unto death." It is some such feeling that is here also to be understood, when, as His betrayer was now on the very point of departing alone, and straightway returning along with his associates, "Jesus was troubled in spirit."

Strong-minded, indeed, are those Christians, if such there are, who experience no trouble at all in the prospect of death; but for all that, are they stronger-minded than Christ? Who would have the madness to say so? And what else, then, does His being troubled signify, but that, by voluntarily assuming the likeness of their weakness, He comforted the weak members in His body, that is in His Church; to the end that, if any of His own are still troubled at the approach of death, they may fix their gaze upon Him, and so be kept from thinking themselves castaways on this account, and being swallowed up in the more grievous death of despair? And how great, then, must be that good which we ought to expect and hope for in the participation of His divine nature, whose very perturbation tranquillizes us, and whose infirmity confirms us? . . . For having by His power assumed our full humanity, by that very power He awoke in Himself our human feelings whenever He judged it becoming.

—St. Augustine, *Tractate LX, On the Gospel of St. John*

Death is no evil, for it frees man from all his ills, and while depriving him of his joys, takes away also his desires.

—Giacomo Leopardi, *Pensieri*

By my troth, I care not; a man can die but once; we owe God a death: I'll ne'er bear a base mind: an 't be my destiny, so; an 't be not, so: no man 's too good to serve 's prince; and let it go which way it will, he that dies this year is quit for the next.

—William Shakespeare, *2 Henry IV*, III, ii

. . . Tell me, what is there in death which is terrible? Is it because it transports thee more quickly to the peaceful haven, and to that life which is free from tumult? Although man should not put thee to death, will not the very law of nature, at length stealing upon thee, separate the body from the soul; and if this event which we fear does not happen now, it will happen shortly.

I speak thus, not anticipating any dread or melancholy event: God forbid! But because I am ashamed for those who are afraid of death. Tell me, whilst expecting such good things as "eye hath not seen, nor ear heard, nor have entered the heart of man," dost thou demur about this enjoyment, and art negligent and slothful; and not only slothful, but fearful and trembling? What is it but shameful? Thou art in pain on account of death, when Paul groaned on account of the present life, and writing to the Romans said, "The creation groaneth together, and ourselves also which have the firstfruits of the Spirit do groan." And he spoke thus, not condemning the things present, but longing for the things to come. "I have tasted," saith he, "of the grace, and I cannot contain myself in the delay. I have the firstfruits of the Spirit, and I press on towards the whole. I have ascended to the third heaven; I have seen that glory which is unutterable; I have beheld the shining palaces; I have learnt what joys I am deprived of, while I linger here, and therefore do I groan." For suppose any one had conducted thee into princely halls, and shewn thee the gold every where glittering on the walls, and all the rest of the glorious show; if from thence he had led thee back afterward to a poor man's hut, and promised that in a short time he would bring thee back to those palaces, and would there give thee a perpetual mansion; tell me, wouldest thou not indeed languish with desire, and feel impatient, even at these few days? Thus think then of heaven, and of earth, and groan with Paul, not because of death, but because of the present life.

But give me, saith one, to be like Paul, and I shall never be afraid of death. Why, what is it that forbids thee, O man, to become like Paul? Was he not a poor man? Was he not a tent maker? Was he not a man of mean rank? For if he had been rich and well born, the poor, when called upon to imitate his zeal, would have had their poverty to plead; but now thou canst say nothing of this sort. For this man was one who exercised a manual art, and supported himself too by his daily labours. And thou, indeed, from the first hast inherited true religion from thy fathers; and from thy earliest age hast been nourished in the study of the sacred writings; but he was "a blasphemer, and a persecutor, and injurious," and ravaged the Church! Nevertheless, he so changed all at once, as to surpass all in the vehemence of his zeal, and he cries out, saying "Be ye followers of me, even as I also am of Christ." He imitated the Lord; and wilt not thou who hast been educated in piety from the first, imitate a fellow-servant; one who by a great change was brought to the faith at a later period of life? Knowest thou not, that they who are in sins are dead whilst they live; and that they who live in righteousness, although they be dead, yet they live? And this is not my word. It is the declaration of Christ speaking to Martha, "He that believeth in me though he were dead yet shall he live." Is our doctrine, indeed, a fable? If thou art a Christian, believe in Christ; if thou believest in Christ, shew me thy faith by thy works. But how mayest thou shew this? By thy contempt of death: for in this we differ from the unbelievers. They may well fear death; since they have no hope of a resurrection. But thou, who art travelling toward better things, and hast the opportunity of meditating on the hope of the future; what excuse hast thou, if whilst assured of a resurrection, thou art yet at the same time as fearful of death, as those who believe not the resurrection?

  —St. John Chrysostom, *Homily V, On the Statues*

You ask why you are afraid of death. It is only human. St. Teresa describes her mental and even bodily sufferings, caused by her violent desire to die and to "be with Christ." And yet, she says, she still had the human fear of death. And our Lord chose to suffer this fear of death for our sakes. The separation of body and soul is a wrench. On the other hand, I know quite well what you mean about the feeling,—when you try to realise death—that there is nothing beyond.

The reason is plainly because *one cannot imagine it.* One tries to *imagine* a pure spiritual imagination of the soul without the body; and naturally one imagines a blank. And then one feels: —"There is no life after death"; and then one says to oneself:—"I am doubting the faith, I am sinning against faith."

All the time, one is only unreasonable,—trying to imagine what can be intellectually conceived, but not pictured.

It is different, I think, if you think of death naturally; not unnaturally.

(1) To die is a violence (as I said) from one point of view; but from another, it is *natural*. And to most people it seems natural to die, when they are dying. Consequently it is easy to imagine yourself on your sick bed, very weak, and faintly hearing prayers around you, and receiving the Sacraments, and gently losing consciousness, and sleeping in God's arms. (This is actually the way death comes to most people,—quite easily and pleasantly.) And looked at in this way, it does not *feel* like an extinction, the going out of a candle; it seems, on the contrary, impossible to feel that this is the end of one's personality. But what comes next? We leave that to God,—we do not try to *imagine* it.

(2) Only in prayer can you get near it—if the world ever falls away, and leaves you in infinity—which you can only describe as nothingness, though it is everything.

The moral of all this is,—do not try to *imagine* "after death," for imagination is only of material and sensible things. Only try to realise what it is to be with God.

One's *terror* of death, after seeing a dead person, is merely because it is unaccustomed. If you were an Undertaker, you wouldn't feel it! Nor even if you were a Nurse in a hospital. It is a thing to laugh yourself out of. But it does not matter much. Some people are afraid of mice or frogs. Some people are afraid of corpses. Some people are afraid of ghosts. Others can't stand the sight of blood. But you can get accustomed to seeing pools of it, and people blown to bits, and be cheerful and joking, and pass by taking no notice. It is all a matter of habit. The Chinese don't mind dying, provided they are sure of having a really nice coffin. I can't say the prospect would appeal to me.

These are gruesome subjects! I think it is much better to be accustomed to them, and to take them as a matter of course. The worst of death is really the blanks it leaves in this world. But it often fills up blanks in the next world; and we must rejoice when some one, dear to us, takes the place prepared "from the foundation of the world," as our Lord tells us, for that soul. . . .

—Dom John Chapman, *Spiritual Letters*

Does He deal hardly with us by shortening our day of sorrow, struggle, temptation, and frailty? What would we have? Prolonged peril, stronger temptation, wherein the very elect themselves might, were it possible, fail? We desire all that fosters our selfishness, in order that we may forget ourselves in our exile. God snatches the poison from us, and we cry like a babe from whom its mother has taken a glistening knife, with which it was fain to pierce itself!

—Archbishop Fénelon, *Letters to Men* (H. L. S. Lear)

CHRISTIAN TRAGEDY

The believing Christian no longer recognizes tragedy as genuine. Redemption has occurred and is perpetually renewed through grace. This untragic approach transforms man's worldly misery and misfortune into a view of the world, a view perhaps utterly pessimistic, seeing the world as but a proving ground where man must earn eternal salvation. The world exists as a flow of events guided by Providence. Here all is but way and transition; here nothing is ultimate reality.

To be sure, every form of tragedy is transparent if caught at the very moment of its transcendence. To be able to stand fast and to die in the midst of nothingness—this is "deliverance," but deliverance within the tragic and through its own efficacy. If there were nothing more than pure immanence, if we were inescapably confined within the limits of our existence, then even to stand fast and hold one's own amidst shipwreck would be meaningless. But when we thus hold our own we do not overcome immanence by bringing in another world. We do so only by the very act of transcending, by the knowledge of our outermost frontiers, and by the insights gained in looking back from those frontiers. Only a faith that knows another reality besides immanent reality can bring deliverance from tragedy. That is the case with Dante, and with Calderón. With them, knowledge of the tragic, the tragic predicaments themselves, and tragic heroism, have all undergone radical change because these poets have included them within the plan of Providence and the operation of Grace, a plan and an operation that deliver man from all the vast nothingness and self-destruction in this world.

—Karl Jaspers, *Tragedy Is Not Enough*
(H. A. T. Reiche, H. T. Moore, and K. W. Deutsch)

RABBI AKIBA

. . . Rabbi Akiba was once travelling through the country, and he had with him an ass, a rooster, and a lamp.

At nightfall he reached a village where he sought shelter for the night without success.

"All that God does is done well," said the Rabbi, and proceeding towards the forest he resolved to pass the night there. He lit his lamp, but the wind extinguished it. "All that God does is done well," he said. The ass and the rooster were devoured by wild beasts; yet still he said no more than "All that God does is done well."

Next day he learned that a troop of the enemy's soldiers had passed through the forest that night. If the ass had brayed, if the rooster had crowed, or if the soldiers had seen his light he would surely have met with death, therefore he said again, "All that God does is done well."

It happened once when Rabbi Gamliel, Rabbi Eleazer, Rabbi Judah, and Rabbi Akiba were walking together, they heard the shouts and laughter and joyous tones of a multitude of people at a distance. Four of the Rabbis wept; but Akiba laughed aloud.

"Akiba," said the others to him, "wherefore laugh? These heathens who worship idols live in peace, and are merry, while our holy city lies in ruins; weep, do not laugh."

"For that very reason I laugh, and am glad," answered Rabbi Akiba. "If God allows those who transgress His will to live happily on earth, how infinitely great must be the happiness which He has stored up in the world to come for those who observe His commands!"

—*The Talmud* (H. POLANO)

Death hath no other ill
Except the thought of dying.
—BATTISTA GUARINI, *Il Pastor Fido,* IV, v

Cowards die many times before their deaths:
The valiant never taste of death but once.
Of all the wonders that I yet have heard,
It seems to me most strange that men should fear;
Seeing that death, a necessary end,
Will come when it will come.
—WILLIAM SHAKESPEARE, *Julius Caesar,* II, ii

Death stands above me, whispering low
I know not what into my ear:

Of his strange language all I know
Is, there is not a word of fear.

—WALTER S. LANDOR

SANTA TERESA'S BOOK-MARK

Let nothing disturb thee,
Nothing affright thee;
All things are passing;
God never changeth;
Patient endurance
Attaineth to all things;
Who God possesseth
In nothing is wanting;
Alone God sufficeth.

(HENRY WADSWORTH LONGFELLOW)

. . . our good Lord answered to all the questions and doubts that I might make, saying full comfortably: *"I may make all thing well; and I can make all thing well; and I shall make all thing well; and I will make all thing well; and thou shalt see thyself that all manner of thing shall be well."* . . . And in these five words, God wills that we be enclosed in rest, and peace. And thus shall the ghostly thirst of Christ have an end; for this is the ghostly thirst of Christ, the love-longing that lasteth and ever shall, till we see that sight at doomsday; for we that shall be safe, and shall be Christ's joy and his bliss, be yet here; and some be to come, and so shall some be into that day. Therefore this is his thirst, and love-longing of us all together here in him to our endless bliss, as to my sight; for we be not now fully as whole in him as we shall be then . . . for the same thirst and longing that he had upon the rood-tree (which desire longing and thirst as to my sight, was in him from without beginning) the same hath he yet, and shall into the time that the last soul that shall be saved is come up to his bliss. . . . And this property of longing and thirst cometh of the endless goodness of God. . . . And in this standeth the point of ghostly thirst, which is lasting in him as long as we be in need, us drawing up to his bliss. And all this was seen in showing of compassion, for that shall cease at doomsday. Thus he hath ruth and compassion on us; and he hath longing to have us; but his wisdom and his love suffer not the same to come till the best time.

—JULIANA OF NORWICH, *Revelations of Divine Love*

My friends, pray to God for gladness. Be glad as children, as the birds of heaven. And let not the sin of men confound you in your doings. Fear not that it will wear away your work and hinder its being accomplished. Do not say, "Sin is mighty, wickedness is mighty, evil environment is mighty, and we are lonely and helpless, and evil environment is wearing us away and hindering our good work from being done." Fly from that dejection, children! There is only one means of salvation, then take yourself and make yourself responsible for all men's sins, that is the truth, you know, friends, for as soon as you sincerely make yourself responsible for everything and for all men, you will see at once that it is really so, and that you are to blame for every one and for all things. But throwing your own indolence and impotence on others you will end by sharing the pride of Satan and murmuring against God.

Of the pride of Satan what I think is this: it is hard for us on earth to comprehend it, and therefore it is so easy to fall into error and to share it, even imagining that we are doing something grand and fine. Indeed many of the strongest feelings and movements of our nature we cannot comprehend on earth. Let not that be a stumbling-block, and think not that it may serve as a justification to you for anything. For the Eternal Judge asks of you what you can comprehend and not what you cannot. You will know that yourself hereafter, for you will behold all things truly then and will not dispute them. On earth, indeed, we are as it were astray, and if it were not for the precious image of Christ before us, we should be undone and altogether lost, as was the human race before the flood. Much on earth is hidden from us, but to make up for that we have been given a precious mystic sense of our living bond with the other world, with the higher heavenly world, and the roots of our thoughts and feelings are not here but in other worlds. That is why the philosophers say that we cannot apprehend the reality of things on earth.

God took seeds from different worlds and sowed them on this earth, and His garden grew up and everything came up that could come up, but what grows lives and is alive only through the feeling of its contact with other mysterious worlds. If that feeling grows weak or is destroyed in you, the heavenly growth will die away in you. Then you will be indifferent to life and even grow to hate it.

—FYODOR DOSTOYEVSKY, *The Brothers Karamazov*
(CONSTANCE GARNETT)

    Since nature's works be good, and death doth serve
As nature's work, why should we fear to die?
    Since fear is vain, but when it may preserve,
Why should we fear that which we cannot fly?
    Fear is more pain than is the pain it fears,
Disarming human minds of native might:
    While each conceit an ugly figure bears,
Which were not evil well view'd in reason's light.
    Our owly eyes, which dimm'd with passions be,
And scarce discern the dawn of coming day,
    Let them be clear'd, and now begin to see
Our life is but a step in dusty way.

Then let us hold the bliss of peaceful mind,
Since this we feel, great loss we cannot find.

—Sir Philip Sidney, *Arcadia*

Fear no more the heat o' the sun,
    Nor the furious winter's rages;
Thou thy worldly task hast done,
    Home art gone, and ta'en thy wages;
Golden lads and girls all must,
As chimney-sweepers, come to dust.
Fear no more the frown o' the great,
    Thou art past the tyrant's stroke:
Care no more to clothe and eat;
    To thee the reed is as the oak:
The sceptre, learning, physic, must
All follow this, and come to dust.
Fear no more the lightning-flash,
    Nor the all-dreaded thunder-stone;
Fear not slander, censure rash;
    Thou hast finish'd joy and moan:
All lovers young, all lovers must
Consign to thee, and come to dust.
No exorciser harm thee!
Nor no witchcraft charm thee!
Ghost unlaid forbear thee!
Nothing ill come near thee!
Quiet consummation have;
And renowned be thy grave!

—William Shakespeare, *Cymbeline*, IV, ii

3. Be Ye Always Ready

Thou shalt no more have the sun for thy light by day, neither shall the brightness of the moon enlighten thee: but the Lord shall be unto thee for an everlasting light, and thy God for thy glory. Thy sun shall go down no more, and thy moon shall not decrease: for the Lord shall be unto thee for an everlasting light, and the days of thy mourning shall be ended. . . . I the Lord will suddenly do this thing in its time.

—Isaias 60:19–20, 22

Lay not up to yourselves treasures on earth: where the rust and moth consume, and where thieves break through, and steal. But lay up to yourselves treasures in heaven: where neither the rust nor moth doth consume, and where thieves do not break through, nor steal. For where thy treasure is, there is thy heart also.

—St. Matthew 6:19–21

Heaven and earth shall pass away, but my word shall not pass away. But of that day or hour no man knoweth, neither the angels in heaven, nor the Son, but the Father. Take ye heed, watch and pray. For ye know not when the time is. Even as a man who, going into a far country, left his house; and gave authority to his servants over every work, and commanded the porter to watch. Watch ye therefore, (for you know not when the Lord of the house cometh:

at even, or at midnight, or at the cock crowing, or in the morning), lest coming on a sudden, he find you sleeping. And what I say to you, I say to all: Watch.

—St. Mark 13:31–37

"Be ye always ready." Our blessed Savior does not tell us to begin to prepare ourselves when death has arrived, but to prepare ourselves beforehand; because the time of death will be a time of confusion, when it will be morally impossible to prepare ourselves in a proper manner to appear for judgment, and to obtain a favorable sentence. "It is a just punishment," says St. Augustine, "upon him who, having it in his power to do good, will not do it, not to be able to do it afterwards when he desires to do it."

No, my God, I will not wait until that time to begin a change of life. Make known to me what I must now do to please Thee, for I desire to do without reserve whatever Thou requirest of me.

—St. Alphonsus de Liguori, *The Way of Salvation*

Almost our whole lives are spent in satisfying foolish curiosities. On the other hand, there are things that ought to provoke men's curiosity to the highest degree—and yet, to judge by the tenor of men's normal lives, inspire them with no curiosity whatsoever.

Where are our friends who have died?

Why are we here?

Do we come from somewhere?

What is freedom?

Can it be reconciled with the law of predestination?

The number of souls, is it finite or infinite?

And the number of inhabitable countries?

—Charles Baudelaire, *My Heart Laid Bare*
(Norman Cameron)

"Teach me to live that I may dread the grave as little as my bed."
This is from the evening hymn that all respectable children are
taught. It sounds well, but it is not moral; it is not desirable that
any living being should live in habitual indifference to death; this
should be kept for worthy occasions, and even then, though death
is gladly faced, it is not healthy that it should be faced as though
it were a mere undressing and going to bed.

—SAMUEL BUTLER, *Notebooks*

As a man, thou art born—art destined to die. Whither wilt thou
go to escape death? What wilt thou do to escape it? That thy Lord
might comfort thee in thy necessary subjection to death, of His
own good pleasure He condescended to die. When thou seest the
Christ lying dead, art thou reluctant to die? Die then thou must;
thou hast no means of escape. Be it to-day, be it to-morrow; it is
to be—the debt must be paid. What, then, does a man gain by
fearing, fleeing, hiding himself from discovery by his enemy? Does
he get exemption from death? No, but that he may die a little
later. He gets not security against his debt, but asks a respite. Put
it off as long as you please, the thing so delayed will come at last.

—ST. AUGUSTINE, *Tractate XLIII,*
On the Gospel of St. John

Men shun the thought of death as sad, but death will only be
sad to those who have no thought of it. It must come sooner or
later, and then he who has refused to see the truth in life will be
forced to face it in death. Death brings a very clear insight as to
all a man has done and all he ought to have done; we shall then
see clearly how we ought to have used past grace, talents, wealth,
health, time, and all the joys and sorrows of life. The thought of
death is the best check we can put upon all our plans and doings.

It is right to wish for it, but we must wait for death with the same absolute submission to God's Will as we accept life. It is right to wish for death, inasmuch as it is the consummation of our repentance, the entrance to blessedness, and our eternal reward. A man has no right to say that he wishes to live to do penance for past sins—death is the fullest of penances; our sins will be expiated in death better than by any other penance. It will be as precious to the good as it will be terrible to the wicked. We ask for death daily in the "Our Father." Every one must ask that the Kingdom of God may come to him. So saying, we must wish for it; for prayer is the heart's desire, and God's Kingdom can only come to us through our death. St. Paul bids Christians "comfort one another" with the thought of death. (I Thess. 4:18)

—Archbishop Fénelon, *Letters to Men* (H. L. S. Lear)

Nearly every man and woman . . . outwardly professes to believe —and a large number unquestionably think they believe— . . . not only that a quite unlimited estate is in prospect for them if they please the Holder of it, but that the infinite contrary of such a possession—an estate of perpetual misery—is in store for them if they displease this great Land-Holder, this great Heaven-Holder. And yet there is not one in a thousand of these human souls that cares to think, for ten minutes of the day, where this estate is or how beautiful it is, or what kind of life they are to lead in it, or what kind of life they must lead to obtain it. . . .

Can you answer a single bold question unflinchingly about that other world?—Are you sure there is a heaven? Sure there is a hell? Sure that men are dropping before your faces through the pavements of these streets into eternal life, or sure that they are not? Sure that at your own death you are going to be delivered from all sorrow, to be endowed with all virtue, to be gifted with all felicity, and raised into perpetual companionship with a King, compared to whom the kings of the earth are as grasshoppers, and the nations

as the dust of His feet? Are you sure of this? or, if not sure, do any
of us so much as care to make it sure? and, if not, how can anything
that we do be right—how can anything we think be wise? what
honor can there be in the arts that amuse us, or what profit in the
possessions that please?

—JOHN RUSKIN, *The Mystery of Life and Its Arts*

A SIMILITUDE OF THE ANT

I wish to give a short similitude to those who live and fare in
the tempest, so that they may valiantly and obediently persist in
this manner of living, and attain to high virtue. There is a little
beast called the ant. She is strong and wise and hard to kill. And
she loves to live in the company of her fellows in a hot, dry land.
And she works in the summer and gathers up food and corn
against the winter; and she splits each grain in two, so that it cannot germinate and spoil, but so that the ants can benefit from it
when there is no other food to be had. And each ant does not make
a separate path, but they all follow the same path. And when the
season comes that she has been willing to wait for, then she is able
to fly. Thus these men ought to do: they should be strong in
awaiting the coming of Christ, wise against the revelations and
suggestions of the devil. They must not wish for death, but always
for the honour of God and to win for themselves fresh virtue. They
must live in the company of their heart and all their powers, and
be obedient to the demands and the compulsion of Divine unity.
They must live in a hot, dry land, which is in the violent tempest
of love and in great impatience, and they must work in their lives'
summer, and gather the fruits of virtue against eternity, and split
them in two. The one portion is that they must evermore desire
the high and delectable unity: the other is that they must restrain
themselves by means of reason, so far as they may, and await the
time that God has ordained: so the fruit of virtues is preserved to

all eternity. And they must not make separate paths or peculiar manners for themselves, but they must follow the path of love through all the storms on the way that love leads them. And while man awaits his time, and furnishes himself with all virtues, he is able to contemplate, and to flee into God's secret refuge.

—JAN VAN RUYSBROEK, *The Spiritual Espousals*
(ERIC COLLEDGE)

REPENT THE DAY BEFORE THY DEATH

The Rabbi who said, "Repent the day before thy death," was asked by his disciples how they could follow his advice, as man was unable to tell upon what day his death would occur. He answered, "Consider *every* day thy last; be ever ready with penitence and good deeds."

—*The Talmud* (H. POLANO)

. . . every day I will be on the watch for death, and will look about me that he take me not by surprise. I will learn how to die; I will turn my thoughts to yonder world. Lord, I see that there is no remaining here; Lord, in sooth, I will not save up my sorrow and repentance till death.

—BLESSED HENRY SUSO, *Eternal Wisdom*

SLEEP

Sleep is that death by which we may be literally said to die daily; a death which Adam died before his mortality; a death whereby we live a middle and moderating point between life and death; in fine, so like death, I dare not trust it without my prayers and an half adieu unto the World, and take my farewell in a Colloquy with God.

> The night is come, like to the day,
> Depart not Thou, great God, away.
> Let not my sins, black as the night,
> Eclipse the lustre of Thy light:
> Keep still in my Horizon; for to me
> The Sun makes not the day, but Thee.
> Thou, whose nature cannot sleep,
> On my temples Sentry keep;
> Guard me 'gainst those watchful foes
> Whose eyes are open while mine close;
> Let no dreams my head infest
> But such as Jacob's temples blest.
> While I do rest, my Soul advance;
> Make my sleep a holy trance;
> That I may, my rest being wrought,
> Awake into some holy thought;
> And with as active vigour run
> My course as doth the nimble Sun.
> Sleep is a death: O make me try,
> By sleeping, what it is to die;
> And as gently lay my head
> On my grave, as now my bed.
> Howe'er I rest, great God, let me
> Awake again at last with Thee;
> And thus assur'd, behold I lie
> Securely, or to awake or die.
> These are my drowsie days; in vain
> I do now wake to sleep again;
> O come that hour, when I shall never
> Sleep again, but wake for ever!

This is the Dormitive I take to bedward; I need no other Laudanum than this to make me sleep; after which I close mine eyes in security, content to take my leave of the Sun, and sleep unto the Resurrection.

—Sir Thomas Browne, *Religio Medici*

Let us do our utmost, dearest brethren, to rouse ourselves, and breaking off the sleep of our past inertia, give our minds to the observance and fulfilment of Our Lord's commands. Let us be such as He told us to be: "Let your loins be girt and your lamps burning, and you yourselves like to men who wait for their lord when he shall come from the wedding; that when he cometh and knocketh they may open to him. Blessed are those servants whom the Lord when He cometh shall find watching." (Lk. 12:35–37) Our loins must be girt, lest when the day comes for the campaign, it find us encumbered with trappings. Let our light shine brightly in good works, so that it may lead us from the darkness of this world into the splendour of eternal light. Let us await the sudden coming of Our Lord, ever attentive and on the alert, so that when He shall knock, our faith may be watching, ready to receive from Our Lord the reward of its vigil. Were but these commands obeyed, were but these warnings and precepts observed—it is impossible that we should be tricked and overcome by the devil in our sleep; from being watchful servants we shall, under Christ's lordship, come to reign ourselves.

—St. Cyprian, *The Unity of the Catholic Church*
(Maurice Bévenot, S.J.)

LOVE IS STRONG AS DEATH

. . . There have been in our time men most famous for virtue and learning, found dead, some in a confessional, others while hearing a sermon: yea some have been seen to fall down dead at their going out of the pulpit, where they had preached with great fervour; and all these deaths were sudden, yet not unprovided. And how many good people do we see die in apoplexy, in a lethargy, and a thousand other ways, very suddenly? And others die in delirium and madness, out of the use of reason; and all these, together with children who are baptized, die in grace and consequently in the love of God. But how could they die in the love of God, since they did not even think of God at the time of their departure?

Learned men, Theotimus, lose not their knowledge while they are asleep; otherwise they would be unlearned at their waking, and have to return to school. The like it is in all the habits of prudence, temperance, faith, hope and charity; they are ever within the just man's heart, though they are not always in action. While a man sleeps it seems that all his habits sleep with him, and when he awakes awake with him; so a just man dying suddenly, whether crushed by a house falling upon him, or killed by thunder, or stifled by an effusion on the lungs, or dying out of his senses by the violence of a burning fever, dies not indeed in the exercise of holy love, yet he dies in the habit thereof. Whereupon the wise man says: *The just man, if he be prevented with death, shall be in rest:* for to obtain eternal life it suffices to die in the state and habit of love and charity.

—St. Francis de Sales, *Treatise on the Love of God*
(Henry Benedict Mackey, O.S.B.)

ON PIETY

Are we disposed to die to be with Christ? St. Augustine says that holiness of life and willingness to die are inseparable dispositions. "The love of this life and of another," says he, "cause an incessant conflict in the imperfect soul. Let not such persons say they wish to live, in order to repair the past: if they examine their hearts, they will find that they cling to life, because they are not sufficiently virtuous to desire the pure joys of heaven." If we only feared the judgments of God upon our entrance into eternity, this fear would be calm and holy. The perfection of our love to God consists in our feeling an entire confidence in him. If we loved him as our father, should we fear him as our judge? Should we fly from his presence, should we tremble thus, when sickness warns us of the approach of death?

But there is a secret infidelity at the bottom of our hearts, that stifles all these sentiments. We weep at the death of those we love, and we tremble at our own, as they who have no hope. Judging from our anxiety about this life, who would believe that we anticipated a happy futurity? How is that they to whom religion has opened the path to another life, they whose hope is full of immortality, how can they reconcile such substantial and glorious hopes with the vain enjoyments that fill their hearts in this world? Our piety must be weak and imperfect, if it do not conquer our fear of death. We must take a very confused and superficial view of the eternal resources of the Christian at the hour of death, and of all that he hopes for beyond this transient life, if our hearts do not kindle with joy at the contemplation of the moment when our sorrows shall pass away and our felicity begin. Let us each ask himself, Am I ready to die? Let me not deceive myself by a false courage. Does the ardour of my love for God overcome my fear of death? Do I use this world as not abusing it? Do I regard it as a passing shadow? Am I unwilling to be subjected to its vanities? Is there nothing here that flatters my self-love and enslaves my affections, making me almost forget eternity? In fine, am I every day preparing for death? Is it by this thought that I regulate my life? And when the last hour shall arrive, shall I be prepared for the fatal stroke? Shall I not shrink from its approach? What will become of my courage when I shall feel myself between this world that is fast vanishing from my sight, and eternity that is opening

to receive me? Whence is it that those who profess not to be lovers
of life do not fear death less than others?

—ARCHBISHOP FÉNELON

The physician sendeth his bill to the apothecary, and therein
writeth sometimes a costly receipt of many strange herbs and roots,
fetched out of far countries, long-lain drugs, all the strength worn
out, and some none such to be got. But this physician sendeth his
bill to thyself, no strange thing therein, nothing costly to buy,
nothing far to fetch, but to be gathered all times of the year in the
garden of thine own soul.

Let us hear, then, what wholesome receipt this is. "Remember,"
saith this bill, "thy last things, and thou shalt never sin in this
world."

Here is first a short medicine containing only four herbs, common and well known, that is to wit, death, doom, pain, and joy.

This short medicine is of a marvellous force, able to keep us all
our life from sin. The physician cannot give no one medicine to
every man to keep him from sickness, but to divers men divers, by
reason of the diversity of divers complexions. This medicine
serveth every man. The physician doth but guess and conjecture
that his receipt shall do good; but this medicine is undoubtedly
sure.

—ST. THOMAS MORE, *The Four Last Things*

THE ART OF DYING

A man is a bubble, said the Greek proverb; which Lucian represents with advantages and its proper circumstances, to this purpose;
saying, that all the world is a storm, and men rise up in their
several generations, like bubbles descending *a Jove pluvio*, from

God and the dew of heaven, from a tear and drop of man, from nature and Providence: and some of these instantly sink into the deluge of their first parent, and are hidden in a sheet of water, having had no other business in the world but to be born that they might be able to die: others float up and down two or three turns, and suddenly disappear, and give their place to others: and they that live longest upon the face of the waters, are in perpetual motion, restless and uneasy; and being crushed with the great drop of a cloud sink into flatness and a froth; the change not being great, it being hardly possible it should be more a nothing than it was before. So is every man: he is born in vanity and sin; he comes into the world like morning mushrooms, soon thrusting up their heads into the air, and conversing with their kindred of the same production, and as soon they turn into dust and forgetfulness: some of them without any other interest in the affairs of the world but that they made their parents a little glad, and very sorrowful: others ride longer in the storm; it may be until seven years of vanity be expired, and then peradventure the sun shines hot upon their heads, and they fall into the shades below, into the cover of death and darkness of the grave to hide them. But if the bubble stands the shock of a bigger drop, and outlives the chances of a child, of a careless nurse, of drowning in a pail of water, of being overlaid by a sleepy servant, or such little accidents, then the young man dances like a bubble, empty and gay, and shines like a dove's neck, or the image of a rainbow, which hath no substance, and whose very imagery and colours are fantastical; and so he dances out the gaiety of his youth, and is all the while in a storm, and endures only because he is not knocked on the head by a drop of bigger rain, or crushed by the pressure of a load of indigested meat, or quenched by the disorder of an ill-placed humour: and to preserve a man alive in the midst of so many chances and hostilities, is as great a miracle as to create him; to preserve him from rushing into nothing, and at first to draw him up from nothing, were equally the issues of an almighty power. And therefore the wise men of the

world have contended who shall best fit man's condition with
words signifying his vanity and short abode. . . . The sum of all
is this: that thou art a man, than whom there is not in the world
any greater instance of heights and declensions, of lights and
shadows, of misery and folly, of laughter and tears, of groans and
death.

* * *

It is a thing that every one suffers, even persons of the lowest
resolution, of the meanest virtue, of no breeding, of no discourse.
Take away but the pomps of death, the disguises and solemn bug-
bears, the tinsel, and the actings by candle-light, and proper and
fantastic ceremonies, the minstrels and the noise-makers, the
women and the weepers, the swoonings and the shriekings, the
nurses and the physicians, the dark room and the ministers, the
kindred and the watchers; and then to die is easy, ready and quitted
from its troublesome circumstances. It is the same harmless thing
that a poor shepherd suffered yesterday, or a maid-servant to-day;
and at the same time in which you die, in that very night a thousand creatures die with you, some wise men, and many fools; and
the wisdom of the first will not quit him, and the folly of the latter
does not make him unable to die.

Of all the evils of the world which are reproached with an evil
character, death is the most innocent of its accusation. For when
it is present, it hurts nobody; and when it is absent, it is indeed
troublesome, but the trouble is owing to our fears, not the affright-
ing and mistaken object: and besides this, if it were an evil, it is
so transient, that it passes like the instant or undiscerned portion
of the present time; and either it is past, or it is not yet; for just
when it is, no man hath reason to complain of so insensible, so
sudden, so undiscerned a change.

* * *

Make no excuses to make thy desires of life seem reasonable;
neither cover thy fear with pretences, but suppress it rather with

arts of severity and ingenuity. Some are not willing to submit to God's sentence and arrest of death till they have finished such a design, or made an end of the last paragraph of their book, or raised such portions for their children, or preached so many sermons, or built their house, or planted their orchard, or ordered their estate with such advantages. It is well for the modesty of these men that the excuse is ready; but if it were not, it is certain they would search one out: for an idle man is never ready to die, and is glad of any excuse; and a busied man hath always something unfinished, and he is ready for every thing but death . . . we must know God's times are not to be measured by our circumstances; and what I value, God regards not: or if it be valuable in the accounts of men, yet God will supply it with other contingencies of His providence. . . . Say no more; but when God calls, lay aside thy papers; and first dress thy soul, and then dress thy hearse.

* * *

After all this, I do not say it is a sin to be afraid of death; we find the boldest spirit, that discourses of it with confidence, and dares undertake a danger as big as death, yet doth shrink at the horror of it when it comes dressed in its proper circumstances. And Brutus, who was as bold a Roman to undertake a noble action as any was since they first reckoned by consuls, yet when Furius came to cut his throat after his defeat by Anthony, he ran from it like a girl, and being admonished to die constantly, he swore by his life that he would shortly endure death. But what do I speak of such imperfect persons? Our blessed Lord was pleased to legitimate fear to us by His agony and prayers in the garden. It is not a sin to be afraid, but it is a great felicity to be without fear; which felicity our dearest Saviour refused to have, because it was agreeable to His purposes to suffer any thing that was contrary to felicity, everything but sin. But when men will by all means avoid death, they are like those who at any hand resolve to be rich; the case may happen in which they will blaspheme, and dishonour providence, or do a base action, or curse God and die: but in all cases they die miserable and ensnared, and in no case do they die the less for it. Nature hath left us the key of the churchyard, and custom hath brought cemeteries and charnel-houses into cities and churches, places most frequented, that we might not carry ourselves strangely in so certain, so expected, so ordinary, so unavoidable an accident. All reluctancy or unwillingness to obey the divine decree is but a snare to ourselves, and a load to our spirits, and is either an entire cause, or a great aggravation, of the calamity. . . . To be angry with God, to quarrel with the divine providence by repining against an unalterable, a natural, an easy sentence, is an argument of a huge folly, and the parent of a great trouble; a man is base and foolish to no purpose, he throws away advice to his own misery, and to no advantages of ease and pleasure. Fear keeps men in bondage all their life, saith St. Paul: and patience makes him his own man, and lord of his own interest and person. Therefore possess yourselves in patience, with reason and religion, and you shall die with ease.

—JEREMY TAYLOR, *Holy Dying*

OVERTURES TO DEATH

For us, born into a world
Of fledged, instinctive trees,
Of lengthening days, snowfall at Christmas
And sentried palaces,

You were the one our parents
Could not forget or forgive—
A remittance man, a very very
Distant relative.

We read your name in the family
Bible.   It was tabu
At meals and lessons, but in church sometimes
They seemed to be praying for you.

You lived overseas, we gathered:
And often lying safe
In bed we thought of you, hearing the indrawn
Breath of the outcast surf.

Later we heard them saying
You had done well in the War.
And, though you never came home to us,
We saw your name everywhere.

When home grew unsympathetic,
You were all the rage for a while—
The favourite uncle with the blank-cheque-book
And the understanding smile.

Some of us went to look for you
In aeroplanes and fast cars:
Some tried the hospitals, some took to vice,
Others consulted the stars.

But now, sir, that you may be going
To visit us any night,
We watch the french windows, picturing you
In rather a different light.

The house, we perceive, is shabby,
There's dry-rot in the wood:
It's a poor welcome and it won't keep you out
And we wish we had been good.

But there's no time now for spring-cleaning
Or mending the broken lock.

We are here in the shrouded drawing-room till
Your first, your final knock.

—C. DAY LEWIS

THAT TO PHILOSOPHIZE
IS TO LEARN HOW TO DIE

Cicero saith, that *to Philosophize is no other thing than for a man to prepare himself to death:* which is the reason that study and contemplation doth in some sort withdraw our soul from us, and severally employ it from the body, which is a kind of apprentisage and resemblance of death; or else it is, that all the wisdom and discourse of the world doth in the end resolve upon this point, to teach us not to fear to die.

. . . Now of all the benefits of virtue, the contempt of death is the chiefest, a mean that furnisheth our life with an ease-full tranquillity, and gives us a pure and amiable taste of it: without which every other voluptuousness is extinguished. Lo, here the reasons why all rules encounter and agree with this article. And albeit they all lead us with a common accord to despise grief, poverty, and other accidental crosses, to which man's life is subject, it is not with an equal care: as well because accidents are not of such a necessity, for most men pass their whole life without feeling any grief or sickness, as *Xenophilus* the Musician, who lived an hundred and six years in perfect and continual health: as also if the worst happen, death may at all times, and whensoever it shall please us, cut off all other inconveniences and crosses. But as for death, it is inevitable.

. . . By the common course of things, long since thou livest by extraordinary favour. Thou hast already over-past the ordinary terms of common life: And to prove it, remember but thy acquaintances and tell me how many more of them have died before they came to thy age, than have either attained or outgone the same:

yea and of those that through renown have ennobled their life, if thou but register them, I will lay a wager, I will find more that have died before they came to five and thirty years, than after. It is consonant with reason and piety, to take example by the humanity of *Jesus Christ,* who ended his human life at three and thirty years. The greatest man that ever was being no more than a man, I mean *Alexander* the great, ended his days, and died also of that age. How many several means and ways hath death to surprise us!

It is uncertain where death looks for us; let us expect her every where: the premeditation of death, is a forethinking of liberty. He who hath learned to die, hath unlearned to serve. There is no evil in life, for him that hath well conceived, how the privation of life is no evil. To know how to die, doth free us from all subjection and constraint.

Our religion hath had no surer human foundation than the contempt of life. Discourse of reason doth not only call and summon us unto it. For why should we fear to lose a thing, which being lost, cannot be moaned? but also, since we are threatened by so many kinds of death, there is no more inconvenience to fear them all, than to endure one: what matter is it when it cometh, since it is unavoidable? . . . *Aristotle* saith, there are certain little beasts alongst the river *Hyspanis* that live but one day; she which dies at 8 a clock in the morning, dies in her youth, and she that dies at 5 in the afternoon, dies in her decrepitude; who of us doth not laugh, when we shall see this short moment of continuance to be had in consideration of good or ill fortune?

Do not all things move as you do, or keep your course? Is there any thing grows not old together with your self? A thousand men, a thousand beasts, and a thousand other creatures die in the very instant that you die.

To what end recoil you from it, if you cannot go back? You have seen many who have found good in death, ending thereby many many miseries. But have you seen any that hath received hurt thereby? Therefore is it mere simplicity to condemn a thing you never proved, neither by your self nor any other. Why doest thou complain of me and of destiny? Do we offer thee any wrong? is it for thee to direct us, or for us to govern thee? Although thy age be not come to her period thy life is. A little man is a whole man as well as a great man. Neither men nor their lives are measured by the Ell. . . . Imagine truly how much an ever-during life would be less tolerable and more painful to a man, than is the life which I have given him: Had you not death, you would then incessantly curse, and cry out against me, that I had deprived you of it. I have of purpose and wittingly blended some bitterness amongst it, that so seeing the commodity of its use, I might hinder you from over-greedily embracing, or indiscreetly calling for it. To continue in this moderation, that is, neither to fly from life, nor to run to death (which I require of you) I have tempered both the one and other between sweetness and sourness. I first taught *Thales* the chiefest of your Sages and Wisemen, that to live and die were indifferent, which made him answer one very wisely, who asked him wherefore he died not; *Because,* said he, *it is indifferent. The water, the earth, the air, the fire, and other members of this my universe, are no more the instruments of thy life, than of thy death. Why fearest thou thy last day? He is no more guilty, and conferreth no more to thy death, than any of the others. It is not the last step that causeth weariness: it only declares it. All days march towards death, only the last comes to it.* Behold here the good precepts of our universal mother Nature. . . .

—MICHEL DE MONTAIGNE, *Essays* (JOHN FLORIO)

Let your desire be to see God; your fear, that you may lose Him; your sorrow, that you are not having fruition of Him; your joy, that He can bring you to Himself. Thus you will live in great peace.

—ST. TERESA OF AVILA, *Maxims of the Mother
Teresa of Jesus Written for Her Nuns*
(E. ALLISON PEERS)

MUSÉE DES BEAUX ARTS

About suffering they were never wrong,
The Old Masters: how well they understood
Its human position; how it takes place
While someone else is eating or opening a window or just walking
    dully along;
How, when the aged are reverently, passionately waiting
For the miraculous birth, there always must be
Children who did not specially want it to happen, skating
On a pond at the edge of the wood:
They never forgot
That even the dreadful martyrdom must run its course
Anyhow in a corner, some untidy spot
Where the dogs go on with their doggy life and the torturer's horse
Scratches its innocent behind on a tree.

In Brueghel's *Icarus,* for instance: how everything turns away
Quite leisurely from the disaster; the ploughman may
Have heard the splash, the forsaken cry,
But for him it was not an important failure; the sun shone
As it had to on the white legs disappearing into the green
Water; and the expensive delicate ship that must have seen
Something amazing, a boy falling out of the sky,
Had somewhere to get to and sailed calmly on.

                                —W. H. AUDEN

LIVE LIKE A NEIGHBOUR UNTO DEATH

    Think not thy time short in this world since the world itself is
not long. The created world is but a small parenthesis in eternity,
and a short interposition for a time between such a state of dura-

tion as was before it and may be after it. And if we should allow of the old tradition, that the world should last six thousand years, it could scarce have the name of old, since the first man lived near a sixth part thereof, and seven Methuselas would exceed its whole duration. However to palliate the shortness of our lives, and somewhat to compensate our brief term in this world, it's good to know as much as we can of it, and also so far as possibly in us lieth to hold such a theory of times past, as though we had seen the same. He who hath thus considered the world, as also how therein things long past have been answered by things present, how matters in one age have been acted over in another, and how there is nothing new under the sun may conceive himself in some manner to have lived from the beginning, and be as old as the world; and if he should still live on, 'twould be but the same thing.

Lastly, if length of days be thy portion, make it not thy expectation. Reckon not upon long life: think every day the last, and live always beyond thy account. He that so often surviveth his expectation lives many lives, and will scarce complain of the shortness of his days. Time past is gone like a Shadow; make times to come, present. Conceive that near which may be far off; approximate thy last times by present apprehensions of them: live like a neighbour unto Death, and think there is but little to come. And since there is something in us that will still live on, join both lives together; unite them in thy thoughts and actions, and live in one but for the other. He who thus ordereth the purposes of this Life will never be far from the next, and is in some manner already in it, by a happy conformity, and close apprehension of it. And if, as we have elsewhere declared, any have been so happy as personally to understand Christian annihilation, extasy, exolution, transformation, the kiss of the Spouse, and ingression into the Divine Shadow, according to mystical theology, they have already had an handsome anticipation of Heaven; the world is in a manner over, and the earth in ashes unto them.

—Sir Thomas Browne, *Christian Morals*

OF HUMAN PRESUMPTION

Among my thoughts I count it wonderful,
   How foolishness in man should be so rife
   That masterly he takes the world to wife
As though no end were set unto his rule:
In labour alway that his ease be full,
   As though there never were another life;
   Till Death throws all his order into strife,
And round his head his purposes doth pull.
And evermore one sees the other die,
   And sees how all conditions turn to change,
      Yet in no wise may the blind wretch be heal'd.
   I therefore say, that sin can even estrange
Man's very sight, and his heart satisfy
      To live as lives a sheep upon the field.
           —GUIDO GUINICELLI (D. G. ROSSETTI)

NOW, THIS BELL TOLLING SOFTLY FOR ANOTHER, SAYS TO ME, THOU MUST DIE

Perchance he for whom this bell tolls may be so ill as that he knows not it tolls for him; and perchance I may think myself so much better than I am, as that they who are about me, and see my state, may have caused it to toll for me, and I know not that. The Church is Catholic, universal, so are all her actions; all that she does belongs to all. When she baptizes a child, that action concerns me; for that child is thereby connected to that Head which is my Head too, and engrafted into that body, whereof I am a member. And when she buries a man, that action concerns me: All mankind is of one Author, and is one volume; when one man dies, one chapter is not torn out of the book, but translated into a better language; and every chapter must be so translated; God employs several translators; some pieces are translated by age, some by sickness, some by war, some by justice; but God's hand is in every translation; and his hand shall bind up all our scattered leaves again, for that Library where every book shall lie open to one another: As therefore the bell that rings to a sermon calls not upon the preacher only, but upon the congregation to come; so this bell calls us all. . . . No man is an island, entire of itself; every man is a piece of the continent, a part of the main; if a clod be washed away by the sea, Europe is the less, as well as if a promontory were, as well as if a manor of thy friends or of thine own were; any man's death diminishes me, because I am involved in Mankind; and therefore never send to know for whom the bell tolls; it tolls for thee.

—JOHN DONNE, *Devotions on Emergent Occasions*

4. Blessed Are They That Mourn

Keep yourselves therefore from murmuring, which profiteth nothing, and refrain your tongue from detraction, for an obscure speech shall not go for nought: and the mouth that belieth, killeth the soul. Seek not death in the error of your life, neither procure ye destruction by the works of your hands. For God made not death, neither hath he pleasure in the destruction of the living. For he created all things that they might be: and he made the nations of the earth for health: and there is no poison of destruction in them, nor kingdom of hell upon the earth. For justice is perpetual and immortal.

—Wisdom 1:11–15

Blessed are the poor in spirit: for theirs is the kingdom of heaven. Blessed are the meek: for they shall possess the land. Blessed are they that mourn: for they shall be comforted. Blessed are they that hunger and thirst after justice: for they shall have their fill. Blessed are the merciful: for they shall obtain mercy. Blessed are the clean of heart: for they shall see God. Blessed are the peacemakers: for they shall be called the children of God. Blessed are they that suffer persecution for justice' sake: for theirs is the kingdom of heaven. Blessed are ye when they shall revile you, and persecute you, and speak all that is evil against you, untruly, for my sake: Be glad and rejoice, for your reward is very great in heaven.

—St. Matthew 5:3–12

At times when you are sad and upset, do not abandon the good works of prayer and penance which you have been in the habit of doing. The devil will try to unsettle you and persuade you to abandon them, but rather than this you should do more of them than usual and you will see how quickly the Lord comes to your aid.

—St. Teresa of Avila, *Maxims of the Mother
Teresa of Jesus Written for Her Nuns*
(E. Allison Peers)

God never strikes but in love, nor takes away save to give again.
—Archbishop Fénelon, *Letters to Men*
(H. L. S. Lear)

After some great sorrow, God usually grants us happiness, as to Abraham He gave "Isaac the desired," which name signifies "laughter." After a while the Almighty plunged the patriarch into grief again, by commanding him to kill the son He had bestowed for his consolation: so does God often deprive His children of their happiness, bidding them sacrifice it and live in sadness. The Apostles felt perfectly safe and confident as they embarked with Christ in their boat; yet they were terrified when the storm arose which seemed likely to drown them, while He, on whose protection they depended, slept, and appeared to have forgotten them. But our Lord had not forgotten them: it was His command that stilled the tempest, and He was as watchful to deliver them as to place them in danger. Why then should you be troubled by the trials your Saviour sends you? Why should you dislike the medicine which comes from the hands of your tender Father? God gives you those sufferings here, to save you from those of eternity. He says of His vineyard: "I keep it night and day, there is no indignation in me against it" (Isaias 27:3, 4). Trust in God's judgment . . . and not in your own, since He understands what is best for you, and knows the present and future state of your soul. Do not weary yourself to death with anxiety, for, as the Gospel says: "You cannot with all your taking thought and caring add one cubit to your stature" (Matt. 6:27). Close your eyes to all that affrights you and trust in the Wounds of Christ, Who received them for your sake, and you will find rest.

Remember that on the eve of their deliverance, God's chosen people were afflicted more than they had ever been; burden after burden was laid upon their shoulders and they were cruelly scourged. So it is that after a night of tempest the day dawns brightest, and when the travail is over, the mother rejoices in the birth of her child. You must believe that your trials are the herald of great joy, for no soul deserves to possess peace and the delights of love until it has been wearied in combat and tasted the bitterness of spiritual desolation. Do not be disturbed if the time seems long in coming, for delay is not refusal especially when the promise has been given by Truth Himself. Your ears will surely one day hear the worlds: "Arise, make haste my love, and come, for winter is now past, the rain is over and gone, the flowers are appearing"— flowers instead of thorns, and your soul shall cast away its mournfulness and bring forth the fruit of love.

—BLESSED JOHN OF AVILA, *In Spiritual Desolation*

ON ANOTHER'S SORROW

Can I see another's woe,
And not be in sorrow too?
Can I see another's grief,
And not seek for kind relief?

Can I see a falling tear,
And not feel my sorrow's share?

Can a father see his child
Weep, nor be with sorrow filled?

Can a mother sit and hear
An infant groan, an infant fear?
No, no! never can it be!
Never, never can it be!

And can He who smiles on all
Hear the wren with sorrows small,
Hear the small bird's grief and care,
Hear the woes that infants bear—

And not sit beside the nest,
Pouring pity in their breast,
And not sit the cradle near,
Weeping tear on infant's tear?

And not sit both night and day,
Wiping all our tears away?
Oh no! never can it be!
Never, never can it be!

He doth give His joy to all:
He becomes an infant small,
He becomes a man of woe,
He doth feel the sorrow too.

Think not thou canst sigh a sigh,
And thy Maker is not by:
Think not thou canst weep a tear,
And thy Maker is not near.

Oh, He gives to us His joy
That our grief He may destroy:
Till our grief is fled and gone
He doth sit by us and moan

—William Blake

Ye good, distressed!
Ye noble few! who here unbending stand
Beneath life's pressure, yet bear up awhile,
And what your bounded view—which only saw
A little part—deemed evil, is no more:
The storms of wintry time will quickly pass,
And one unbounded Spring encircle all.

—JAMES THOMSON, *The Seasons* (*Winter*)

Those who die are, in respect of us, but as absent for a few years, it may be only months. Their seeming loss should tend to loosen our hold on the world, where we must lose everything, and draw us to that other world where we shall find all again.

—ARCHBISHOP FÉNELON, *Letters to Men*
(H. L. S. LEAR)

When the righteous dies 'tis earth that meets with loss. The jewel will ever be a jewel, but it has passed from the possession of its former owner. . . .

Life is a passing shadow, say the Scriptures. The shadow of a tower or a tree; the shadow which prevails for a time? No; even as the shadow of a bird in its flight, it passeth from our sight. . . .

Mourn for those who are left; mourn not for the one taken by God from earth. He has entered into the eternal rest, while we are bowed with sorrow.

—*The Talmud* (H. POLANO)

O my God, let me never forget that seasons of consolation are refreshments here, and nothing more; not our abiding state. They will not remain with us, except in heaven. Here they are only intended to prepare us for doing and suffering. I pray Thee, O my God, to give them to me from time to time. Shed over me the sweetness of Thy Presence, lest I faint by the way; lest I find religious service wearisome, through my exceeding infirmity, and give over prayer and meditation; lest I go about my daily work in a dry spirit, or am tempted to take pleasure in it for its own sake, and not for Thee. Give me Thy Divine consolations from time to time; but let me not rest in them. Let me use them for the purpose for which Thou givest them. Let me not think it grievous, let me not be downcast, if they go. Let them carry me forward to the thought and the desire of heaven.

—JOHN HENRY NEWMAN, *Meditations and Devotions*

ALL GRIEVOUS THINGS ARE TO BE ENDURED FOR THE SAKE OF ETERNAL LIFE

"My son, be not discouraged by the labours which thou hast undertaken for My sake, nor let tribulations ever wholly cast thee down; but let My promise strengthen and comfort thee under every circumstance. I am well able to reward thee, above all measure and degree. Thou shalt not long toil here, nor always be oppressed with griefs. Wait a little while, and thou shalt see a speedy end of thine evils. There will come an hour when all labour and trouble shall cease. Poor and brief is all that which passeth away with time. Do in earnest what thou doest; labour faithfully in My vineyard; I will be thy recompence. Write, read, chant, mourn, keep silence, pray, endure crosses manfully; life everlasting is worth all these conflicts, and greater than these. Peace shall come in one day which is known unto the Lord, and it shall be not day nor night (that is, of this present time), but unceasing light, infinite brightness, steadfast peace, and secure rest. Then thou shalt not say, 'Who shall deliver me from the body of this death?' nor cry, 'Woe is me, that my sojourning is prolonged!' for death shall be cast down headlong, and there shall be salvation which can never fail, no more anxiety, blessed joy, society sweet and noble. O if thou hadst seen the everlasting crowns of the Saints in Heaven, and with how great glory they now rejoice, who once were esteemed by the world as contemptible, and in a manner unworthy of life itself; truly thou wouldst forthwith humble thyself even to the earth, and wouldst rather seek to be under all, than to have command so much as over one. Neither wouldst thou long for this life's pleasant days, but rather wouldst rejoice to suffer affliction for God, and esteem it thy greatest gain to be reputed as nothing amongst men. O if thou hadst a relishing of these things, and didst suffer them to sink into the bottom of thy heart, how couldst thou dare so much as once to complain? Are not all painful labours to be endured for the sake of life eternal? It is no small matter, to lose or to gain the Kingdom of God. Lift up thy face therefore unto Heaven; behold, I and all My Saints with Me, who in this world had great conflicts, do now rejoice, are now comforted, now secure, now at rest, and shall remain with Me everlastingly in the Kingdom of My Father."

—Thomas a Kempis, *The Imitation of Christ*

HOW VERY PLEASING TO GOD IS THE WILLING DESIRE TO SUFFER FOR HIM

"Very pleasing to Me, dearest daughter, is the willing desire to bear every pain and fatigue, even unto death, for the salvation of souls, for the more the soul endures, the more she shows that she loves Me; loving Me she comes to know more of My truth, and the more she knows, the more pain and intolerable grief she feels at the offences committed against Me. Thou didst ask Me to sustain thee, and to punish the faults of others in thee, and thou didst not remark that thou wast really asking for love, light, and knowledge of the truth, since I have already told thee that, by the increase of love, grows grief and pain, wherefore he that grows in love grows in grief. Therefore, I say to you all, that you should ask, and it will be given you, for I deny nothing to him who asks of Me in truth. Consider that the love of divine charity is so closely joined in the soul with perfect patience, that neither can leave the soul without the other. For this reason (if the soul elect to love Me) she should elect to endure pains for Me in whatever mode or circumstance I may send them to her. Patience cannot be proved in any other way than by suffering, and patience is united with love as has been said. Therefore bear yourselves with manly courage, for, unless you do so, you will not prove yourselves to be spouses of My Truth, and faithful children, nor of the company of those who relish the taste of My honour, and the salvation of souls."

—St. Catherine of Siena, *A Treatise
of Divine Providence*

Suffering changes an earthly man into a heavenly man.

* * *

Suffering draws and forces men to God, whether they like it or not. He who is always cheerful in suffering, has for his servants joy and sorrow, friend and foe.

* * *

If suffering gave no pain, it could not be called suffering. There is nothing more painful than suffering, and nothing more joyful than to have suffered. Suffering is a short pain and a long joy. Suffering gives to the sufferer pain here and joy hereafter. Suffering kills suffering. Suffering is ordained that the sufferer may not suffer eternally.

* * *

Suffering is a safeguard against grievous falls; it makes a man know himself, rely on himself, and have faith in his neighbour.

Suffering keeps the soul humble and teaches patience. It is the guardian of purity, and confers the crown of eternal salvation. There is probably no man living but who derives good from suffering, whether he be in a state of sin, or on the eve of conversion, or in the fruition of grace, or on the summit of perfection; for it purges the soul as fire purges iron and purifies gold; it adorns the wrought jewel. Suffering takes away sin, lessens the fire of purgatory, expels temptation, consumes imperfections, and renovates the spirit.

* * *

Patience in suffering is a living sacrifice, it is a sweet smell of balsam before the divine face, it is an appealing wonder before the entire host of heaven. Never was a skilful knight in a tournament so gazed at as a man who suffers well is gazed at by all the heavenly court. All the saints are on the side of the suffering man; for, indeed, they have all partaken of it before him, and they call out to him with one voice that it contains no poison, but is a wholesome beverage. Patience in suffering is superior to raising the dead, or the performing of other miracles. It is a narrow way which leads direct to the gates of heaven. Suffering makes us companions of the martyrs, it carries honour with it, and leads to victory against every foe. Suffering clothes the soul in garments of rose colour, and in the brightness of purple; in suffering she wears the garland of red roses, and carries the sceptre of green palms. Suffering is for her as a shining ruby in a young maiden's necklace. Adorned with it, she sings with a sweet voice and a free heart a new song which not all the angelic choirs could ever sing, because they never knew suffering.

—BLESSED HENRY SUSO, *Eternal Wisdom*

The books of the Sacred Scripture contain much more than what is written in them. Our soul also has depths unknown to us. On the sacred pages and in our soul, there are melodies we do not hear. In the spaces of the world there are melodies which no one catches because no one listens. How I weep for this beauty which is lost to us! How I long for songs without words, sweet harmonies that could be ours and are not! There are echoes of songs that are as many songs. There are groans that no one hears, tears that no one sees or wipes away. There are tables at which no one sits. There are sanctuaries where no one prays. There is a nostalgia which no one shares. There are symphonies that no one hears, something resounding within us and smothered by us—words not written that nevertheless mean so much. There are words without echo, questions without answers.

Every word of the prophets, every saying of Christ, is full of celestial harmonies. We do not treasure what is so near us; perhaps the Lord's words and our souls have much to say to us, but we are distracted. Often we are near God and yet far from God. Near the Book and yet far off. From afar we perceive a Voice, a Divine Message, and we do not understand it. A Voice is calling us from afar and we cannot follow it. A ray of Light invites us and we do not see it.

It may be that the sadness which invades us and pervades our soul is due to all that we have lost before we ever possessed it. It is perhaps the regret of the best and highest part of our life that we have not lived. Perhaps we are now seeking what has died and has never been lived.

In the silence of solitary nights there is still a knock at the door of my soul. It is the Pilgrim whose call I had not understood. He ought to have been my Guest, Guest of my soul. Perhaps He has gone, I see Him no more.

The day is far spent. The hour of sunset is not far away. It comes. The harvest is miserable, the flowers to decorate the Lord's altar are few.

Will the Lord gather the tears not yet shed, the harmonies suspended in the air, the songs not yet sung? Will the Lord receive my soul's weeping?

I have nothing except what I have lost, except what I shall never have and what I regret. This regret and this weeping are the only thing that I could still, although unworthily, offer to my Lord. It is the better part of myself.

In the soul of each one of us Christ lives, Christ who is the way to God, the life of God, the truth of God. He lives in us and we deny Him. When I feel the burden of my life, when I am conscious of the immense nostalgia of tears not wept, of beauties which have perished unnoticed, I weep over Christ crucified by me and in me. My true self is not the ego that crucified Christ in me, but the "I" who weep and long for Him, who call upon Him, who long to be one with Him.

—EUGENIO ZOLLI, *Before the Dawn*

When from the world I shall be ta'en
And from earth's necessary pain,
Then let no blacks be worn for me,
Not in a ring, my dear, by thee.
But this bright diamond, let it be
Worn in remembrance of me.
And when it sparkles in your eye,
Think 'tis my shadow passeth by.
For why, more bright you shall me see,
Than that or any gem can be.
Dress not the house with sable weed,
As if there were some dismal deed
Acted to be when I am gone:
There is no cause for me to mourn.
And let no badge of herald be
The sign of my antiquity.
It was my glory I did spring
From heaven's eternal powerful King;
To his bright palace heir am I,
It is his promise, he'll not lie.

By my dear brother pray lay me,
It was a promise made by thee,
And now I must bid thee adieu,
For I am parting now from you.

—ANONYMOUS (1652)

. . . there is no such thing as feeling pity for death. Death causes no pain to the dead. The living may pity themselves, for what they have lost . . .

—PAUL-LOUIS LANDSBERG, *The Experience of Death*
(CYNTHIA ROWLAND)

When some one dies, the family group to which he belongs feels itself lessened and, to react against this loss, it assembles. A common misfortune has the same effects as the approach of a happy event: collective sentiments are renewed which then lead men to seek one another and to assemble together. We have even seen this need for concentration affirm itself with a particular energy: they embrace one another, put their arms round one another, and press as close as possible to one another. But the affective state in which the group then happens to be only reflects the circumstances through which it is passing. Not only do the relatives, who are affected the most directly, bring their own personal sorrow to the assembly, but the society exercises a moral pressure over its members, to put their sentiments in harmony with the situation. To allow them to remain indifferent to the blow which has fallen upon it and diminished it, would be equivalent to proclaiming that it does not hold the place in their hearts which is due it; it would be denying itself. A family which allows one of its members to die without being wept for shows by that very fact that it lacks moral unity and cohesion: it abdicates; it renounces its existence. An individual, in his turn, if he is strongly attached to the society of which he is a member, feels that he is morally held to participating in its sorrows and joys; not to be interested in them would be equivalent to breaking the bonds uniting him to the group; it would be renouncing all desire for it and contradicting himself.

—ÉMILE DURKHEIM, *The Elementary Forms of the Religious Life* (JOSEPH WARD SWAIN)

A Power is passing from the earth
To breathless Nature's dark abyss;
But when the great and good depart
What is it more than this—

That Man, who is from God sent forth,
Doth yet again to God return?—
Such ebb and flow must ever be,
Then wherefore should we mourn?

—WILLIAM WORDSWORTH: *Lines composed at Grasmere, the Author having just read in a Newspaper of the expected death of a friend.*

Our nature coveteth preservation from things hurtful. Hurtful things being present do breed heaviness, being future do cause fear. Our Saviour, to abate the one, speaketh thus unto his disciples, "Let not your hearts be troubled"; and to moderate the other, addeth, "Fear not." Grief and heaviness in the presence of sensible evils cannot but trouble the minds of men. It may therefore seem that Christ required a thing impossible. Be not troubled. Why, how could they choose? But we must note, this being natural and therefore simply not reprovable, is in us good or bad according to the causes for which we are grieved, or the measure of our grief. . . .

When Christ the life of the world was led unto cruel death, there followed a number of people and women, which women bewailed much his heavy case. It was natural compassion which caused them, where they saw undeserved miseries, there to pour forth unrestrained tears. Nor was this reproved. But in such readiness to lament where they less needed, their blindness in not discerning that for which they ought much rather to have mourned, this our Saviour a little toucheth, putting them in mind that the tears which were wasted for him might better have been spent upon themselves; "Daughters of Jerusalem, weep not for me, weep for yourselves and for your children." It is not, as the Stoics have imagined, a thing unseemly for a wise man to be touched with grief of mind; but to be sorrowful when we least should, and where we should lament there to laugh, this argueth our small wisdom. . . .

Now though the cause of our heaviness be just, yet may not our affections herein be yielded unto with too much indulgence and favour. The grief of compassion whereby we are touched with the feeling of other men's woes is of all other least dangerous. Yet this is a let unto sundry duties; by this we are [apt] to spare sometimes where we ought to strike. The grief which our own sufferings do bring, what temptations have not risen from it? . . . Whether we be therefore moved vainly with that which seemeth hurtful and is not; or have just cause of grief, being pressed indeed with those things which are grievous, our Saviour's lesson is, touching the one, Be not troubled, nor over-troubled for the other. For, though to have no feeling of that which merely concerneth us were stupidity, nevertheless, seeing that as the Author of our salvation was himself consecrated by affliction, so the way which we are to follow him by is not strewed with rushes, but set with thorns, be it never so hard to learn, we must learn to suffer with patience even that which seemeth almost impossible to be suffered; that in the hour when God shall call us unto our trial, and turn this honey of peace

and pleasure wherewith we swell into that gall and bitterness
which flesh doth shrink to taste of, nothing may cause us in the
troubles of our souls to storm and grudge and repine at God, but
every heart be enabled with divinely inspired courage to inculcate
unto itself, Be not troubled; and in those last and greatest conflicts
to remember it, that nothing may be so sharp and bitter to be
suffered, but that still we ourselves may give ourselves this encouragement, Even learn also patience, O my soul.

　　　　　—RICHARD HOOKER, *A Remedy Against Sorrow and*
　　　　　　　　　　　　Fear: Delivered in a Funeral Sermon

GRAVES OF INFANTS

Infants' gravemounds are steps of angels, where
　　Earth's brightest gems of innocence repose.
God is their parent, so they need no tear;
　　He takes them to his bosom from earth's woes—
　　A bud their lifetime and a flower their close.
Their spirits are the Iris of the skies,
　　Needing no prayer; a sunset's happy close.
Gone are the bright rays of their soft blue eyes;
Flow'rs weep in dew-drops o'er them, and the gale gently sighs.

Their lives were nothing but a sunny shower,
　　Melting on flowers as tears melt from the eye.
Each death
　　Was toll'd on flowers as summer gales went by:
　　They bow'd and trembled, yet they heaved no sigh;
And the sun smiled to show the end was well.
　　Infants have naught to weep for ere they die,
All prayers are needless, beads they need not tell;
White flowers their mourners are, Nature their passing bell.

　　　　　　　　　　　　　　　—JOHN CLARE

Hast thou lost a child? Thou hast angels, with whom thou shalt dance about the throne of God, and shalt be glad with everlasting joy. Set expected joys over against present griefs, and thus thou wilt preserve for thyself that calm and quiet of the soul whither the injunction of the Apostle calls us. Let not the brightness of human success fill thy soul with immoderate joy; let not grief bring low thy soul's high and lofty exaltation through sadness and anguish. Thou must be trained in the lessons of this life before thou canst live the calm and quiet life to come. Thou wilt achieve this without difficulty, if thou keep ever with thee the charge to rejoice always. Dismiss the worries of the flesh. Gather together the joys of the soul. Rise above the sensible perception of present things. Fix thy mind on the hope of things eternal. Of these the mere thought suffices to fill the soul with gladness, and to plant in our hearts the happiness of angels.

—ST. BASIL: *Homily IV, On The Giving of Thanks*

CONSOLATION IN
LOSS OF CHILDREN

... the deceased has removed into a better country, and bounded away to a happier inheritance; ... thou hast not lost thy son, but bestowed him henceforward in an inviolable spot. Say not then, I pray thee, I am no longer called "father," for why art thou no longer called so, when thy son abideth? For surely thou didst not part with thy child, nor lose thy son? Rather thou hast gotten him, and hast him in greater safety. Wherefore, no longer shalt thou be called "father" here only, but also in heaven; so that thou hast not lost the title "father," but hast gained it in a nobler sense; for henceforth thou shalt be called father not of a mortal child, but of an immortal; of a noble soldier; on duty continually within (the palace). For think not, because he is not present, that therefore he is lost; for had he been absent in a foreign land, the title of thy relationship had not gone from thee with his body. Do not then gaze on the countenance of what lieth there, for so thou dost but kindle afresh thy grief; but away with thy thought from him that lieth there, up to heaven. That is not thy child which is lying there, but he who hath flown away, and sprung aloft into boundless height. When then thou seest the eyes closed, the lips locked together, the body motionless, O be not these thy thoughts, "These lips no longer speak, these eyes no longer see, these feet no longer walk, but are all on their way to corruption!" O say not so: but say the reverse of this, "These lips shall speak better, and the eyes see greater things, and the feet shall mount upon the clouds; and this body which now rotteth away shall put on immortality, and I shall receive my son back more glorious. But if what thou seest distress thee, say to thyself the while, This is (only) clothing, and he has put it off to receive it back more precious; this is an house, and it is taken down to be restored in greater splendour. For like as we, when purposing to take houses down, allow not the inmates to stay, that they may escape the dust and noise; but causing them to remove a little while, when we have built up the tenement securely, admit them freely; so also doth God; Who taking down this His decaying tabernacle, hath received him the while into His paternal dwelling and unto Himself, that when it hath been taken down and built anew, He may then return it to him more glorious.

Say not then, "He is perished, and shall no more be"; for these be the words of unbelievers; but say, "He sleepeth, and will rise again," "He is gone a journey, and will return with the King." Who sayeth this? He that hath Christ speaking in him. *For,* saith he, *if we believe that Jesus died and rose again* and revived, *even so them also which sleep in Jesus will God bring with Him.* (Paul: I Thess. 4:14) If then thou seek thy son, there seek him, where the King is, where is the army of the Angels; not in the grave; not in the earth. . . .

—St. John Chrysostom, *Homily I, On the Second Epistle of St. Paul the Apostle to the Corinthians*

FOR A CHILD BORN DEAD

What ceremony can we fit
You into now? If you had come
Out of a warm and noisy room
To this, there'd be an opposite
For us to know you by. We could
Imagine you in lively mood

And then look at the other side,
The mood drawn out of you, the breath
Defeated by the power of death.
But we have never seen you stride
Ambitiously the world we know.
You could not come and yet you go.

But there is nothing now to mar
Your clear refusal of our world.
Not in our memories can we mould
You or distort your character.
Then all our consolation is
That grief can be as pure as this.

—Elizabeth Jennings

ON OUR ETERNAL HOPES

"Eye hath not seen, nor ear heard, neither hath it entered into the heart of man, what things God hath prepared for them that love him."   *I Cor. 2:9*

What a disproportion there is between what we endure here and what we hope for in heaven! The first Christians rejoiced without ceasing at the hope placed before them; for they believed that they saw the heavens opening to them. The cross, disgrace, punishment, the most cruel death could not discourage them. They trusted to that infinite goodness that would compensate them for all their sufferings. They were transported with joy at being counted worthy to suffer; while we, cowardly spirits, cannot endure, because we cannot hope; we are overwhelmed by the least sorrow, and often by those troubles that spring from our own pride, or imprudence, or effeminacy.

"They who sow in tears shall reap in joy." We must sow in order to reap. This life is the seed-time; we shall enjoy the fruits of our labors in another. Earthly-minded men, weak and impatient as they are, would reap before they have sowed.

We desire that God would please us, that he would smooth the way that leads to him. We are willing to serve him, if it does not cost us much. To hope for a great reward, and suffer but little for it, this is what our self-love proposes. Blind that we are, shall we never know that the kingdom of heaven must suffer violence, that it is only strong and courageous souls that shall be counted worthy of victory? Weep then, since blessed are they who mourn, for God shall wipe away all tears from their eyes.

—Archbishop Fénelon; *Reflections for Every Day
in the Month, Fifteenth Day.*

Say, if as we sit together, the Emperor were to send and invite some one of us to the palace, would it be right, I ask, to weep and mourn? Angels are present, commissioned from heaven and come from thence, sent from the King Himself to call their fellow servant, and say, dost thou weep? Knowest thou not what a mystery it is that is taking place, how awful, how dread, and worthy indeed of hymns and lauds? Wouldest thou learn, that thou mayest know, that this is no time for tears? For it is a very great mystery of the Wisdom of God. As if leaving her dwelling, the soul goes forth, speeding on her way to her own Lord, and dost thou mourn? Why then, thou shouldest do this on the birth of a child: for this in fact

is also a birth, and a better than that. For here she goes forth to a
very different light, is loosed as from a prison-house, comes off as
from a contest. . . . Say, what canst thou have to condemn in the
little child? Why dost thou mourn for it? What in the newly baptized? for he too is brought into the same condition: why dost thou
mourn for him? For as the sun arises clear and bright, so the soul,
leaving the body with a pure conscience, shines joyously. Not such
the spectacle of Emperor as he comes in state to take possession of
the city, not such the hush of awe, as when the soul having quitted
the body is departing in company with Angels. Think what the
soul must then be! in what amazement, what wonder, what delight!

—St. John Chrysostom, *Homily XXI*
On the Acts of the Apostles

The various rites of burial give us the inestimable comfort of feeling that we can still do something for them, of having at our dis-
posal ways of approaching their being.

—Paul-Louis Landsberg, *The Experience of Death*
(Cynthia Rowland)

THE RESPONSIBILITIES AND
PRIVILEGES OF MOURNERS

For signification of love towards them that are departed mourning is not denied to be a thing convenient. As in truth the Scripture
everywhere doth approve lamentation made unto this end. The
Jews by our Saviour's tears therefore, gathered in this case that his
love towards Lazarus was great. And that as mourning at such
times is fit, so likewise that there may be a kind of attire suitable
to a sorrowful affection and convenient for mourners to wear, how

plainly doth David's example show, who being in heaviness went up to the mount with his head covered and all the people that were with him in like sort? White garments being fit to use at marriage feasts and such other times of joy, whereunto Salomon alluding when he requireth continual cheerfulness of mind speaketh in this sort, "Let thy garments be always white"; what doth hinder the contrary from being now as convenient in grief as this heretofore in gladness hath been? "If there be no sorrow" they say "it is hypocritical to prevent it, and if there be to provoke it" by wearing such attire "is dangerous." Nay if there be, to show it is natural, and if there be not, yet the signs are meet to show what should be, especially sith it doth not come oftentimes to pass that men are fain to have their mourning gowns pulled off their backs for fear of killing themselves with sorrow that way nourished.

The honour generally due unto all men maketh a decent interring of them to be convenient even for very humanity's sake. And therefore so much as is mentioned in the burial of the widow's son, the carrying of him forth upon a bier and the accompanying of him to the earth, hath been used even amongst infidels, all men accounting it a very extreme destitution not to have at the least this honour done them. Some man's estate may require a great deal more according as the fashion of the country where he dieth doth afford. And unto this appertained the ancient use of the Jews to embalm the corpse with sweet odours, and to adorn the sepulchres of certain.

In regard of the quality of men it hath been judged fit to commend them unto the world at their death, amongst the heathen in funeral orations, amongst the Jews in sacred poems; and why not in funeral sermons also amongst Christians? Us it sufficeth that the known benefit hereof doth countervail millions of such inconveniences as are therein surmised, although they were not surmised only but found therein. The life and death of saints is precious in God's sight. Let it not seem odious in our eyes if both the one and the other be spoken of then especially, when the present occasion doth make men's minds the more capable of such speech. The care no doubt of the living both to live and to die well must needs be somewhat increased, when they know that their departure shall not be folded up in silence but the ears of many be made acquainted with it. Besides when they hear how mercifully God hath dealt with their brethren in their last need, besides the praise which they give to God and the joy which they have or should have by reason of their fellowship and communion with saints, is not their hope also much confirmed against the day of their own dissolution? Again the sound of these things doth not so pass the ears of them that are most loose and dissolute in life but it causeth them one time or other to wish, "O that I might die the death of the righteous and that my end might be like his!" Thus much peculiar good there doth grow at those times by speech concerning the dead, besides the benefit of public instruction common unto funeral with other sermons.

For the comfort of them whose minds are through natural affection pensive in such cases no man can justly mislike the custom which the Jews had to end their burials with funeral banquets, in reference whereunto the prophet Jeremy spake concerning the people whom God had appointed unto a grievous manner of destruction, saying that men should not "give them the cup of consolation to drink for their father or for their mother," because it should not be now with them as in peaceable times with others, who bringing their ancestors unto the grave with weeping eyes have notwithstanding means wherewith to be recomforted. "Give wine," said Salomon, "unto them that have grief of heart." Surely he that ministereth unto them comfortable speech doth much more than give them wine.

But the greatest thing of all other about this duty of Christian burial is an outward testification of the hope which we have touching the resurrection of the dead. For which purpose let any man of reasonable judgment examine, whether it be more convenient for a company of men as it were in a dumb show to bring a corpse to the place of burial, there to leave it covered with earth, and so end, or else to have the exequies devoutly performed with solemn recital of such lectures, psalms and prayers, as are purposely framed for the stirring up of men's minds unto a careful consideration of their estate both here and hereafter.

—RICHARD HOOKER, *Of the Laws of Ecclesiastical Polity,* V, 75

At every turn beautify it [the corpse]; in every move, remove it farther away; with the lapse of time return to the ordinary course of life. For the way (*Tao*) of death is thus; if it is not made beautiful, it becomes ugly; if it is ugly, there is no mourning; if it is near, it becomes wearisome; if wearisome, then it becomes distasteful; if distasteful, then it becomes neglected; if neglected, then it is not done reverently. Suppose on one morning I should lose both parents, and the mourners in the funeral should not mourn nor be respectful, then I should be loathed by the birds and beasts . . . the rites provide for beautiful adornment, but do not go so far as to be fascinating; they provide for coarse mourning clothes, but do not go so far as to be stingy and neglectful; they provide for music and contentment, but do not go so far as licentiousness or laziness; they provide for weeping and sorrow, but do not go so far as an undue degree of distress and self-injury.

—HSÜNTZE, *On the Rules of Proper Conduct*
(HOMER H. DUBS)

Humanity is accustomed to death. But no man is accustomed to death, to any death that touches him closely or even distantly, and even perhaps if it does not touch him. For there is a residue of mystery in death, a centre, an abyss, a revelation of mystery—and quite independent of whose death, be it your father or your mother —every man is gripped . . . the deafest hear, and the blindest see, and the closed are opened and even those who are armoured in insensibility bow their heads for a moment at a funeral.

—CHARLES PÉGUY, *Clio I* (ALEXANDER DRU)

THE BURIAL OF THE DEAD

Why hew the rocky tomb so deep,
   Why raise the monument so fair,
   Save that the form we cherish there
Is no dead thing, but laid to sleep?

This is the faithful ministry
   Of Christian men, who hold it true
   That all shall one day live anew
Who now in icy slumber lie.

       *   *   *

Take now, O earth, the load we bear,
   And cherish in thy gentle breast
   This mortal frame we lay to rest,
The poor remains that were so fair.

For they were once the soul's abode,
   That by God's breath created came;
   And in them, like a living flame,
Christ's precious gift of wisdom glowed.

Guard thou the body we have laid
   Within thy care, till He demand
   The creature fashioned by His hand
And after His own image made. . . .

       *   *   *

We trust the words our Saviour said
   When, victor o'er grim Death, he cried
   To him who suffered at His side
"In Mine own footsteps shalt thou tread."

See, open to the faithful soul,
   The shining paths of Paradise;
   Now may they to that garden rise
Which from mankind the Serpent stole.

Guide him, we pray, to that blest bourn,
   Who served Thee truly here below;
   May he the bliss of Eden know,
Who strayed in banishment forlorn.

But we will honour our dear dead
   With violets and garlands strown,
   And o'er the cold and graven stone
Shall fragrant odours still be shed.
                    —Prudentius (R. M. Pope and R. F. Davis)

. . . what shall we say of those who mourn out of pure love and tenderness? Blessed, a thousand times blessed are they! Their hearts melt within them, and (as the Scriptures tell us) seem to make their eyes a fountain of tears. But who shall tell me the cause of these tears? Who shall tell me? Those who have shed them, often cannot tell, cannot explain what it is that moves them, that stirs such passionate emotion. Sometimes it is the goodness of a Father; sometimes the condescension of a King; sometimes the absence of a Divine Bridegroom; sometimes the darkness left in the soul by His departure; and sometimes it is His tender voice when He draws near and calls His faithful spouse to Him: but, oftenest of all, it is—I know not what—something unspeakable.
        —Bishop Bossuet, *The Eight Beatitudes: The Mourners*
                                    (Rev. D. O'Mahony)

5. The Consummation of Life

A good name is better than precious ointments: and the day of death than the day of one's birth. It is better to go to the house of mourning, than to the house of feasting: for in that we are put in mind of the end of all, and the living thinketh what is to come. Anger is better than laughter: because by the sadness of the countenance the mind of the offender is corrected. The heart of the wise is where there is mourning, and the heart of fools where there is mirth. It is better to be rebuked by a wise man, than to be deceived by the flattery of fools.

—Ecclesiastes 7:2–6

Amen, amen I say to you, unless the grain of wheat falling into the ground die, itself remaineth alone. But if it die, it bringeth forth much fruit. He that loveth his life shall lose it, and he that hateth his life in this world, keepeth it unto life eternal.

—St. John 12:24–25

To him who is dead to self bodily death is but the consummation of the work of grace.

—ARCHBISHOP FÉNELON, *Letters to Men* (H. L. S. LEAR)

[Death] is the gateway of all knowledge. Men live and toil to discover knowledge and learning. They go as boys to school to learn all the world has to teach them. In their old age, when death comes, they are still learning. So slow is the amassing of our little knowledge. Then death comes, and suddenly they know all.

—BEDE JARRETT, O.P., *Holy Week*

It is so difficult to realize that all verification lies ahead, that death is the ultimate verification of life, that to live means to die. He who withdraws from life may think that he has avoided death; however, he has merely foregone life, and death, instead of being avoided, closes in from all sides and creeps into one's very heart, a petrified heart. If he is to be restored to life he must recognize the sovereignty of death.

He must direct his life to no other goal but death. Only then does life become simple, inasmuch as it no longer seeks to elude death, being willing to chant the dirge at any moment, while advancing in the face of death. He must know that at the end of the path of graves, a grave is already being prepared for him.

There is no remedy for death; not even health. A healthy man, however, has the strength to continue towards the grave. The sick man invokes death and lets himself be carried away in mortal fear. In health, even death comes at the "proper" time. Health is on good terms with Death. It knows that when the Grim Reaper comes he will remove his stone mask and catch the flickering torch from the anxious and weary and disappointed hands of Brother Life; it knows that he will dash it on the ground and extinguish it, but it also knows that only then the full brilliance of the nocturnal sky will brightly glow. It knows that it will be accepted into the open arms of Death. Life's eloquent lips are put to silence and the eternally Taciturn One will speak: "Do you finally recognize me? I am your brother."

—FRANZ ROSENZWEIG, *Understanding
the Sick and the Healthy*

Jesus came not to negate life but to give it more abundantly. Christianity is not a decadent worship of death for its own sake, but the discovery that including death within life is the secret of the fullest life. Even the extremest types of Christian other-worldliness, ascetic hermits and monks, have lived this truth. By giving up a part of the world before they died bodily, they placed death in the middle of life as an encouragement. They proved that death is an essential element of living, in fact its sharpest ingredient. But there are more forms of other-worldliness as well. Any father, manager, or teacher has to practice resignation and let the young learn by doing things he could do better himself; for he knows that one day he must die and they must take his place. The New Testament is full of such heroic resignation; Jesus voluntarily forewent saying many truths that the second or third generation needed to discover for themselves. All such acts from the beyond stem not from our instinct of life but from our wisdom of death. Man as an animal organism lives forward from birth toward death, but, as a soul who knows beforehand that he will die, he molds his life looking backward from its end.

—EUGEN ROSENSTOCK-HUESSY, *The Christian Future*

THE DEATH OF THE JUST

. . . the death of such souls is ever sweeter and gentler than was their whole life; for they die amid the delectable encounters and impulses of love, like the swan, which sings most sweetly when it is about to die and is at the point of death. For this reason David said: "Precious is the death of the just"; for at such a time the rivers of love of the soul are about to enter the sea, and they are so broad and dense and motionless that they seem to be seas already. The beginning and the end unite together to accompany the just man as he departs and goes forth to his kingdom, and praises are heard from the ends of the earth, which are the glory of the just man.

When, at that time, amid these glorious encounters, the soul feels itself very near to going forth in abundance to the perfect possession of its kingdom, since it sees itself to be pure and rich and prepared for this, God permits it in this state to see His beauty, and entrusts it with the gifts and virtues that He has given it, and all this turns into love and praise, since there is no leaven to corrupt the mass. And when it sees that it has only now to break the frail web of this human condition of natural life wherein it feels itself to be enmeshed and imprisoned, and its liberty to be impeded, it desires to be loosed and to see itself with Christ, and to burst these bonds of spirit and of flesh, which are of very different kinds, so that each may receive its deserts, the flesh remaining upon the earth and the spirit returning to God that gave it.

—St. John of the Cross, *Living Flame of Love*
(E. Allison Peers)

How miserable is the wisdom of mortal man! How uncertain is his foresight! Do Thou, Who foreseest all, provide the necessary means whereby my soul may serve Thee according to Thy will and not to its own. Punish me not by giving me what I wish or desire, if Thy love (and may it ever live in me!) desire not this. May this self of mine die, and may Another, greater than myself and better for me than myself, live in me, so that I may serve Him. May He live and give me life; may He reign and may I be His captive, for my soul desires no other freedom. How can one be free who is separated from the Most High? What harder or more miserable captivity is there than for the soul to have escaped from the hand of its Creator? Happy are they who find themselves laden with the strong fetters and chains of the gifts of God's mercy, so that they are unable to gain the power to set themselves free. Strong as death is love and hard as hell. Oh that one might die at the hands of love and be cast into this Divine hell, whence there is no hope of escape, or rather, no fear of finding oneself cast forth from it! But alas, Lord, for as long as this mortal life endures our eternal life is all the time in danger.

O life, that art the enemy of my welfare, would that one were permitted to end thee! I endure thee because God endures thee; I sustain thee because thou art His. Betray me not; be not ungrateful to me! And yet, Lord, alas, my exile is long; and time itself is short in exchange for Thine eternity; a single day, even an hour, is very long for one who knows not if he is offending Thee and fears lest he may do so. O free-will, thou art the slave of thine own freedom, unless thou be pierced through with fear and love for Him Who created thee! Oh, when will come that happy day in which thou shalt find thyself engulfed in that infinite ocean of supreme truth, wherein thou shalt not be free to sin, nor wish to be so, since thou shalt be secure from all misery, and made of one nature with the life of thy God!

God is happy, since He knows and loves and rejoices in Himself without the possibility of doing otherwise. He is not, nor can He be, free to forget Himself and to cease to love Himself, nor would it be perfection in Him were He to be so. Thou wilt not enter into thy rest, my soul, until thou becomest inwardly one with this Highest Good, knowing what He knows, loving what He loves and enjoying what He enjoys. Then shalt thou see the end of the mutability of thy will; then, then shall there be an end of mutability. For the grace of God will have wrought so much in thee that it will have made thee a partaker of His Divine nature, with such perfection that thou wilt neither desire nor be able to forget the Highest Good, nor cease to rejoice in Him and in His love.

Blessed are those whose names are written in the book of that life. But if thou art among them, my soul, why art thou sad and why dost thou trouble me? Hope in God, for even now I will confess to Him my sins and His mercies and of them all I will make a song of praise and will breathe perpetual sighs to my Saviour and my God. It may be that a day will come when my glory shall sing to Him and my conscience shall be no more afflicted, when at last all sighs and fears shall cease. But meanwhile, in silence and in hope shall my strength be. Rather would I live and die in the expectation and hope of eternal life than possess all created things and all the blessings which belong to them, since these must pass away. Forsake me not, Lord; since I hope in Thee, may my hope not be confounded; may I ever serve Thee; do with me what Thou wilt.

—St. Teresa of Avila, *Exclamations of the Soul to God*
(E. Allison Peers)

("Vivo sin vivir en mí . . .")

I live, yet no true life I know,
And, living thus expectantly,
I die because I do not die.

Since this new death-in-life I've known,
Estrang'd from self my life has been,
For now I live a life unseen:
The Lord has claim'd me as His own.
My heart I gave Him for His throne,
Whereon He wrote indelibly:
"I die because I do not die."

Within this prison-house divine,
Prison of life whereby I live,
My God Himself to me doth give,
And liberate this heart of mine.
And, as with love I yearn and pine,
With God my prisoner, I sigh:
"I die because I do not die."

How tedious is this life below,
This exile, with its griefs and pains,
This dungeon and these cruel chains
In which the soul is forced to go!
Straining to leave this life of woe,
With anguish sharp and deep I cry:
"*I die because I do not die.*"

How bitter our existence ere
We come at last the Lord to meet!
For, though the soul finds loving sweet,
The waiting-time is hard to bear.
Oh, from this leaden weight of care,
My God, relieve me speedily,
Who die because I do not die.

I only live because I know
That death's approach is very sure,
And hope is all the more secure
Since death and life together go.
O death, thou life-creator, lo!
I wait upon thee, come thou nigh:
I die because I do not die.

Consider, life, love's potency,
And cease to cause me grief and pain.
Reflect, I beg, that, thee to gain,
I first must lose thee utterly.
Then, death, come pleasantly to me.
Come softly: undismay'd am I
Who die because I do not die.

That life, with life beyond recall,
Is truly life for evermore:
Until this present life be o'er
We cannot savour life at all.

So, death, retreat not at my call,
For life through death I can descry
Who die because I do not die.

O life, what service can I pay
Unto my God Who lives in me
Save if I first abandon thee
That I may merit thee for aye?
I'd win thee dying day by day,
Such yearning for my Spouse have I,
Dying because I do not die.

       —St. Teresa of Avila (E. Allison Peers)

It is as natural to die as to be born; and to a little infant, perhaps, the one is as painful as the other. He that dies in an earnest pursuit is like one that is wounded in hot blood, who for the time scarce feels the hurt; and, therefore, a mind fixt and bent upon somewhat that is good, doth avert the sadness of death. But above all, believe it, the sweetest canticle is, *Nunc Dimittis,* when a man hath obtained worthy ends and expectations. Death hath this also; that it openeth the gate to good fame, and extinguisheth envy.

       —Francis Bacon, *Of Death*

We see how essential is the rôle of death in the Christian idea of progress. The death of the world gives progress its being and its justice; individual death is the enduring spur. We should examine closely the way in which this ending of progress determines its structure. Progress, as we see it, is not a process of regular accumulation, an automatism which would recall the Greek version of eternity, in the form of some sort of expansive immobility or mechanical fatality. Péguy considered that this automatic view of progress was a cosmic generalisation of bourgeois capitalism, with its mystique of savings. This is a clue to its very soul. Progress, for the Christian, is not an accumulation of possessions such as goods, power or comfort, but a journey towards perfection of being. If I die, it is because this possession requires the dispossession of all having, and death is dispossession itself.

—EMMANUEL MOUNIER, *Be Not Afraid*
(CYNTHIA ROWLAND)

Heaven is Glory, and heaven is Joy; we cannot tell which most; we cannot separate them; and this comfort is joy in the Holy Ghost. This makes all Job's states alike; as rich in the first chapter of his Book, where all is suddenly lost, as in the last, where all is abundantly restored. This consolation from the Holy Ghost makes my midnight noon, mine Executioner a Physician, a stake and pile of fagots, a bonfire of triumph; this consolation makes a satire, and slander, and libel against me, a panegyric, an elegy in my praise; it makes a *Tolle* an *Ave,* a *Voe* an *Euge,* a *Crucifige* an *Hosanna;* it makes my death-bed, a marriage-bed, and my passing-bell, an Epithalamion.

—JOHN DONNE, *Sermon XXXVI*

They are all gone into the world of light!
    And I alone sit ling'ring here;
Their very memory is fair and bright,
    And my sad thoughts doth clear.

It glows and glitters in my cloudy breast
    Like stars upon some gloomy grove,
Or those faint beams in which this hill is drest,
    After the Sun's remove.

I see them walking in an Air of glory,
　　Whose light doth trample on my days:
My days, which are at best but dull and hoary,
　　Mere glimering and decays.

O holy hope! and high humility,
　　High as the Heavens above!
These are your walks, and you have shew'd them me
　　To kindle my cold love.

Dear, beauteous death! the Jewel of the Just,
　　Shining nowhere, but in the dark;
What mysteries do lie beyond thy dust;
　　Could man outlook that mark!

He that hath found some fledg'd birds nest, may know
　　At first sight, if the bird be flown;
But what fair Well, or Grove he sings in now,
　　That is to him unknown.

And yet, as Angels in some brighter dreams
　　Call to the soul, when man doth sleep:
So some strange thoughts transcend our wonted themes,
　　And into glory peep.

If a star were confin'd into a tomb
　　Her captive flames must needs burn there;
But when the hand that lockt her up, gives room,
　　She'l shine through all the sphaere.

O Father of eternal life, and all
　　Created glories under thee!
Resume thy spirit from this world of thrall
　　Into true liberty.

Either disperse these mists, which blot and fill
　　My perspective (still) as they pass,

Or else remove me hence unto that hill,
    Where I shall need no glass.
                —HENRY VAUGHAN, *Silex Scintillans*

. . . One glimpse of glory on the saints bestow'd,
With eager longings fills the courts of God
For deeper views, in that abyss of light,
While mortals slumber here, content with night:
Though nought, we find, below the moon, can fill
The boundless cravings of the human will.
And yet, what fierce desire the fancy wings
To gain a grasp of perishable things;
Although one fleeting hour may scatter far
The fruit of many a year's corroding care;
Those spacious regions where our fancies roam,
Pain'd by the past, expecting ills to come,
In some dread moment, by the fates assign'd,
Shall pass away, nor leave a rack behind;
And Time's revolving wheels shall lose at last
The speed that spins the future and the past;
And, sovereign of an undisputed throne,
Awful eternity shall reign alone.
Then every darksome veil shall fleet away
That hides the prospects of eternal day:
Those cloud-born objects of our hopes and fears,
Whose air-drawn forms deluded memory bears
As of substantial things, away so fast
Shall fleet, that mortals, at their speed aghast,
Watching the change of all beneath the moon,
Shall ask, what once they were, and will be soon?
The time will come when every change shall cease,
This quick revolving wheel shall rest in peace:
No summer then shall glow, nor winter freeze;

Nothing shall be to come, and nothing past,
But an eternal now shall ever last.
Though time shall be no more, yet space shall give
A nobler theatre to love and live;
The wingèd courier then no more shall claim
The power to sink or raise the notes of Fame,
Or give its glories to the noontide ray:
True merit then, in everlasting day,
Shall shine for ever, as at first it shone
At once to God and man and angels known.
Happy are they who in this changing sphere
Already have begun the bright career
That reaches to the goal which, all in vain,
The Muse would blazon in her feeble strain:
    —PETRARCH, *The Triumph of Eternity* (HUGH BOYD)

Come, lovely and soothing Death,
Undulate round the world, serenely arriving, arriving,
In the day, in the night, to all, to each,
Sooner or later, delicate Death.

Praised be the fathomless universe
For life and joy, and for objects and knowledge curious;
And for love, sweet love—But praise! O praise and praise
For the sure-enwinding arms of cool-enfolding Death.
    —WALT WHITMAN, *When Lilacs
    Last in the Dooryard Bloomed*

ELEGY,

*Wrote in the Tower while confined with
the Princess Elizabeth, 1554.*

The life is long that lothsomely doth last,
   The doleful days draw slowly to their date,
The present pang, or painful plague, scarce past,
   But some new grief, still green, doth mar our state,
In all we find 'midst this world's storm and strife,
Sure death is sweet that shorteth such a life.

The pleasant years that some so swiftly run,
   The merry days to end so fast that fleet,
The riot-night which day draws on so soon,
   The happy hours which more do miss than meet,
Do all consume, like snow kiss'd by the sun,
And death soon ends all that vain life begun.

Death is a port whereby we pass to joy;
   Life is a lake that drowneth all in pain;
Death is so dear, it killeth all annoy;
   Life is so lewd that all it yields is vain;
For, as by life to bondage man was brought,
Even so by death all freedom too was wrought.

—JOHN HARRINGTON

Leave me, O Love, which reachest but to dust;
And thou, my mind, aspire to higher things;
Grow rich in that which never taketh rust;
Whatever fades, but fading pleasures brings.
Draw in thy beams, and humble all thy might
To that sweet yoke, where lasting freedoms be;
Which breaks the clouds, and opens forth the light
That doth both shine, and give us sight to see.
O take fast hold; let that light be thy guide
In this small course which birth draws out to death,
And think how evil becometh him to slide,

Who seeketh heav'n, and comes of heav'nly breath.
Then farewell, world; thy uttermost I see:
Eternal Love, maintain thy life in me.
—SIR PHILIP SIDNEY, *Astrophel and Stella*

Living the kingdom, bringing it back from the end of time and embodying some of it here and now, is the process by which man, ever since Jesus, consciously participates in his own creation. Man is initiated into his destiny. He has acquired partnership in God's deepest wisdom: when to let go, when to say farewell, when to end a chapter of evolution. In the flowering of the great pagan cultures he had shown himself a master of brilliantly creative beginnings; through Christianity he has become master of creative endings, of the termination of himself and all his enterprises. Able now to say *both* no and yes, to die in part and survive in part, he is made *whole* and enters the full freedom of the children of God.

He that would save his life shall lose it, and he who loses his life for Christ's sake shall find it: death has paradoxically become the key to everlasting life. By learning to anticipate the inevitable end which the pagan fights off, man has robbed death of its paralyzing doom.

—EUGEN ROSENSTOCK-HUESSY, *The Christian Future*

THAT THE HAPPINESS OF DYING IN HEAVENLY CHARITY IS A SPECIAL GIFT OF GOD

In fine, the heavenly King having brought the soul which he loves to the end of this life, he assists her also in her blessed departure, by which he draws her to the marriage-bed of eternal glory, which is the delicious fruit of holy perseverance. And then, dear Theotimus, this soul, wholly ravished with the love of her well-beloved, putting before her eyes the multitude of favours and succours wherewith she was prevented and helped while she was yet in her pilgrimage, incessantly kisses this sweet helping hand, which conducted, drew and supported her in the way; and confesses, that it is of this divine Saviour that she holds her felicity, seeing he has done for her all that the patriarch Jacob wished for his journey, when he had seen the ladder to heaven. O Lord, she then says, thou wast with me, and didst guide me in the way by which I came. Thou didst feed me with the bread of thy sacraments, thou didst clothe me with the wedding garment of charity, thou hast happily conducted me to this mansion of glory, which is thy house, O my eternal Father. Oh! what remains, O Lord, save that I should protest that thou art my God for ever and ever! Amen.

—St. Francis de Sales, *Treatise on the Love of God*
(Henry Benedict Mackey)

6. The Death of Death

He shall cast death down headlong for ever: and the Lord God shall wipe away tears from every face, and the reproach of his people he shall take away from off the whole earth: for the Lord hath spoken it. And they shall say in that day: Lo, this is our God, we have waited for him, and he will save us: this is the Lord, we have patiently waited for him, we shall rejoice and be joyful in his salvation.

—Isaias 24:8–9

I will deliver them out of the hand of death. I will redeem them from death: O death, I will be thy death; O hell, I will be thy bite. . . .

—Osee 13:14

For by a man came death, and by a man the resurrection of the dead. And as in Adam all die, so also in Christ all shall be made alive. But every one in his own order: the firstfruits, Christ: then they that are of Christ, who have believed in his coming. Afterwards the end, when he shall have delivered up the kingdom to God and the Father, when he shall have brought to nought all principality, and power, and virtue. For he must reign, until he hath put all his enemies under his feet. And the enemy death shall be destroyed last: For he hath put all things under his feet. And whereas he saith, All things are put under him; undoubtedly, he is excepted, who put all things under him. And when all things shall be subdued unto him, then the Son also himself shall be subject unto him that put all things under him, that God may be all in all.

—St. Paul I Corinthians 15:21–28

And when Jesus, the slayer of Death, came, and clothed Himself in a Body from the seed of Adam, and was crucified in His Body, and tasted death; and when (Death) perceived thereby that He had come down unto him, he was shaken from his place and was agitated when he saw Jesus; and he closed his gates and was not willing to receive Him. Then He burst his gates, and entered into him, and began to despoil all his possessions. But when the dead saw light in the darkness, they lifted up their heads from the bondage of death, and looked forth, and saw the splendor of the King Messiah. Then the powers of the darkness of Death sat in mourning, for he was degraded from his authority. Death tasted the medicine that was deadly to him, and his hands dropped down, and he learned that the dead shall live and escape from his sway. And when He had afflicted Death by the despoiling of his possessions, he wailed and cried aloud in bitterness and said, "Go forth from my realm and enter it not. Who then is this that comes in alive into my realm?" And while Death was crying out in terror (for he saw that his darkness was beginning to be done away, and some of the righteous who were sleeping arose to ascend with Him), then He made known to him that when He shall come in the fullness of time, He will bring forth all the prisoners from his power, and they shall go forth to see the light. . . .

So Jesus dead was the bringer to nought of Death; for through Him life is made to reign, and through Him Death is abolished, to whom it is said:—*O Death, where is thy victory?*

—Aphrahat, *Select Demonstrations:*
Of Death and the Latter Times

THE KILLING

That was the day they killed the Son of God
On a squat hill-top by Jerusalem.
Zion was bare, her children from their maze
Sucked through the gates. The very halt and blind
Had somehow got themselves up to the hill.

After the ceremonial preparation,
The scourging, nailing against the wood,
Erection of the main-trees with their burden,
While from the hill rose an orchestral wailing,
They were there at last, high up in the soft spring day.
We watched the writhings, heard the moanings, saw
The three heads turning on their separate axles
Like broken wheels left spinning. Round *his* head
Was loosely bound a crown of plaited thorn
That hurt at random, stinging temple and brow
As the pain swung into its envious circle.
In front the wreath was gathered in a knot
That as he gazed looked like the last stump left
Of a death-wounded deer's great antlers. Some
Who came to stare grew silent as they looked,
Indignant or sorry. But the hardened old
And the hard-hearted young, although at odds
From the first morning, cursed him with one curse,
Having prayed for a Rabbi or an armed Messiah
And found the Son of God. What use to them
Was a God or a Son of God? Of what avail
For purposes such as theirs? Beside the cross-foot,
Alone, four women stood and did not move
All day. The sun revolved, the shadow wheeled,
The evening fell. His head lay on his breast,

But in his breast they watched his heart move on
By itself alone, accomplishing its journey.
Their taunts grew louder, sharpened by the knowledge
That he was walking in the park of death,
Far from their rage. Yet all grew stale at last,
Spite, curiosity, envy, hate itself.
They waited only for death and death was slow
And came so quietly they scarce could mark it.
They were angry then with death and death's deceit.

I was a stranger, could not read these people
Or this outlandish deity. Did a God
Indeed in dying cross my life that day
By chance, he on his road and I on mine?

—EDWIN MUIR

Life was slain and rose again,
    In fairhead may we fare,
And death is brought till little or nought,
    And cast in endless care.
On him that thee bought, have all thy thought,
    And lead thee in his lare,
Give all thy heart till Christ thy quart,
    And love him evermare.

—RICHARD ROLLE

Death was struck with dismay on beholding a new visitant descending into Hades, not bound by the chains of that place. Wherefore, O ye porters of Hades, when ye saw Him, were ye scared?

What unwonted fear seized you? Death fled, and his flight betrayed his cowardice. The holy prophets ran unto Him, and Moses the Lawgiver, and Abraham, and Isaac, and Jacob; David also, and Samuel, and Isaias, and John the Baptist, who bore witness when he asked, *Art Thou He that should come, or do we look for another?* (Mt. 11:3) All the Just were ransomed, whom death had devoured; for it behoved the King who had been heralded, to become the redeemer of His noble heralds. Then each of the Just said, *O death, where is thy sting? O grave, where is thy victory?* (I Cor. 15:55) For the Conqueror hath redeemed us.

—St. Cyril of Jerusalem, *Catechetical Lectures,* XIV

. . . He took upon Him the flesh in which we have sinned that by wearing our flesh He might forgive sins; a flesh which He shares with us by wearing it, not by sinning in it. He blotted out through death the sentence of death, that by a new creation of our race in Himself He might sweep away the penalty appointed by the former Law. . . . For Scripture had foretold that He Who is God should die; that the victory and triumph of them that trust in Him lay in the fact that He, Who is immortal and cannot be overcome by death, was to die that mortals might gain eternity. . . .

In this calm assurance of safety did my soul gladly and hopefully take its rest, and feared so little the interruption of death, that death seemed only a name for eternal life. And the life of this present body was so far from seeming a burden or affliction that it was regarded as children regard their alphabet, sick men their draught, shipwrecked sailors their swim, young men the training for their profession, future commanders their first campaign; that is, as an endurable submission to present necessities, bearing the promise of a blissful immortality. . . .

—St. Hilary of Poitiers, *On the Trinity, Book I*

IN LOVE, TO LOVE, BY LOVE, FOR LOVE, AND OF LOVE

... this divine lover *died* amongst the flames and ardours of love, by reason of the infinite charity which he had towards us, and by the force and virtue of love: that is he died in love, by love, for love, and *of love,* for though his cruel torments were sufficient to have killed any one, yet could death never make entry into his life who keeps the keys of life and death, unless divine love, which handles those keys, had opened the gates to death, to let it ravage that divine body and despoil it of life. Love was not content to have only made him subject to death for us unless it made him dead. It was by choice, not by force of torment, that he died. *No man taketh my life away from me: but I lay it down of myself, and I have power to lay it down, and I have power to take it up again. He was offered,* says Isaias, *because it was his own will.* And therefore it is not said that his spirit went away, forsook him, or separated itself from him, but, contrariwise, that he gave up his spirit, breathed it out, yielded and commended it into the hands of his eternal Father; so that St. Athanasius remarks that he bowed his head to die, that he might consent to and bend to death's approach, which otherwise durst not have come near him; and crying out with a loud voice he gives up his spirit into his Father's hands, to show that as he had strength and breath enough not to die, so had he love so great that he could no longer live, but would by his death revive those who without it could never escape death, nor have the chance of true life. Wherefore our Saviour's death was a true sacrifice, and a sacrifice of holocaust, which himself offered to his Father for our redemption: for though the pains and dolours of his passion were so great and violent that any but he had died of them, yet had he never died of them unless he himself had pleased, and unless the fire of his infinite charity had consumed his life. He was then the sacrificer himself, who offered himself unto his Father and immolated himself, dying in love, to love, by love, for love, and of love.

—St. Francis de Sales, *Treatise on the Love of God*
(Henry Benedict Mackey)

THE SPARROW

I was returning from hunting, and walking along an avenue of the garden, my dog running in front of me.

Suddenly he took shorter steps, and began to steal along as though tracking game.

I looked along the avenue, and saw a young sparrow, with yellow about its beak and down on its head. It had fallen out of the nest (the wind was violently shaking the birch-trees in the avenue) and sat unable to move, helplessly flapping its half-grown wings.

My dog was slowly approaching it, when, suddenly darting down from a tree close by, an old dark-throated sparrow fell like a stone right before his nose, and all ruffled up, terrified, with despairing and pitiful cheeps, it flung itself twice towards the open jaws of shining teeth.

It sprang to save; it cast itself before its nestling . . . but all its tiny body was shaking with terror; its note was harsh and strange. Swooning with fear, it offered itself up!

What a huge monster must the dog have seemed to it! And yet it could not stay on its high branch out of danger. . . . A force stronger than its will flung it down.

My Trésor stood still, drew back. . . . Clearly he too recognised this force.

I hastened to call off the disconcerted dog, and went away, full of reverence.

Yes; do not laugh. I felt reverence for that tiny heroic bird, for its impulse of love.

Love, I thought, is stronger than death or the fear of death.
Only by it, by love, life holds together and advances.

—Ivan Turgenev, *Poems in Prose* (Constance Garnett)

A DIALOGUE-ANTHEM

CHRISTIAN. Alas, poor death! where is thy glory?
　　　　　　Where is thy famous force, thy ancient sting?
DEATH. Alas, poor mortal, void of story,
　　　　　　Go spell and read how I have kill'd thy King.
CHRISTIAN. Poor death! and who was hurt thereby?
　　　　　　Thy curse being laid on him makes thee accurst.
DEATH. Let losers talk, yet thou shalt die;
　　　　　　These arms shall crush thee.
CHRISTIAN.　　　　　　　Spare not, do thy worst.
　　　　　　I shall be one day better than before:
　　　　　　Thou so much worse, that thou shalt be no more.

—George Herbert

DEATH

Death, thou wast once an uncouth hideous thing,
　　　　Nothing but bones,
　　　The sad effect of sadder groans:
Thy mouth was open, but thou couldst not sing.

For we consider'd thee as at some six
　　　　Or ten years hence,
　　　After the loss of life and sense,
Flesh being turn'd to dust, and bones to sticks.

We lookt on this side of thee, shooting short;
Where we did find
The shells of fledge souls left behind,
Dry dust, which sheds no tears, but may extort.

But since our Saviour's death did put some blood
Into thy face;
Thou art grown fair and full of grace,
Much in request, much fought for, as a good.

For we do now behold thee gay and glad,
As at doomsday;
When souls shall wear their new array.
And all thy bones with beauty shall be clad.

Therefore we can go die as sleep, and trust
Half that we have
Unto an honest faithful grave;
Making our pillows either down, or dust.

—GEORGE HERBERT

MY BAPTISMAL BIRTH-DAY

God's child in Christ adopted,—Christ my all,—
What that earth boasts were not lost cheaply, rather
Than forfeit that blest name, by which I call
The Holy One, the Almighty God, my Father?—
Father! in Christ we live, and Christ in Thee—
Eternal Thou, and everlasting we.
The heir of heaven, henceforth I fear not death:
In Christ I live! in Christ I draw the breath
Of the true life!—Let then earth, sea, and sky
Make war against me! On my front I show
Their mighty master's seal. In vain they try
To end my life, that can but end its woe.—

Is that a death-bed where a Christian lies?—
Yes! but not his—'tis Death itself there dies.
                                    —SAMUEL TAYLOR COLERIDGE

THAT MOUNT CALVARY IS
THE ACADEMY OF LOVE

And at last, as our conclusion,—the death and passion of Our
Lord is the sweetest and most constraining motive that can animate
our hearts in this mortal life: and it is the very truth, that mystical
bees make their most excellent honey within the wounds of this
Lion of the tribe of Judah, slain, rent and torn upon the Mount
of Calvary. And the children of the cross glory in their admirable
problem, which the world understands not: Out of death, the eater
of all, has come forth the meat of our consolation; and out of
death, strong above all, has come forth the sweetness of the honey
of our love. O Jesus, my Saviour, how love-worthy is thy death,
since it is the sovereign effect of thy love!

So, in the glory of heaven above, next to the Divine goodness
known and considered in itself, Our Saviour's death shall most
powerfully ravish the blessed spirits in the loving of God. As a
sign whereof, in the Transfiguration, where we have a glimpse of
heaven, Moses and Elias talked with Our Saviour of the Excess
which he was to accomplish in Jerusalem. But of what excess, if
not of that excess of love by which life was forced from the lover,
to be bestowed on the well-beloved? So that in the eternal canticle
I imagine to myself that this joyous exclamation will be repeated
every moment:

Live, Jesus live, whose death doth prove,
The might supreme of heavenly love.

Theotimus, Mount Calvary is the mount of lovers. All love that
takes not its beginning from Our Saviour's Passion is frivolous and

dangerous. Unhappy is death without the love of the Saviour, unhappy is love without the death of the Saviour! Love and death are so mingled in the Passion of Our Saviour that we cannot have the one in our heart without the other. Upon Calvary one cannot have life without love, nor love without the death of Our Redeemer. But, except there, all is either eternal death or eternal love: and all Christian wisdom consists in choosing rightly. . . .

During this mortal life we must choose eternal love or eternal death, there is no middle choice.

O eternal love, my soul desires and makes choice of thee eternally! Ah! come, Holy Spirit and inflame our hearts with thy love! To love or to die! To die and to love! To die to all other love in order to live in Jesus's love, that we may not die eternally, but that, living in thy eternal love, O Saviour of our souls we may eternally sing: Vive Jésus! I love Jesus. Live Jesus whom I love! I love Jesus, who lives and reigns for ever and ever. Amen.

—St. Francis de Sales, *Treatise on the Love of God*
(Henry Benedict Mackey)

7. The Immortality of the Soul

But at that time shall Michael rise up, the great prince, who standeth for the children of thy people: and a time shall come such as never was from the time that nations began even until that time. And at that time shall thy people be saved, every one that shall be found written in the book. And many of those that sleep in the dust of the earth, shall awake: some unto life everlasting, and others unto reproach, to see it always. But they that are learned shall shine as the brightness of the firmament: and they that instruct many to justice, as stars for all eternity.

—Daniel 12:1–3

Behold, I tell you a mystery. We shall all indeed rise again: but we shall not all be changed. In a moment, in the twinkling of an eye, at the last trumpet: for the trumpet shall sound, and the dead shall rise again incorruptible: and we shall be changed. For this corruptible must put on incorruption; and this mortal must put on immortality. And when this mortal hath put on immortality, then shall come to pass the saying that is written: *Death is swallowed up in victory. O death, where is thy victory? O death, where is thy sting?* Now the sting of death is sin: and the power of sin is the law. But thanks be to God, who hath given us the victory through our Lord Jesus Christ. Therefore, my beloved brethren, be ye steadfast and unmoveable; always abounding in the work of the Lord, knowing that your labor is not in vain in the Lord.

—St. Paul I Corinthians 15:51–58

IMMORTALITY

... by way of preface I say that of all stupidities that is the most foolish, the basest, and the most pernicious, which believes that after this life there is no other; for if we turn over all the scriptures both of the philosophers and of the other sage writers, all agree in this, that within us there is a certain part that endures. And this we see is the earnest contention of Aristotle, in that *Of the Soul*, this is the earnest contention of all the Stoics, this the contention of Tully, especially in that booklet *Of Old Age;* this we see spoken according to the faith of the Gentiles; this the contention of every religion, Jews, Saracens, and Tartars, and all others who live according to any law. So that if all of them were deceived there would follow an impossibility which it would be horrible even to handle. Everyone is assured that human nature is the most perfect of all other natures here below; and this is denied of none; and Aristotle averreth it when he saith in the twelfth *Of the Animals* that man is the most perfect of all the animals. Whence, inasmuch as many living creatures are entirely mortal, as are the brute beasts; and are all, so long as they live, without this hope, to wit of another life; if our hope were vain the flaw in us would be greater than in any other animal; because there have been many ere now who have surrendered this life for the sake of that; and so it would follow that the most perfect animal, to wit man, was the most imperfect, which is impossible; and that part, to wit the reason, which is his chief perfection, would be the cause to him of having this greater flaw; which seemeth a strange thing indeed to aver. Further it would follow that nature had set this hope in the human mind in opposition to herself, since we have said that many have hastened to the death of the body, for to live in the other life; and this is also impossible.

Further we witness unbroken experience of our immortality in the divination of our dreams, which might not be if there were not some immortal part in us; inasmuch as the revealer, whether corporeal or incorporeal, must needs be immortal if we think it out subtly. . . .

And further we are assured of it by the most truthful teaching of Christ, which is the way, the truth and the light; the way, because in it we advance unimpeded to the blessedness of this very immortality; the truth, because it suffereth no error; the light, because it lighteth us in the darkness of earthly ignorance. This teaching, I say, assureth us above all other reasons; because he hath given it to us who seeth and measureth our immortality, the which we ourselves may not perfectly see, so long as our immortal part is mingled with our mortal part; but by faith we see it perfectly, and by reason we see it with a shadow of obscurity, which cometh about because of the mingling of the mortal with the immortal. And this should be the most potent argument that both the two exist in us; and so I believe, so aver, and so am assured, of the passage after this life to another better life. . . .

—DANTE, *Convivio,* Canto II, 9 (PHILIP H. WICKSTEED)

The world was made by God, that men might be born; again, men are born, that they may acknowledge God as a Father, in whom is wisdom; they acknowledge Him, that they may worship Him, in whom is justice; they worship Him, that they may receive the reward of immortality; they receive immortality, that they may serve God for ever.

—LACTANTIUS, *Epitome of the Divine Institutes, LXIX*
(REV. WILLIAM FLETCHER)

INTIMATIONS OF IMMORTALITY

The immortality of the soul is a thing which concerns us so potently and touches us so deeply, that a man who is indifferent to the knowledge of religion must be dead to all feeling. All our thoughts and actions should follow such different lines, according as there will be a hope of eternal blessings or no, that it is impossible to take any step with sense or judgment except with regard to the consideration of this point, which should be our ultimate object.

Thus our first interest and our first duty is to enlighten ourselves on the subject on which all our condition depends. And this is why, regarding the people who are not persuaded of it, I make a great difference between those who labour with all their might to instruct themselves concerning it, and those who live without troubling or thinking about the matter.

I can have nought but compassion for those who honestly bewail this doubt, who regard it as the last misfortune, and who, sparing nothing in order to be rid of it, make this research their principal and most serious occupation.

But as for those who pass their life without thinking of life's last end, and who, solely because they do not find in themselves the lights which persuade them of it, neglect to seek them elsewhere, and to examine thoroughly if this opinion is of those that the people receive through a credulous simplicity, or of those which, although obscure in themselves, have nevertheless a very solid and unshakable foundation,—I consider them in a wholly different manner.

This apathy in a matter which concerns themselves, their eternity, their all, irritates me more than it softens me; it surprises and affrights me; it is to me a monstrosity. I do not say this from the pious zeal of a spiritual devotion. On the contrary, I mean that one should have this feeling from a principle of human interest, and by the interest of self-love . . .

*   *   *

Nothing is so important to man as his condition; nothing is so fearful to him as eternity. And thus, if there are men indifferent to the loss of their existence and to the peril of an eternity of miseries, it is not at all natural. They are quite otherwise as regards other things: they fear even the slightest, they foresee them, they feel them: and the very man who passes so many days and nights in rage and despair at the loss of a post or at some imagined offence to his honour, is the same who without inquietude or emotion knows that he will lose all by death. It is a monstrous thing to see in the same heart, and at the same time, this sensibility to small things and this strange insensibility to the greatest things. It is an incomprehensible enchantment, and a supernatural lethargy . . .

*   *   *

. . . as for those who live without knowing Him and without seeking Him, they judge themselves so little worthy of their own care that they are not worthy of the care of others, and it is necessary to have all the charity of the religion they despise, in order not to despise them to the extent of abandoning them to their folly. But because this religion requires us always to consider them, as long as they are in this life, as capable of the grace which can enlighten them, and to believe that in a short time they may be fuller of grace than we are, and that we, on the other hand, may fall into the blindness in which they are, we must do for them that which we would have them do for us were we in their place, and call them to pity themselves and to take at least some steps to try if they cannot find light. Let them give to this reading some of the hours which they spend so uselessly elsewhere; whatever aversion they may have for it, it may be that they will light upon something, and at any rate they will not lose much. But for those who bring to it a perfect sincerity and a real desire to find the truth, I hope that they will have satisfaction, and that they will be convinced by the proofs of a religion so divine . . .

—BLAISE PASCAL, *Pensées* (G. B. RAWLINGS)

A belief not by any means confined to the more dogmatic adherents of religion is that there is a future non-material existence in store for us. Heaven is nowhere in space, but it is in time. (All the meaning of the belief is bound up with the word *future;* there is no comfort in an assurance of bliss in some *former* state of existence.) On the other hand the scientist declares that time and space are a single continuum, and the modern idea of a Heaven in time but not in space is in this respect more at variance with science than the pre-Copernican idea of a Heaven above our heads. The question I am now putting is not whether the theologian or the scientist is right, but which is trespassing on the domain of the other? Cannot theology dispose of the destinies of the human soul in a nonmaterial way without trespassing on the realm of science? Cannot science assert its conclusions as to the geometry of the space-time continuum without trespassing on the realm of theology?

—Sir Arthur Eddington, *The Nature of the*
Physical World

At the root of all being there is an act, the *affirmation of the self.* In each personality, aware of its uniqueness, we find the affirmation of this uniqueness, moving towards its realisation, an affirmation which implies the tendency to surpass the limits of time. Faith in a personal survival is not merely a comforting thought, it is above all the expression, the actual shape given to this ontological factor. Death considered as finality, physical death considered as the universal negation of our existence, is only the reflection of a despairing unbelief, a negation of the *person* by the *person.*

—Paul-Louis Landsberg, *The Experience of Death*
(Cynthia Rowland)

AN ACCLAMATION

Oh what is Man, great Maker of mankind,
That Thou to him so great respect dost bear,

That Thou adornst him with so bright a mind,
Mak'st him a king, and even an angel's peer!

Oh what a lively life, what heavenly power,
What spreading virtue, what a sparkling fire!
How great, how plentiful, how rich a dower
Dost Thou within this dying flesh inspire!

Thou leav'st Thy print in other works of Thine,
But Thy whole image Thou in Man hast writ;
There cannot be a creature more divine
Except, like Thee, it should be infinite.

But it exceeds Man's thought to think how high
God hath rais'd Man since God a Man became:
The angels do admire this mystery,
And are astonished when they view the same.

Nor hath He given these blessings for a day,
Nor made them on the body's life depend;
The Soul, though made in time, survives for aye,
And, though it hath beginning, sees no end.

Her only end is never-ending bliss,
Which is the eternal face of God to see
Who Last of Ends and First of Causes is:
And, to do this, she must eternal be.

How senseless then and dead a soul hath he
Which thinks his soul doth with his body die!
Or thinks not so, but so would have it be,
That he might sin with more security.

For though these light and vicious persons say
Our Soul is but a smoke or airy blast
Which during life doth in our nostrils play,
And when we die doth turn to wind at last:

Although they say "Come let us eat and drink:
Our life is but a spark which quickly dies!"
Though thus they say, they know not what to think,
But in their minds ten thousand doubts arise.

Therefore no heretics desire to spread
Their light opinions, like these Epicures:
For so the staggering thoughts are comforted,
And other men's assent their doubt assures.

Yet though these men against their conscience strive,
There are some sparkles in their flinty breasts
Which cannot be extinct, but still revive,
That though they would, they cannot quite, be beasts.

But whoso makes a mirror of his mind,
And doth with patience view himself therein,
His Soul's eternity shall clearly find,
Though the other beauties be defaced with sin.

—SIR JOHN DAVIES, *Nosce Teipsum*

THE IMMORTALITY OF MAN

. . . A scientist risks his life for a new discovery in the realm of matter, a pioneer to establish a new settlement, an aviator to improve our means of communication, a miner to extract coal from the earth, a pearl fisher to filch from the ocean an ornament for the beauty of some unknown woman, a traveler to contemplate new landscapes, a mountain climber to conquer a bit of earth. What comparison is there between the result to be obtained, be it momentous or slight, and the price of human life which is thus wagered, the value of that being, full of promise, endowed with so many gifts and whom many hearts may love? Well, at each corner of human activity death lies in ambush. Every day we trust our lives and those of our beloved to the unknown driver of a subway train, of a plane, of a bus or a taxi. Where there is no risk, there is no life. A wisdom or a civilization based on the avoidance of risk, by virtue of a misinterpretation of the value of the human being, would run the greatest of all risks, that of cowardice and of deadly stupidity. That perpetual risk which man takes is the very condition of his life. That squandering of the human being is a law of nature; it is also the proof of the confidence, the trust and the elementary love we give every day to the divine principle from which we proceed, the very law of which is superabundance and generosity.

Now we face a paradox: on the one hand nothing in the world is more precious than one single human person; on the other hand nothing in the world is more squandered, more exposed to all kinds of dangers, than the human being—and this condition must be. What is the meaning of this paradox? It is perfectly clear. We have here a sign that man knows very well that death is not an end, but a beginning. He knows very well, in the secret depths of his own being, that he can run all risks, spend his life and scatter his possessions here below, because he is immortal. The chant of the Christian liturgy before the body of the deceased is significant: Life is changed, life is not taken away.

—JACQUES MARITAIN (The Garvin Lecture for 1941)

SONG

Love lives beyond the tomb
And earth, which fades like dew;
   I love the fond,
The faithful, and the true.

   Love lives in sleep:
'Tis happiness of healthy dreams;
   Eve's dews may weep,
But love delightful seems.

'Tis seen in flowers,
And in the morning's pearly dew;
  In earth's green bowers,
And in the heaven's eternal blue.

'Tis heard in Spring;
When light and sunbeams, warm and kind,
  On angel's wing
Bring love and music to the mind.

And where's the voice
So young, so beautiful, and sweet,
  As Nature's choice
Where Spring and lovers meet?

Love lives beyond the tomb
And earth, which fades like dew:
  I love the fond,
The faithful, and the true.

—JOHN CLARE

It is very difficult for us to take stock of the fact that the localization of the personality, of the conscious mind, inside the body is only symbolic, just an aid for practical use. Let us, with all the knowledge we have about it, follow such a "tender look" inside the body. We do hit there on a supremely interesting bustle or, if you like, machinery. We find millions of cells of very specialized build in an arrangement that is unsurveyably intricate but quite obviously serves a very far-reaching and highly consummate mutual communication and collaboration; a ceaseless hammering of regular electrochemical pulses which, however, change rapidly in their configuration, being conducted from nerve-cell to nerve-cell, tens of thousands of contacts being opened and blocked within every split second, chemical transformations being induced and

maybe other changes as yet undiscovered. All this we meet and, as
the science of physiology advances, we may trust that we shall come
to know more and more about it. But now let us assume that in a
particular case you eventually observe several efferent bundles of
pulsating currents, which issue from the brain and through long
cellular protrusions (motor nerve-fibres), are conducted to certain
muscles of the arm, which, as a consequence, tends a hesitating,
trembling hand to you to bid you farewell—for a long, heart-
rending separation; at the same time you may find that some other
pulsating bundles produce a certain glandular secretion so as to
veil the poor sad eye with a crape of tears. But nowhere along this
way from the eye through the central organ to the arm muscles
and the tear glands—nowhere, you may be sure, however far
physiology advances, will you ever meet the personality, will you
ever meet the dire pain, the bewildered worry within this soul,
though their reality is to you so certain as though you suffered
them yourself—as in actual fact you do! The picture that physio-
logical analysis vouchsafes to us of any other human being, be it
our most intimate friend, strikingly recalls to me Edgar Allan
Poe's masterly story, which I am sure many a reader remembers
well; I mean *The Masque of the Red Death.* A princeling and his
retinue have withdrawn to an isolated castle to escape the pestilence of the red death that rages in the land. After a week or so of
retirement they arrange a great dancing feast in fancy dress and
mask. One of the masks, tall, entirely veiled, clad all in red and
obviously intended to represent the pestilence allegorically, makes
everybody shudder, both for the wantonness of the choice and for
the suspicion that it might be an intruder. At last a bold young
man approaches the red mask and with a sudden jolt tears off the
veil and head-gear. It is found empty.

Now our skulls are not empty. But what we find there, in spite
of the keen interest it arouses, is truly nothing when held against
the life and the emotions of the soul.

To become aware of this may in the first moment upset one. To
me it seems, on deeper thought, rather a consolation. If you have

to face the body of a deceased friend whom you sorely miss, is it not soothing to realize that this body was never really the seat of his personality but only symbolically "for practical reference"?

—ERWIN SCHRÖDINGER, *Mind and Matter*

We cannot blow hot and cold with the same breath. If we would retain personal identity at all, we must continue it beyond what we call death; in which case death ceases to be what we have hitherto thought it, that is to say, the end of our being. We cannot have both personal identity and death too.

—SAMUEL BUTLER, *Notebooks*

AN ARGUMENT FOR
THE IMMORTALITY OF THE SOUL

The object of a will that is capable of being determined by the moral law, is the production in the world of the highest good. Now, the supreme condition of the highest good is the perfect harmony of the disposition with the moral law. Such a harmony must be possible, not less than the object of the will, for it is implied in the command to promote that object. Perfect harmony of the will with the moral law is *holiness,* a perfection of which no rational being existing in the world of sense is capable at any moment of his life. Yet holiness is demanded as practically necessary, and it can be found only in an infinite progress toward perfect harmony with the moral law. Pure practical reason therefore forces us to assume such a practical progress towards perfection as the real object of our will.

Now, this infinite progress is possible only if we presuppose that the existence of a rational being is prolonged to infinity, and that he retains his personality for all time. This is what we mean by the immortality of the soul. The highest good is therefore practically possible, only if we presuppose the immortality of the soul. Thus immortality is inseparably bound up with the moral law. It is a *postulate* of pure practical reason, that is, a proposition that cannot be proved *theoretically*, but depends upon an *a priori practical* law of unconditioned validity.

A finite rational being is capable only of an infinite progress from lower to higher stages of moral perfection. The Infinite Being, who is free from the limits of time, sees in this series, which for us has no end, a whole that is in harmony with the moral law. Holiness He demands inexorably as a duty in order to assign to everyone his exact share in the highest good; and this holiness lies completely before Him in a single intellectual perception of rational beings. Created beings can hope to share in the highest good only in so far as they are conscious of having stood the test of the moral law. If in the past they have advanced from lower to higher degrees of morality, and have thus proved the strength of their resolution, they may hope to make unbroken progress in the future as long as they live here, and even beyond the present life. They can never hope in this life, or, indeed, at any imaginable point of time in the future life, to be in perfect harmony with the will of God, but they may hope for this harmony in the infinite duration of their existence as it is surveyed by God alone.

—IMMANUEL KANT, *The Critique of Practical Reason*
(JOHN WATSON)

THE THREE POWERS
OF THE SOUL

The first life in the mother's womb is spent,
Where she her nursing power doth only use;
Where, when she finds defect of nourishment,
She expels her body, and this world she views.

This we call *birth;* but if the child could speak
He *death* would call it, and of Nature plain
That she would thrust him out naked and weak
And in his passage pinch him with such pain.

Yet, out he comes, and in this world is placed
Where all his senses in perfection be,
Where he finds flowers to smell, and fruits to taste,
And sounds to hear and sundry forms to see.

When he hath past some time upon this stage,
His Reason then a little seems to wake,
Which, though she spring, when sense doth fade with age,
Yet can she here no perfect practice make.

Then doth the aspiring Soul the body leave:
Which we call death, but, were it known to all
What life our souls do by this death receive,
Men would it birth or jail-delivery call.

In this third life, Reason will be so bright
As that her spark will like the sunbeams shine,
And shall of God enjoy the real sight,
Being still increast by influence divine.

—SIR JOHN DAVIES, *Nosce Teipsum*

... The iniquity of oblivion blindly scattereth her poppy, and deals with the memory of men without distinction to merit of perpetuity. Who can but pity the founder of the pyramids? ... In vain we compute our felicities by the advantage of our good names, since bad have equal durations, and Thersites is like to live as long as Agamemnon. Who knows whether the best of men be known, or whether there be not more remarkable persons forgot, than any that stand remembered in the known account of time? Without the favor of the everlasting register, the first man had been as unknown as the last, and Methuselah's long life had been his only chronicle.

Oblivion is not to be hired. The greater part must be content to be as though they had not been, to be found in the register of God, not in the record of man. . . .

In vain do individuals hope for immortality, or any patent from oblivion, in preservations below the moon; men have been deceived even in their flatteries above the sun, and studied conceits to perpetuate their names. . . .

There is nothing strictly immortal, but immortality. Whatever hath no beginning may be confident of no end (all others have a dependent being and within the reach of destruction); which is the peculiarity of that necessary Essence that cannot destroy itself; and the highest strain of omnipotency, to be so powerfully constituted as not to suffer even from the power of itself. But the sufficiency of Christian immortality frustrates all earthly glory, and the quality of either state after death makes a folly of posthumous memory. . . .

To subsist in lasting monuments, to live in their productions, to exist in their names and predicament of chimeras, was large satisfaction unto old expectations, and made one part of their Elysiums. But all this is nothing in the metaphysics of true belief. To live indeed, is to be again ourselves, which being not only an hope, but an evidence in noble believers, 'tis all one to lie in St. Innocents' church-yard as in the sands of Egypt. Ready to be anything, in the ecstasy of being ever, and as content with six foot as the moles of Adrianus.

—Sir Thomas Browne, *Urn-Burial*

How uncertain is fame! how slippery! Many have promised immortality to themselves, and have not been able to retain fame for their lifetime, as e.g. Apion, the grammarian, who, as we read in

Pliny, said, That he had endowed with immortality those to whom he had addressed some of his works, yet of his own books, not even a single letter is extant. Nay, also, how unfortunate is the fame of those who have done deserving work! The works of Ovid remain, but not those of Chrysippus or Crantor. The works of Vincent of Beauvais have come to us complete; but not so those of Titus Livius, not those of Polybius, not those of Marcus Varro, not even those of Marcus Tullius Cicero! As Martial not inaptly said, "If a book is going to have a long life, it must have a [protecting] genius." We must add, how changeful a book's fame is! The same book seems beautiful at one time and in certain places, and at another time and in other places, detestable. Many splendid discoveries become obscure by the natural powers and diligence of posterity, so that the later books block up by their size many of the earlier books, just as lights are darkened by the heights of surrounding buildings. But, put the case that you have obtained renown, praise, glory; what good will it be to you when you come to die? For then you will perceive none of these things, which are happening here, no more than the horse, when he is proclaimed victor in the Olympian games, or the picture of Apelles, which we study closely with admiration. What is all the renown of his name, to Cicero? or to Aristotle? So with others, how does their glory now affect them though they were once illustrious in arms or in letters? Or in life itself, if out of public view, what glory does a man feel? What glory affects him when he is asleep? If you are present when you are praised then it necessarily follows that those who praise you to your face, are vain; or else that you willingly listen to words of praise said in your presence. What can in that case be said with propriety? O learned, O eloquent man (nay, rather, O light and empty-minded man!),—not even if you consider a slight meed of praise the due reward of your literary labour. But if you take no note of the praise of men, and desire to obey faithfully your own conscience, and through it, to serve God, how much more lasting and solid glory will be yours, if the living God praises you in your life, if the Ever-Present praises the man before Him; the Immortal

God, the mortal man. He who ever looks on thee, He who will pronounce no false judgment, but who will judge you from your own evidence! "Not he that commendeth himself is approved," says Paul, "but whom the Lord commendeth."

A learned man must often reflect on the migration of our temporal life, and on the eternal life, and by meditating often and deeply, make the thought of death familiar, so as not to be terrified by the mention of it. Then will come into his mind, that Judge, the Rewarder of his actions, one by one, before Whom, in a short time, he must appear, when he has left the stage and the hypocrisy of life. To be approved of God will then become the sole aim of his life. For to whom else would the accused person or the patron desire to vindicate himself, if he were wise, but to his Judge?

—JUAN LUIS VIVES, *The Transmission of Knowledge*
(FOSTER WATSON)

Were there not another life that I hope for, all the vanities of this World should not entreat a moment's breath from me: could the Devil work my belief to imagine I could never die, I would not outlive that very thought. I have so abject a conceit of this common way of existence, this retaining to the sun and elements, I cannot think this is to be a man, or to live according to the dignity of humanity. In expectation of a better, I can with patience embrace this life, yet in my best meditations do often defy death; I honour any man that contemns it, nor can I highly love any that is afraid of it: this makes me naturally love a soldier, and honour those tattered and contemptible regiments that will die at the command of a sergeant. For a pagan there may be some motives to be in love with life; but for a Christian to be amazed at death, I see not how he can escape this dilemma, that he is too sensible of this life, or hopeless of the life to come.

—SIR THOMAS BROWNE, *Religio Medici*

THAT IMMORTALITY IS
THE CHIEF GOOD

What, then, will be the advantage of justice and virtue, if they shall have nothing but evil in life? But if virtue, which despises all earthly goods, most wisely endures all evils, and endures death itself in the discharge of duty, cannot be without a reward, what remains but that immortality alone is its reward? For if a happy life falls to the lot of man, as the philosophers will have it, and in this point alone they do not disagree, therefore also immortality falls to him. For that only is happy which is incorruptible; that only is incorruptible which is eternal. Therefore immortality is the chief good, because it belongs both to man, and to the soul, and to virtue. We are only directed to this; we are born to the attainment of this. Therefore God proposes to us virtue and justice, that we may obtain that eternal reward for our labours.

*   *   *

Therefore God is to be worshipped, that by means of religion, which is also justice, man may receive from God immortality, nor is there any other reward of a pious mind; and if this is invisible, it cannot be presented by the invisible God with any reward but that which is invisible.

—LACTANTIUS, *Epitome of The Divine Institutes,* XXXV
(WILLIAM FLETCHER)

THE PARADOX

Our death implicit in our birth,
We cease, or cannot be;
And know when we are laid in earth
We perish utterly.

And equally the spirit knows
The indomitable sense
Of immortality, which goes
Against all evidence.

See faith alone, whose hand unlocks
All mystery at a touch,
Embrace the awful Paradox
Nor wonder overmuch.

—RUTH PITTER

8. Eternal Life

The earth is the Lord's and the fulness thereof: the world, and all they that dwell therein. For he hath founded it upon the seas; and hath prepared it upon the rivers. Who shall ascend into the mountain of the Lord: or who shall stand in his holy place? The innocent in hands, and clean of heart, who hath not taken his soul in vain, nor sworn deceitfully to his neighbour. He shall receive a blessing from the Lord, and mercy from God his saviour. This is the generation of them that seek him, of them that seek the face of the God of Jacob. Lift up your gates, O ye princes, and be ye lifted up, O eternal gates: and the King of Glory shall enter in. Who is this King of Glory? the Lord who is strong and mighty: the Lord mighty in battle. Lift up your gates, O ye princes, and be ye lifted up, O eternal gates: and the King of Glory shall enter in. Who is this King of Glory? the Lord of hosts, he is the King of Glory.

—Psalm 23

And behold a certain lawyer stood up, tempting him, and saying, Master, what must I do to possess eternal life? But he said to him: What is written in the law? how readest thou? He answering, said: Thou shalt love the Lord thy God with thy whole heart, and with thy whole soul, and with all thy strength, and with all thy mind: and thy neighbour as thyself.

—St. Luke 10:25–27

"The present life of man, O king, seems to me, in comparison of that time which is unknown to us, like to the swift flight of a sparrow through the room wherein you sit at supper in winter, with your commanders and ministers, and a good fire in the midst, whilst the storms of rain and snow prevail abroad; the sparrow, I say, flying in at one door, and immediately out at another, whilst he is within, is safe from the wintry storm; but after a short space of fair weather, he immediately vanishes out of your sight, into the dark winter from which he had emerged. So this life of man appears for a short space, but of what went before, or what is to follow, we are utterly ignorant. If, therefore, this new doctrine contains something more certain, it seems justly to deserve to be followed."

—Courtier to King Edwin, in BEDE's
Ecclesiastical History of the English Nation
(J. STEVENS)

I have learned
To look on nature, not as in the hour
Of thoughtless youth; but hearing oftentimes
The still, sad music of humanity,
Nor harsh nor grating, though of ample power
To chasten and subdue. And I have felt
A presence that disturbs me with the joy
Of elevated thoughts; a sense sublime
Of something far more deeply interfused,
Whose dwelling is the light of setting suns,
And the round ocean and the living air,
And the blue sky, and in the mind of man:
A motion and a spirit, that impels
All thinking things, all objects of all thought,
And rolls through all things. Therefore am I still
A lover of the meadows and the woods,

And mountains; and of all that we behold
From this green earth; of all the mighty world
Of eye, and ear,—both what they half create,
And what perceive; well pleased to recognise
In nature and the language of the sense
The anchor of my purest thoughts, the nurse,
The guide, the guardian of my heart, and soul
Of all my moral being.
　　　　—WILLIAM WORDSWORTH, *Lines Written*
　　　　　　a Few Miles Above Tintern Abbey

ANNUAL AND PERENNIAL

The sweet pea like an atheist
Has but one life to give:
What's missed
No heaven will give.

With Christian fortitude the rose
Endures each winter storm:
She knows
June will be warm.
　—WILHELMINE GERBER WRIGHT, *The Haunted*
　　　　Mountain and Other Poems

. . . Even in these times of intoxication mingled with anxiety, amidst the most pressing necessities, it is the rôle of the Christian, a man among his brother men, buoyed up by the same aspirations and cast down by the same anxieties, to raise his voice and remind those who forget it of their own nobility; man is only himself, he only exists for himself *here and now* if he can discover within himself, in silence, some untouched region, some mysterious background which, whether gloomy or cheerful, commonplace or tragic, is not encroached upon by the cares of the present. To seek to give him back an understanding of this is not to plunge him in the water of Lethe, to stupefy him with opium, or to give him Dutch courage. And to call back to the duties of the day one who lives entirely in a future which he sees rising out of his own creative energy is by no means to try to snatch from him his faith in man. On the contrary, it is to make him have a respect for man wherever he is found. It is to forbid his ever making use of the man of to-day as a mere instrument for the purposes of the man of to-morrow. Above all, it is to prevent him, both now or in the future, whether rich or poor, successful or unsuccessful, from being entirely absent, completely estranged from himself. . . .

There is in man an eternal element, a "germ of eternity," which already "breathes the upper air," which always, *hic et nunc,* evades the temporal society. The truth of his being evades his being itself. For he is made in the image of God, and in the mirror of his being the Trinity is ever reflected. But it is only a mirror, an image. If man, by an act of sacrilege, inverts the relationship, usurps God's attributes, and declares that God was made to man's image, all is over with him. The transcendence that he repudiates was the sole warrant of his own immanence. Only by acknowledging himself to be a reflexion could he obtain completeness, and only in his act of adoration could he find his own inviolable depths. Henceforth, then, he is estranged from himself, *dispersed,* separated from himself. . . .

How grateful must we be to the Church for reminding us always, *opportune, importune,* of the essential condition of our existence, for that continual *sursum,* that continual *redi ad cor,* which she presses upon us. Nothing is more superficial than the charge made against her of losing sight of immediate realities, of neglecting man's urgent needs, by speaking to him always of the hereafter. For in truth the hereafter is far nearer than the future, far nearer than what we call the present. It is the Eternal found at the heart of all temporal development which gives it life and direction. It is the authentic Present without which the present itself is like the dust which slips through our hands. If modern men are so absent from each other, it is primarily because they are absent from themselves, since they have abandoned this Eternal which alone establishes them in being and enables them to communicate with one another.

—HENRI DE LUBAC, S.J., *Catholicism*
(LANCELOT C. SHEPPARD)

The universe is deathless,
Is deathless because, having no finite self,
It stays infinite.
A sound man by not advancing himself
Stays the further ahead of himself,
By not confining himself to himself
Sustains himself outside himself:
By never being an end in himself
He endlessly becomes himself.

—LAO-TSE (WITTER BYNNER)

He who builds a house for himself takes great pains to make it commodious, airy, and handsome, and says: "I labor and give myself a great deal of trouble about this house, because I shall have to live in it all my life." And yet how little is the house of eternity thought of! When we shall have arrived at eternity there will be no question of our residing in a house more or less commodious, or more or less airy: the question will be of our dwelling in a palace overflowing with delights, or in a gulf of endless tor-

ments. And for how long a time? Not for forty or fifty years, but
forever, as long as God shall be God.

—St. Alphonsus de Liguori,
The Way of Salvation

The human person is not, in its true essence, an *existence towards
death*. Like every other existence, after its own fashion, it is a
movement towards self-realisation and towards eternity. It tends
towards its own perfection, even if this means passing through the
strait and narrow gate of death. It can only change its outer ontological aspect by turning death into the means of its own fulfilment.

—Paul-Louis Landsberg, *The Experience of Death*
(Cynthia Rowland)

The Door of Death is made of Gold,
That Mortal Eyes cannot behold;
But, when the Mortal Eyes are clos'd,
And cold and pale the Limbs repos'd,
The Soul awakes; and, wond'ring, sees
In her mild Hand the golden Keys:
The Grave is Heaven's golden Gate,
And rich and poor around it wait;
O Shepherdess of England's Fold,
Behold this Gate of Pearl and Gold!

—William Blake

The source of life
Is as a mother.

Be fond of both mother and children but know the mother dearer
And you outlive death.
Curb your tongue and senses
And you are beyond trouble,
Let them loose
And you are beyond help.
Discover that nothing is too small for clear vision,
Too insignificant for tender strength,
Use outlook
And insight,
Use them both
And you are immune:
For you have witnessed eternity.

—LAO-TSE (WITTER BYNNER)

If in the hour of my death I shall see how good God is to me,
how He intends to heap His affection upon me for a whole eternity
—and that I can never again prove mine to Him by sacrifices—
how impossible that will be to bear if on earth I had not done
everything in my power to give Him joy!

—ST. THÉRÈSE OF LISIEUX, *Story of a Soul*
(unedited notes)

How simple was the time of Cain
Before the latter Man-made Rain
Washed away all loss and gain
And the talk of right and wrong—
Murdered now and gone.

And the ghost of Man is red
With the sweep of the world's blood. . . .

In this late equality
Would you know the ghost of Man
From the ghost of a Flea?

But still the fires of the great Spring
In the desolate fields proclaim
Eternity . . . those wild fires shout
Of Christ the new song.

Run those fires from field to field!
I walk alone and ghostily
Burning with Eternity's
Fires, and quench the Furies' song
In flame that never tires.

—EDITH SITWELL, *Song:*
Now that Fate is dead and gone

THE INVISIBLE WORLD

There are two worlds, "the visible and the invisible," as the
Creed speaks,—the world we see, and the world we do not see;
and the world which we do not see as really exists as the world
we do see. It really exists, though we see it not. The world that we
see we know to exist, *because* we see it. We have but to lift up our
eyes and look around us, and we have proof of it: our eyes tell us.
We see the sun, moon and stars, earth and sky, hills and valleys,
woods and plains, seas and rivers. And again, we see men, and
the works of men. We see cities, and stately buildings, and their
inhabitants; men running to and fro, and busying themselves to
provide for themselves and their families, or to accomplish great
designs, or for the very business' sake. All that meets our eyes
forms one world. It is an immense world; it reaches to the stars.

Thousands on thousands of years might we speed up the sky, and though we were swifter than the light itself, we should not reach them all. They are at distances from us greater than any that is assignable. So high, so wide, so deep is the world; and yet it also comes near and close to us. It is every where; and it seems to leave no room for any other world.

And yet in spite of this universal world which we see, there is another world, quite as far-spreading, quite as close to us, and more wonderful; another world all around us, though we see it not, and more wonderful than the world we see, for this reason if for no other, that we do not see it. All around us are numberless objects, coming and going, watching, working or waiting, which we see not: this is that other world, which the eyes reach not unto, but faith only.

. . . Do you ask what it is, and what it contains? I will not say that all that belongs to it is vastly more important than what we see, for among things visible are our fellow-men, and nothing created is more precious and noble than a son of man. But still, taking the things which we see altogether, and the things we do not see altogether, the world we do not see is on the whole a much higher than that which we do see. For, first of all, He is there who is above all beings, who has created all, before whom they all are as nothing, and with whom nothing can be compared. Almighty God, we know, exists more really and absolutely than any of those fellow-men whose existence is conveyed to us through the senses; yet we see Him not, hear Him not, we do but "feel after Him," yet without finding Him. It appears, then, that the things which are seen are but a part, and but a secondary part of the beings about us, were it only on this ground, that Almighty God, the Being of beings, is not in their number, but among "the things which are not seen.". . .

And in that other world are the souls also of the dead. They too, when they depart hence, do not cease to exist, but they retire from this visible scene of things; or, in other words, they cease to act towards us and before us *through our senses.* They live as they lived before; but that outward frame, through which they were able to hold communion with other men, is in some way, we know not how, separated from them, and dries away and shrivels up as leaves may drop off a tree. They remain, but without the usual means of approach towards us, and correspondence with us. As when a man loses his voice or hand, he still exists as before, but cannot any longer talk or write, or otherwise hold intercourse with us; so when he loses not voice and hand only, but his whole frame, or is said to die, there is nothing to show that he is gone, but we have lost our means of apprehending him.

Again: Angels also are inhabitants of the world invisible, and concerning them much more is told us than concerning the souls of the faithful departed, because the latter "rest from their labours"; but the Angels are actively employed among us in the Church. They are said to be "ministering spirits, sent forth to minister for them who shall be heirs of salvation." No Christian is so humble but he has Angels to attend on him, if he lives by faith and love. Though they are so great, so glorious, so pure, so wonderful, that the very sight of them (if we were allowed to see them) would strike us to the earth, as it did the prophet Daniel, holy and righteous as he was; yet they are our "fellow-servants" and our fellow-workers, and they carefully watch over and defend even the humblest of us . . .

*   *   *

O blessed they indeed, who are destined for the sight of those wonders in which they now stand, at which they now look, but which they do not recognize! Blessed they who shall at length behold what as yet mortal eye hath not seen and faith only enjoys! Those wonderful things of the new world are even now as they shall be then. They are immortal and eternal; and the souls who shall then be made conscious of them, will see them in their calmness and their majesty where they ever have been. But who can express the surprise and rapture which will come upon those, who then at last apprehend them for the first time, and to whose perceptions they are new! Who can imagine by a stretch of fancy the feelings of those who having died in faith, wake up to enjoyment! The life then begun, we know, will last for ever; yet surely if memory be to us then what it is now, that will be a day much to be observed unto the Lord through all the ages of eternity. We may increase indeed for ever in knowledge and in love, still that first waking from the dead, the day at once of our birth and our espousals, will ever be endeared and hallowed in our thoughts. When we find ourselves after long rest gifted with fresh powers, vigorous with the seed of eternal life within us, able to love God as we wish, conscious that all trouble, sorrow, pain, anxiety, bereavement, is over for ever, blessed in the full affection of those earthly friends whom we loved so poorly, and could protect so feebly, while they were with us in the flesh, and above all, visited by the immediate visible ineffable Presence of God Almighty, with his Only-begotten Son our Lord Jesus Christ, and His Co-equal Co-eternal Spirit, that great sight in which is the fulness of joy and pleasure for evermore,—what deep, incommunicable, unimaginable thoughts will be then upon us! what depths will be stirred up within us! what secret harmonies awakened, of which human nature seemed incapable! Earthly words are indeed all worthless to minister to such high anticipations. Let us close our eyes and keep silence.

—JOHN HENRY NEWMAN, *Parochial and Plain Sermons*

CHURCHYARDS

Oh why do people waste their breath
Inventing dainty names for death?
On the old tombstones of the past
We do not read "At peace at last"

But simply "died" or plain "departed."
It's no good being chicken-hearted.
We die; that's that; our flesh decays
Or disappears in other ways.
But since we're Christians, we believe
That we new bodies will receive
To clothe our souls for us to meet
Our Maker at his Judgement Seat.
And this belief's a gift of faith
And, if it's true, no end is death.

   Mid-Lent is passed and Easter's near
The greatest day of all the year
When Jesus, who indeed had died,
Rose with his body glorified.
And if you find believing hard
The primroses in your churchyard
And modern science too will show
That all things change the while they grow,
And we, who change in Time will be
Still more changed in Eternity.

—JOHN BETJEMAN

Eternity is a mysterious absence of times and ages: an endless length of ages always present, and forever perfect. For as there is an immovable space wherein all finite spaces are enclosed, and all motions carried on, and performed: so is there an immovable duration, that contains and measures all moving durations. Without which first the last could not be; no more than finite places and bodies moving without infinite space. All ages being but successions corresponding to those parts of that Eternity wherein they abide, and filling no more of it than ages can do. Whether they are commensurate with it or not is difficult to determine. But the infinite immovable duration is Eternity, the place and duration of all things, even of infinite space itself: the Cause and End, the Author and Beautifier, the Life and Perfection of all.

* * *

Eternity magnifies our joys exceedingly, for whereas things in themselves began and quickly end, before they came were never in being, do service but for few moments, and after they are gone pass away and leave us forever, Eternity retains the moments of their beginning and ending within itself: and from everlasting to everlasting those things were in their times and places before God, and in all their circumstances eternally will be, serving Him in those moments wherein they existed, to those intents and purposes for which they were created. The swiftest thought is present with Him eternally: the Creation and the Day of Judgment, His first consultation, choice and determination, the result and end of all just now in full perfection, ever beginning, ever passing, ever ending: with all the intervals of space between things and things. As if those objects that arise many thousand years one after the other were all together. We also were ourselves before God eternally, and have the joy of seeing ourselves eternally beloved, and eternally blessed, and infinitely enjoying all the parts of our blessedness, in all the durations of eternity appearing at once before ourselves, when perfectly consummated in the Kingdom of light and glory. The smallest thing, by the influence of Eternity, is made infinite and eternal. We pass through a standing continent or region of ages that are already before us, glorious and perfect while we come to them. Like men in a ship we pass forward, the shores and marks seeming to go backward, though we move and they stand still. We are not with them in our progressive motion, but prevent the swiftness of our course, and are present with them in our understandings. Like the sun we dart our rays before us, and occupy those spaces with light and contemplation, which we move towards but possess not with our bodies. And seeing all things in the Light of Divine Knowledge eternally serving God, rejoice unspeakably in that service, and enjoy it all.

*   *   *

His Omnipresence is an ample territory or field of joys, a transparent temple of infinite luster, a strong tower of defense, a castle of repose, a bulwark of security, a palace of delights, an immediate help, and a present refuge in the needful time of trouble, a broad and a vast extent of fame and glory, a theatre of infinite excellence, an infinite ocean by means whereof every action, word and thought is immediately diffused like a drop of wine in a pail of water, and everywhere present everywhere seen and known, infinitely delighted in, as well as filling infinite spaces. It is the Spirit that pervades all His works, the life and soul of the universe, that in every point of space from the center to the Heavens, in every kingdom in the world in every city, in every wilderness, in every house, every soul, every creature, in all the parts of His infinity, and Eternity sees our persons, loves our virtues, inspires us with itself, and crowns our actions with praise and glory. It makes our honor infinite in extent, our glory immense, and our happiness eternal. The rays of our light are by this means darted from everlasting to everlasting. This spiritual region makes us infinitely present with God, angels and men in all places from the utmost bounds of the everlasting hills, throughout all the unwearied durations of His endless infinity, and gives us the sense and feeling of all the delights and praises we occasion, as well as of all the beauties and powers and pleasures and glories which God enjoys or creates.

*   *   *

Our Bridegroom and our King being everywhere, our Lover and Defender watchfully governing all worlds, no danger or enemy can arise to hurt us, but is immediately prevented and suppressed, in all the spaces beyond the utmost borders of those unknown habitations which He possesses. Delights of inestimable value are there preparing. For everything is present by its own existence.

The Essence of God therefore being all Light and Knowledge, Love and Goodness, Care and Providence, Felicity and Glory, a Pure and Simple Act; it is present in its operations and by those acts which it eternally exerts, is wholly busied in all parts and places of His dominion, perfecting and completing our bliss and happiness.

—THOMAS TRAHERNE, *The Fifth Century*

9 Judgment

But the souls of the just are in the hand of God, and the torment of death shall not touch them. In the sight of the unwise they seemed to die: and their departure was taken for misery: and their going away from us, for utter destruction: but they are in peace. And though in the sight of men they suffered torments, their hope is full of immortality. Afflicted in few things, in many they shall be well rewarded: because God hath tried them, and found them worthy of himself. As gold in the furnace he hath proved them, and as a victim of a holocaust he hath received them, and in time there shall be respect had to them. The just shall shine, and shall run to and fro like sparks among the reeds. They shall judge nations, and rule over people, and their Lord shall reign for ever. They that trust in him shall understand the truth: and they that are faithful in love shall rest in him: for grace and peace is to his elect. But the wicked shall be punished according to their own devices: who have neglected the just, and have revolted from the Lord. For he that rejecteth wisdom, and discipline, is unhappy: and their hope is vain, and their labors without fruit, and their works unprofitable.

—Wisdom 3:1–11

Again the kingdom of heaven is like to a net cast into the sea, and gathering together of all kinds of fishes. Which, when it was filled, they drew out, and sitting by the shore, they chose out the good into vessels, but the bad they cast forth. So shall it be at the end of the world. The angels shall go out, and shall separate the wicked from among the just.

—St. Matthew 13:47–49

What a sweet joy it is to think that the Lord is just, which means that He takes our weaknesses into account and is perfectly aware of the frailty of our nature! What, then, need I fear? The good God who is infinitely just and deigns in His great mercy to pardon the faults of the prodigal son, must He not be *just* to me also. . . .

—St. Thérèse of Lisieux, *Story of a Soul*

I know one must be most pure to appear before the God of all holiness, but I know too that the Lord is infinitely just; and it is this justice, which terrifies so many souls, that is the basis of my joy and trust. To be just means not only to exercise severity in punishing the guilty, but also to recognize right intentions and to reward virtue. I hope as much from the good God's justice as from His mercy—because He is "compassionate and merciful, long-suffering and plenteous in mercy."

—St. Thérèse of Lisieux, *Novissima Verba*

He that believes, says Christ, is not judged. And is there any need to judge a believer? Judgment arises out of ambiguity, and where ambiguity ceases, there is no call for trial and judgment. Hence not even unbelievers need be judged, because there is no doubt about their being unbelievers; but after exempting believers and unbelievers alike from judgment, the Lord added a case for judgment and human agents upon whom it must be exercised. For some there are who stand midway between the godly and the ungodly, having affinities to both, but strictly belonging to neither class, because they have come to be what they are by a combination of the two. They may not be assigned to the ranks of belief, because there is in them a certain infusion of unbelief; they may not be ranged with unbelief, because they are not without a certain portion of belief. For many are kept within the pale of the church by the fear of God; yet they are tempted all the while to worldly faults by the allurements of the world. They pray, because they are afraid; they sin, because it is their will. The fair hope of future life makes them call themselves Christians; the allurements of present pleasure make them act like heathen. They do not abide in ungodliness, because they hold the name of God in honor; they are not godly because they follow after things contrary to godliness. And they cannot help loving those things best which can never enable them to be what they call themselves, because their desire to do such works is stronger than their desire to be true to their name. And this is why the Lord, after saying that believers would not be judged and that unbelievers had been judged already, added that *This is the judgment, that the light is come into the world, and men loved the darkness rather than the light.*

These, then, are they whom the judgment awaits which unbelievers have already had passed upon them and believers do not need: because they have loved darkness more than light; not that they did not love the light too, but because their love of darkness is the more active. For when two loves are matched in rivalry, one always wins the preference; and their judgment arises from the fact that, though they loved Christ, they yet loved darkness more. These then will be judged; they are neither exempted from judgment like the godly, nor have they already been judged like the ungodly; but judgment awaits them for the love which they have deliberately preferred.

—St. Hilary of Poitiers, *Homily on Psalm I*

Although your days are numbered, and the following darkness sure, is it necessary that you should share the degradation of the brute, because you are condemned to its mortality; or live the life of the moth, and of the worm, because you are to companion them in the dust? Not so; we may have but a few thousands of days to spend, perhaps hundreds only—perhaps tens; nay, the longest of our time and best, looked back on, will be but as a moment, as the twinkling of an eye; still we are men, not insects; we are living spirits, not passing clouds. "He maketh the winds His messengers; the momentary fire, His minister"; and shall we do less than *these?* Let us do the work of men while we bear the form of them; and, as we snatch our narrow portion of time out of Eternity, snatch also our narrow inheritance of passion out of Immortality—even though our lives *be* as a vapor, that appeareth for a little time, and then vanisheth away.

But there are some of you who believe not this—who think this cloud of life has no such close—that it is to float, revealed and illumined, upon the floor of heaven, in the day when He cometh with clouds, and every eye shall see Him. Some day, you believe, within these five, or ten, or twenty years, for every one of us the judgment will be set, and the books opened. If that be true, far more than that must be true. Is there but one day of judgment? Why, for us every day is a day of judgment—every day is a Dies Irae, and writes its irrevocable verdict in the flame of its West. Think you that judgment waits till the doors of the grave are opened? It waits at the doors of your houses—it waits at the corners of your streets; we are in the midst of judgment—the insects that we crush are our judges—the elements that feed us, judge, as they indulge. Let us, for our lives, do the work of Men while we bear the form of them, if indeed those lives are *Not* as a vapor, and do *Not* vanish away.

—JOHN RUSKIN, *The Mystery of Life and Its Arts*

A certain man had three friends. One of these he loved dearly; the second he loved also, but not as intensely as the first; but towards the third one he was quite indifferently disposed.

Now the king of the country sent an officer to this man, commanding his immediate appearance before the throne. Greatly terrified was the man at this summons. He thought that somebody had been speaking evil of him, or probably accusing him falsely before his sovereign, and being afraid to appear unaccompanied before the royal presence, he resolved to ask one of his friends to go with him. First, he naturally applied to his dearest friend, but he at once declined to go, giving no reason and no excuse for his lack of friendliness. So the man applied to his second friend, who said to him:

"I will go with thee as far as the palace gates, but I will not enter with thee before the king."

In desperation the man applied to his third friend, the one whom he had neglected, but who replied to him at once:

"Fear not; I will go with thee, and I will speak in thy defence. I will not leave thee until thou art delivered from thy trouble."

The "first friend" is a man's wealth, which he must leave behind him when he dies. The "second friend" is typified by the relatives who follow him to the grave and leave him when the earth has covered his remains. The "third friend," he who entered with him into the presence of the king, is as the good deeds of a man's life, which never desert, but accompany him to plead his cause before the King of kings. . . .

—*The Talmud* (H. POLANO)

. . . "Blessed are those whose iniquities are forgiven, and whose sins are covered," not those in whom no sins are found. The sins are covered, they are smothered, they are wiped out. If God covers sins, it means he doesn't want to notice them; if he doesn't want to notice them, he doesn't want to punish them; if he doesn't want to punish them, he prefers to forgive them. Don't misunderstand this about sins being covered, as though they lived on under cover, still there to burden the conscience. He uses this phrase about sins being covered, to indicate that they are no longer seen. And God's seeing or not seeing sins is only a way of putting his punishing or not punishing them. So it says in another psalm, "Turn away your face from my sins" (Ps. 50:11). May he not see your sins, but see you instead—as he saw Nathanael under the fig-tree. The shade of the fig-tree wasn't too thick for the eyes of God's mercy to see through.

—St. Augustine, *Sermon on Psalm 31 (32)*
(Edmund Hill)

THE WEDDING OF CANA IN GALILEE

"His mother saith unto the servants: Whatsoever he saith unto you, do it". . .

"Do it. . . . Gladness, the gladness of some poor, very poor, people. . . . Of course they were poor, since they hadn't wine enough even at a wedding. . . . The historians write that, in those days, the people living about the Lake of Gennesaret were the poorest that can possibly be imagined . . . and another great heart, that other great being, His Mother, knew that He had come not only to make His great terrible sacrifice. She knew that His heart was open even to the simple, artless merry-making of some obscure and unlearned people, who had warmly bidden Him to their poor wedding. 'Mine hour is not yet come,' He said, with a soft smile (He must have smiled gently to her). And indeed was it to make wine abundant at poor weddings He had come down to earth? And yet He went and did as she asked Him. . . . Ah, he is reading again". . .

"Jesus saith unto them, Fill the waterpots with water. And they filled them up to the brim.

"And he saith unto them, Draw out now and bear unto the governor of the feast. And they bare it.

*"When the ruler of the feast had tasted the water that was made
wine, and knew not whence it was; [but the servants which drew
the water knew] the governor of the feast called the bridegroom,*

*"And saith unto him: Every man at the beginning doth set forth
good wine; and when men have well drunk, that which is worse;
but thou hast kept the good wine until now."*

"But what's this, what's this? Why is the room growing wider?
. . . Ah, yes . . . It's the marriage, the wedding couple sitting, and
the merry crowd and . . . Where is the wise governor of the feast?
But who is this? Who? Again the walls receding. . . . Who is getting
up there from the great table? What! . . . He here, too? But he's in
the coffin . . . but he's here, too. He has stood up, he sees me, he
is coming here. . . . God!" . . .

Yes, he came up to him, to him, he, the little, thin old man,
with tiny wrinkles on his face, joyful and laughing softly. There
was no coffin now, and he was in the same dress as he had worn
yesterday sitting with them, when the visitors had gathered about
him. His face was uncovered, his eyes were shining. How was this
then, he, too, had been called to the feast. He, too, at the marriage
of Cana in Galilee. . . .

"Yes, my dear, I am called, too, called and bidden," he heard a
soft voice saying over him. "Why have you hidden yourself here,
out of sight? You come and join us too."

It was his voice, the voice of Father Zossima. And it must be he,
since he called him!

The elder raised Alyosha by the hand and he rose from his knees.

"We are rejoicing," the little, thin old man went on. "We are
drinking the new wine, the wine of new, great gladness; do you see
how many guests? Here are the bride and bridegroom, here is the
wise governor of the feast, he is tasting the new wine. Why do you
wonder at me? I gave an onion to a beggar, so I, too, am here. And
many here have given only an onion each—only one little onion.
. . . What are all our deeds? And you, my gentle one, you, my kind
boy, you too have known how to give a famished woman an onion

to-day. Begin your work, dear one, begin it, gentle one! . . . Do you see our Sun, do you see Him?"

"I am afraid . . . I dare not look," whispered Alyosha.

"Do not fear Him. He is terrible in His greatness, awful in His sublimity, but infinitely merciful. He has made Himself like unto us from love and rejoices with us. He is changing the water into wine that the gladness of the guests may not be cut short. He is expecting new guests, He is calling new ones unceasingly for ever and ever. . . . There they are bringing new wine. Do you see they are bringing the vessels . . ."

Something glowed in Alyosha's heart, something filled it till it ached, tears of rapture rose from his soul. . . . He stretched out his hands, uttered a cry and waked up.

Again the coffin, the open window, and the soft, solemn, distinct reading of the Gospel. But Alyosha did not listen to the reading. It was strange, he had fallen asleep on his knees, but now he was on his feet, and suddenly, as though thrown forward, with three firm rapid steps he went right up to the coffin. His shoulder brushed against Father Païssy without his noticing it. Father Païssy raised his eyes for an instant from his book, but looked away again at once, seeing that something strange was happening to the boy. Alyosha gazed for half a minute at the coffin, at the covered, motionless dead man that lay in the coffin, with the ikon on his breast and the peaked cap with the octangular cross, on his head. He had only just been hearing his voice, and that voice was still ringing in his ears. He was listening, still expecting other words, but suddenly he turned sharply and went out of the cell.

He did not stop on the steps either, but went quickly down; his soul, overflowing with rapture, yearned for freedom, space, openness. The vault of heaven, full of soft, shining stars, stretched vast and fathomless above him. The Milky Way ran in two pale streams from the zenith to the horizon. The fresh, motionless, still night enfolded the earth. The white towers and golden domes of the cathedral gleamed out against the sapphire sky. The gorgeous autumn flowers, in the beds round the house, were slumbering till morning. The silence of earth seemed to melt into the silence of the heavens. The mystery of earth was one with the mystery of the stars. . . .

Alyosha stood, gazed, and suddenly threw himself down on the earth. He did not know why he embraced it. He could not have told why he longed so irresistibly to kiss it, to kiss it all. But he kissed it weeping, sobbing and watering it with his tears, and vowed passionately to love it, to love it for ever and ever. "Water the earth with the tears of your joy and love those tears," echoed in his soul.

What was he weeping over?

Oh! in his rapture he was weeping even over those stars, which were shining to him from the abyss of space, and "he was not ashamed of that ecstasy." There seemed to be threads from all those innumerable worlds of God, linking his soul to them, and it was trembling all over "in contact with other worlds." He longed to forgive every one and for everything, and to beg forgiveness. Oh, not for himself, but for all men, for all and for everything. "And others are praying for me too," echoed again in his soul. But with every instant he felt clearly and, as it were, tangibly, that something firm and unshakable as that vault of heaven had entered into his soul. It was as though some idea had seized the sovereignty of his mind—and it was for all his life and for ever and ever. He had fallen on the earth a weak boy, but he rose up a resolute champion, and he knew and felt it suddenly at the very moment of his ecstasy. And never, never, all his life long, could Alyosha forget that minute.

—FYODOR DOSTOYEVSKY, *The Brothers Karamazov*
(CONSTANCE GARNETT)

And the Life-giver shall come, the Destroyer of Death, and shall bring to nought his power, from over the just and from over the wicked. And the dead shall arise with a mighty shout, and Death shall be emptied and stripped of all the captivity. And for judgment shall all the children of Adam be gathered together, and each shall go to the place prepared for him. The risen of the righteous shall go unto life, and the risen of the sinners shall be delivered unto death.

—APHRAHAT, *Select Demonstrations: Of Death and the Latter Times*

I saw *three* manner of longings in God, and all to one end. The *first* is, for that he longeth to learn us to know him and to love him ever more and more, as it is convenient and speedful to us. The *second* is, that he longeth to have us up into bliss, as souls are when they be taken out of pain into heaven. The *third* is, to fulfill us of bliss, and that shall be on the last day fulfilled ever to last. For I saw, as it is known to our faith, that then pain and sorrow shall be ended to all that shall be saved. And not only we shall receive the same bliss that souls afore have had in heaven, but also we shall receive a new, which plenteously shall flie out of God into us, and fulfill us. And those be the goods which he hath ordained to give us fro without beginning. These goods are treasured and hid in himself; for into that time [the] creature is not mighty, nor worthy to receive them. In this we should see verily the cause of all the deeds that God hath done. And over-more we should see the cause of all thing that he hath suffered: and the bliss, and the fulfilling shall be so deep and so high, that for wonder and marvel all creatures should have to God so great reverence and dread, over-passing that hath been seen and felt before that the pillars of heaven shall travel and quake. But this manner of trembling and dread shall have no manner of pain; but it longeth to the worthy majesty of God, thus to be beholden of his creatures, dreadfully trembling and quaking: for much more of joy, endlessly marvelling of the greatness of God the Maker, and of the least part of all that is made.

—JULIANA OF NORWICH, *Revelations of Divine Love*

To know the course of heaven, is to see the secret predestinations of the heavenly disposals. But to set down the reason thereof on the earth is to lay open before the hearts of men the causes of such secrets. To set down, namely, the reason of heaven on the earth, is either to examine the mysteries of the heavenly judgments, by consideration, or to make them manifest in words. Which certainly no one can do who is placed in this life. . . . Who can understand why one man, who plots for the deaths of his neighbours, survives, and another, who would be likely to preserve the lives of many, dies? One man, who is only eager to do hurt, attains the height of power, another only desires to defend the injured, and yet he himself is lying under oppression. One man wishes for leisure, and is involved in innumerable occupations, another wishes to be engaged in employments, and is compelled to be disengaged. One beginning badly is drawn on from worse to worse, even to the end of his life; another beginning well, proceeds through a long period of time to the increase of his merits. . . . One, who has been born in the error of unbelief, perishes in his error; another, who has been born in the soundness of the Catholic faith, is perfected in the soundness of the Catholic faith. But, on the other hand, one, who has come forth from the womb of a Catholic Mother, is swallowed up, at the close of his life, in the gulf of error, but another terminates his life in Catholic piety, who, born in misbelief, had sucked in the poison of error with his mother's milk. One both wishes, and is able, to aim at the loftiness of holy living; another is neither willing nor able. One wishes, and is not able; another is able, and is not willing. Who then can examine into these secrets of the heavenly judgments? Who can understand the secret balance of hidden equity? For no one attains to understand these recesses of secret judgments. Let this be said then to a man, that he may learn his own ignorance; let him know his own ignorance, that he may fear; let him fear, that he may be humbled; let him be humbled, that he may not trust in himself; let him trust not in himself, that he may seek for the assistance of his Creator, and that he who is dead from trusting in himself, may seek the assistance of his Maker, and live.

—St. Gregory the Great, *Morals on the Book of Job* (Book XXIX)

O dark dark dark. They all go into the dark,
The vacant interstellar spaces, the vacant into the vacant,
The captains, merchant bankers, eminent men of letters,
The generous patrons of art, the statesmen and the rulers,
Distinguished civil servants, chairmen of many committees,
Industrial lords and petty contractors, all go into the dark,
And dark the Sun and Moon, and the Almanach de Gotha
And the Stock Exchange Gazette, the Directory of Directors,
And cold the sense and lost the motive of action.
And we all go with them, into the silent funeral,
Nobody's funeral, for there is no one to bury.
I said to my soul, be still, and let the dark come upon you
Which shall be the darkness of God.   As, in a theatre,
The lights are extinguished, for the scene to be changed
With a hollow rumble of wings, with a movement of darkness
      on darkness,
And we know that the hills and the trees, the distant pano-
      rama
And the bold imposing façade are all being rolled away—
Or as, when an underground train, in the tube, stops too long
      between stations

And the conversation rises and slowly fades into silence
And you see behind every face the mental emptiness deepen
Leaving only the growing terror of nothing to think about;
Or when, under ether, the mind is conscious but conscious of
      nothing—
I said to my soul, be still, and wait without hope
For hope would be hope for the wrong thing; wait without
      love
For love would be love of the wrong thing; there is yet faith
But the faith and the love and the hope are all in the waiting.
Wait without thought, for you are not ready for thought:
So the darkness shall be the light, and the stillness the dancing.

Whisper of running streams, and winter lightning.
The wild thyme unseen and the wild strawberry,
The laughter in the garden, echoed ecstasy
Not lost, but requiring, pointing to the agony
Of death and birth.

                  You say I am repeating
Something I have said before. I shall say it again.
Shall I say it again? In order to arrive there,
To arrive where you are, to get from where you are not,
   You must go by a way wherein there is no ecstasy.
In order to arrive at what you do not know
   You must go by a way which is the way of ignorance.
In order to possess what you do not possess
   You must go by the way of dispossession.
In order to arrive at what you are not
   You must go through the way in which you are not.
And what you do not know is the only thing you know
And what you own is what you do not own
And where you are is where you are not.
                —T. S. Eliot, *Four Quartets* (*East Coker*)

MAGDALEN

Magdalen at Michael's gate
　Tirlèd at the pin;
On Joseph's thorn sang the blackbird,
　"Let her in! Let her in!"

"Hast thou seen the wounds?" said Michael,
　"Know'st thou thy sin?"
"It is evening, evening," sang the blackbird,
　"Let her in! Let her in!"

"Yes, I have seen the wounds,
　And I know my sin."
"She knows it well, well, well," sang the blackbird,
　"Let her in! Let her in!"

"Thou bringest no offerings," said Michael.
　"Nought save sin."
And the blackbird sang, "She is sorry, sorry, sorry,
　"Let her in! Let her in!"

When he had sung himself to sleep,
　And night did begin,
One came and open'd Michael's gate,
　And Magdalen went in.

　　　　　　　　　　　—Henry Kingsley

DOOMSDAY

　Lo! at midnight, unawares, the great day of the Lord omnip-
otent shall mightily overtake the dwellers on earth, the bright
creation; as oft a daring robber, a crafty thief, prowling about in

darkness, in the murky night, suddenly comes upon careless men bound in sleep, and sorely assails them unprepared.

Then together unto Mount Zion shall ascend a great multitude, radiant and joyful, the faithful of the Lord; glory shall be theirs. Thereupon from the four corners of the world, from the uttermost regions of earth, angels all-shining shall with one accord blow their crashing trumpets; the earth shall tremble under men. Glorious and steadfast they shall sound together over against the course of the stars, chanting in harmony and making melody from south and from north, from east and from west, throughout the whole creation; all mankind shall they wake from the dead unto the last judgment; they shall rouse the sons of men all aghast from the ancient earth, bidding them straightway arise from their deep sleep.

There one may hear a sorrowing people, sad of heart and greatly disquieted, sorely afraid and pitifully bewailing the deeds done in the body. This shall be the greatest forewarning ever shown unto men before or since. There all the hosts of angels and of devils shall mingle, the fair and the swart; there shall be a coming of both the white and the black, according as an abode is prepared all unlike for saints and sinners.

Then suddenly upon Mount Zion a blaze of the sun, shining clear from the southeast, shall come forth from the Creator, gleaming more brightly than the mind of man can conceive, when the Son of God shall appear hither through the vault of heaven. All glorious from the eastern skies shall come the presence of Christ, the aspect of the noble King, gentle in spirit toward His own, bitter toward the wicked, wondrously varied, diverse to the blessed and the forlorn. Unto the good, the host of the holy, He shall be joyful of countenance, radiant, winsome, loving, gracious, and fair. Sweet and pleasant shall it be for His loved ones, for those who in days of old pleased Him well by their words and deeds, to gaze upon that shining face, winningly benign, upon the advent of the King, the Lord of might. But unto the evil and wicked, unto those who shall come to Him undone by sin, He shall be terrible and awful to behold.

—Cynewulf, *Christ* (Charles Huntington Whitman)

ON THE DAY OF JUDGMENT

Father Unoriginate, Only-begotten Son,
Life-giving Spirit,
merciful, pitiful, long-suffering,
full of pity, full of kind yearnings,
who lovest the just and pitiest the sinful,
who passest by sins and grantest petitions,
God of penitents,
Saviour of sinners,
I have sinned before Thee, O Lord,
and thus and thus have I done.
Alas, alas! woe, woe.
How was I enticed by my own lust!
How I hated instruction!
Nor felt I fear nor shame
at Thy incomprehensible glory,
Thy awful presence,
Thy fearful power,
Thy exact justice,
Thy winning goodness.
I will call if there be any that will answer me;
to which of the saints shall I turn?
O wretched man that I am,
who shall deliver me from the body of this death?
how fearful is Thy judgment, O Lord?
when the thrones are set
and Angels stand around,
and men are brought in,

the books opened,
the works enquired into,
the thoughts examined,
and the hidden things of darkness.
What judgment shall be upon me?
who shall quench my flame?
who shall lighten my darkness,
if Thou pity me not?
Lord, as Thou art loving,
give me tears,
give me floods, give me to-day.
For then will be the incorruptible Judge,
the horrible judgment-seat,
the answer without excuses,
the inevitable charges,
the shameful punishment,
the endless Gehenna,
the pitiless Angels,
the yawning hell,
the roaring stream of fire,
the unquenchable flame,
the dark prison,
the rayless darkness,
the bed of live coals,
the unwearied worm,
the indissoluble chains,
the bottomless chaos,
the impassable wall,
the inconsolable cry,
none to stand by me,
none to plead for me,
none to snatch me out.
But I repent, Lord, O Lord, I repent,
help Thou mine impenitence,
and more, and still more,

pierce, rend, crush my heart.
Behold, O Lord, that I am
indignant with myself,
for my senseless, profitless,
hurtful, perilous passions;
that I loathe myself,
for these inordinate, unseemly,
deformed, insincere,
shameful, disgraceful
passions,
that my confusion is daily before me,
and the shame of my face hath covered me.
Alas! woe, woe—
O me, how long?
Behold, Lord, that I sentence myself
to punishment everlasting,
yea, and all miseries of this world.
Behold me, Lord, self-condemned;
Behold, Lord, and enter not into judgment
with Thy servant.
And now, Lord,
I humble myself under Thy mighty hand.
I bend to Thee, O Lord, my knees,
I fall on my face to the earth.
Let this cup pass from me!
I stretch forth my hands unto Thee;
I smite my breast, I smite on my thigh.
Out of the deep my soul crieth unto Thee,
as a thirsty land;
and all my bones,
and all that is within me.
Lord, hear my voice.

—LANCELOT ANDREWES, *Private Devotions*
(JOHN HENRY NEWMAN)

DAY OF JUDGMENT

When through the North a fire shall rush
        And roll into the East,
And like a fiery torrent brush
        And sweep up South and West,

When all shall stream and lighten round
        And with surprising flames
Both stars and elements confound
        And quite blot out their names,

When Thou shalt spend Thy sacred store
        Of thunders in that heat
And low as ere they lay before
        Thy six-days' buildings beat,

When like a scroll the heavens shall pass
        And vanish clean away,
And naught must stand of that vast space
        Which held up night and day,

When one loud blast shall rend the deep
        And from the womb of earth
Summon up all that are asleep
        Unto a second birth,

When Thou shalt make the clouds Thy seat,
        And in the open air
Thy quick and dead, both small and great,
        Must to Thy bar repair;

O then it will be all too late
        To say, What shall I do?

Repentance there is out of date
    And so is mercy too;

Prepare, prepare me then, O God!
    And let me now begin
To feel my loving Father's rod
    Killing the man of sin!

Give me, O give me crosses here,
    Still more afflictions lend;
That pill, though bitter, is most dear
    That brings health in the end;

Lord, God! I beg nor friends nor wealth,
    But pray against them both;
Three things I'd have, my soul's chief health!
    And one of these seem loath,

A living faith, a heart of flesh,
    The world an enemy;
This last will keep the first two fresh,
    And bring me where I'd be.
                I Pet. 4:7
Now the end of all things is at hand; be you therefore sober,
and watching in prayer.
                    —HENRY VAUGHAN, *Silex Scintillans*

A SONG FOR
ST. CECILIA'S DAY, 1687

From harmony, from heav'nly harmony
    This universal frame began.

When Nature underneath a heap
Of jarring atoms lay,
And cou'd not heave her head,
The tuneful voice was heard from high,
Arise ye more than dead.
Then cold, and hot, and moist, and dry,
In order to their stations leap,
and Music's pow'r obey.
From harmony, from heav'nly harmony
This universal frame began:
From harmony to harmony
Through all the compass of the notes it ran,
The diapason closing full in Man.

.   .   .   .

As from the pow'r of sacred lays
The spheres began to move,
And sung the great Creator's praise
To all the bless'd above;
So when the last and dreadful hour
This crumbling pageant shall devour,
The trumpet shall be heard on high,
The dead shall live, the living die,
And music shall untune the Sky.

—JOHN DRYDEN

10. The Resurrection of the Dead

I know that my Redeemer liveth, and in the last day I shall rise out of the earth. And I shall be clothed again with my skin, and in my flesh I shall see my God. Whom I myself shall see, and my eyes shall behold, and not another: this my hope is laid up in my bosom.

—Job 19:25–27

And you shall know that I am the Lord, when I shall have opened your sepulchres, and shall have brought you out of your graves, O my people: And shall have put my spirit in you, and you shall live. . . .

—Ezechiel 37:13–14

But some man will say: How do the dead rise again? or with what manner of body shall they come? Senseless man, that which thou sowest is not quickened, except it die first. And that which thou sowest, thou sowest not the body that shall be; but bare grain, as of wheat, or of some of the rest. But God giveth it a body as he will: and to every seed its proper body. All flesh is not the same flesh: but one is the flesh of men, another of beasts, another of birds, another of fishes. And there are bodies celestial, and bodies terrestrial: but, one is the glory of the celestial, and another of the terrestrial. One is the glory of the sun, another the glory of the moon, and another the glory of the stars. For star differeth from star in glory. So also is the resurrection of the dead. It is sown in corruption, it shall rise in incorruption. It is sown in dishonor, it shall rise in glory. It is sown in weakness, it shall rise in power. It is sown a natural body, it shall rise a spiritual body.

—St. Paul I Corinthians 15:35–44

The word "resurrection" is as strange to modern feeling as the idea that death is not necessary. We still use it as an inheritance from the age of faith, but in a different sense. In contemporary language, it signifies the return of life in spring after the torpor of winter, or some new accession of energy in a man after a period of stagnation. Resurrection has come to mean an impulse in the rhythm of life, a rise after a preceding descent. There is nothing of this in the resurrection of Christ, and through Him of redeemed mankind. It has another, a more exact, a revolutionary meaning.

It means that Christ, after His death, raised Himself up by the sovereign power of the living God to a new and truly human life. It does not mean merely that His soul was immortal, and received divine glory in eternity; or merely that His image and His Gospel attained a life-giving power in the hearts of those that believed in Him. But it means that His body, after it had died, lived on in a higher way; that His soul, by the power of the Holy Spirit, penetrated and transformed His body; that He entered upon eternal glory in the fullness of His divine and human nature. This doctrine is not a legendary apotheosis, not a later, mythical structure put on a purely human life, but is found everywhere in the original sources. Christ's resurrection is as essential a part of the Gospel, throughout, as His redeeming death. The fact that He rose is as much a fact as that He lived at all. Paul leaves us in no doubt: "And if Christ be not risen again, then is our preaching vain . . . If Christ be not risen [and through him we ourselves] . . . if in this life only we have hope in Christ, we are of all men most miserable" (I Cor. 15:14–19). Without the resurrection of Christ there is no Christianity. Without the resurrection Christianity would become something apt to make anyone capable of serious and profound reasoning "of all men the most miserable."

With Christ's death and resurrection something happened to death. It ceased to be the mere executing of God's justice, the bitter end with beyond it only the "indestructibility of the soul." Christ's death has given it a new character, which does not change its form but does alter its meaning and restore it to what it should have been for the first man—the passage into a new, eternally human life.

—ROMANO GUARDINI, *The Last Things*
(C. E. FORSYTH AND G. B. BRANHAM)

What right have they [atheists] to say that one cannot rise from the dead? Which is the more difficult, to be born, or to rise again; that that which has never been, be, or that that which has been, be again? Is it more difficult to come into being than to return to being? Custom makes the one seem easy, the absence of custom makes the other seem impossible: a popular method of judging!

—BLAISE PASCAL, *Pensées* (G. B. RAWLINGS)

THE TRIUMPH OF CHRIST

As the bird, among the beloved leaves, reposing on the nest of her sweet brood through the night which hides things from us, who, in order to see their longed-for looks and to find the food wherewith she may feed them, in which heavy toils are pleasing to her, anticipates the time upon the open twig, and with ardent affection awaits the sun, fixedly looking till the dawn may break;

thus my Lady was standing erect and attentive, turned toward the region beneath which the sun shows least haste; so that I, seeing her rapt and eager, became such as he who in desire should wish for something, and in hope is satisfied. But short while was there between one and the other *when:* that of my awaiting, I mean, and of my seeing the heavens become brighter and brighter. And Beatrice said, "Behold the hosts of the triumph of Christ, and all the fruit harvested by the revolution of these spheres." It seemed to me her face was all aflame, and her eyes were so full of joy that I must needs pass it over without description.

*   *   *

O Beatrice, sweet guide and dear!

She said to me, "That which overcomes thee is a power from which naught defends itself. Here is the Wisdom and the Power that opened the roads between heaven and earth, for which there had already been such long desire."

—DANTE, *Paradiso,* Canto XXIII (C. E. NORTON)

. . . can we not preserve something at least of the imposing explanation that Origen gives of Ezechiel's vision? As at Jahwe's command, when he breathed upon them, the bones strewn about on the plain came together and were covered with flesh, and life entered into them, and the House of Israel, "an exceeding great army," was thus re-made, so will it be at the last day when death shall be overcome. "When shall come the resurrection of the real, whole body of Christ, then the members of Christ will be knitted together, joint to joint, each one in his place, and the multitude of members will form at last, completely and in full reality, one single Body." For the divine inbreathing which is the very source of resurrection and of life has ever appeared as the source of unity, so much so, in fact, that the resurrection of the dead can be described by the word already used for the formation of the Church —*congregatio.*

Finally, if it is obviously wrong to speak of a real deprivation, a doubt, an anxiety in the glorified Christ, would it not be possible, on the other hand, to consider that as long as the work given him to do by the Father is not complete there is room in heaven for a certain hope on Christ's part? As he still suffers in his earthly members, so, according to this view, Christ hopes in himself and in his heavenly members: and taken together this suffering and this hope complete the redemption. . . .

. . . it matters little really that "hope" hardly seems the right term if we follow to the letter the most current but not necessarily best-founded definitions. It is not surprising that our language should fail in some point in dealing with these subjects. But the idea more or less successfully conveyed by this term is, on the contrary, of the highest importance. The work of God, the work of Christ, is one. In these different states—militant, suffering, triumphant—there is, all the same, but one Church. We can never realize this too keenly. We can differentiate better than many of our forebears between the temporal and the eternal, so that there is no longer any temptation to deny to the elect their essential blessedness. But if we take our stand, as we must, in the temporal order which is ours here below, we must surely affirm that the one and only Church will remain incomplete until the last day. We may conclude with Bossuet: "Jesus Christ will not be whole until the number of the saints is complete. Our gaze must ever be fixed on this consummation of God's work."

—Henri de Lubac, S.J., *Catholicism*
(Lancelot C. Sheppard)

The law of death divides the Universal Church itself into two parts, the one visible upon the earth, the other invisible in the heavens. The dominion of death is established. The heavens and the earth are separated by Man's desire for immediate and material enjoyment of earthly reality and finite existence. Man de-

sired to experience or taste everything by external sensation. He
desired to unite his heavenly spirit to the dust of the earth by a
superficial union of mere contact. But such a union could not last;
it was bound to end in death. In order to reunite the spirit of
humanity to material humanity and to conquer death, Man must
be linked to the Whole, not by the sensible surface of his being but
by its absolute centre which is God. Universal Man is reintegrated
by divine Love which not only raises Man to God, but by identify-
ing him inwardly with the Godhead causes him to embrace in It
all that is, and thus unites him to every single creature by an indissoluble and eternal union. This love brings down divine grace
into earthly nature and triumphs not only over moral evil but
also over its physical consequences, sickness and death. Its work
is the final resurrection. And the Church, which teaches this resurrection in her revealed doctrine, formulated in the last article of
her creed, foreshadows and inaugurates it in the last of her sacraments. In face of sickness and the danger of death, Extreme Unc-
tion is the symbol and pledge of our immortality and of our future
integrity. The cycle of the sacraments, like the cycle of universal
life, is completed by the resurrection of the flesh, the integration of
the whole of humanity, the final incarnation of the divine Wisdom.

—Vladimir Solovyev, *Russia and the
Universal Church* (Herbert Rees)

God made the first Marriage, and man made the first Divorce; God
married the Body and Soul in the Creation, and man divorced the
Body and Soul by death through sin, in his fall. God doth not admit, not justify, not authorize such super-inductions upon such
divorces, as some have imagined; that the soul departing from one
body should become the soul of another body, in a perpetual revolution and transmigration of souls through bodies, which hath
been the giddiness of some philosophers to think; or that the body
of the dead should become the body of an evil spirit, that that

spirit might at his will, and to his purposes inform and inanimate that dead body; God allows no such super-inductions, no such second marriages upon such divorces by death, no such disposition of soul or body, after their dissolution by death. But because God hath made the band of Marriage indissoluble but by death, farther than man can die, this divorce cannot fall upon man; as far as man is immortal, man is a married man still, still in possession of a soul, and a body too; and man is forever immortal in both; immortal in his soul by preservation, and immortal in his body by reparation in the Resurrection. For, though they be separated *à Thoro et Mensa,* from bed and board, they are not divorced; though the soul be at the Table of the Lamb, in Glory, and the body but at the table of the Serpent, in dust; though the soul be *in lecto florido,* in that bed which is always green, in an everlasting spring, in Abraham's Bosom; and the body but in that green-bed whose covering is but a yard and a half of turf and a rug of grass, and the sheet but a winding sheet, yet they are not divorced; they shall return to one another again, in an inseparable re-union in the Resurrection.

—JOHN DONNE, *Sermon LXXX*

After the ascension of the Lord eternal, triumph came to God's servants through grace of the Spirit.

Of this sang Solomon, the son of David, ruler of nations, versed in the hidden things of song, and these words he spake: "This shall be made known, that the Saviour, the King of angels, strong in might, shall ascend the mountains, leaping the lofty downs; He shall encompass the mountains and hills with His glory, and by that noble leap He shall redeem the world and all the inhabitants of earth."

The first leap was when He descended unto the virgin, that spotless maid, and took on Him the likeness of man, yet without sin; that was for the comfort of all the dwellers on earth. The second leap was the birth of the infant, when the Glory of all glories, in the likeness of a child, lay in the manger wrapped in (swaddling) clothes. The third leap, the bound of the King of heaven, was when He ascended the cross, the Father, the Spirit of comfort. The fourth leap was into the grave, when He came down from the tree, (and was held) fast in the sepulchre. The fifth leap was when He cast the host of hell into living torment, and with fiery fetters bound their king within, that fierce spokesman of fiends, where he lieth yet in prison, fastened with chains, bound by his sins. The sixth leap was the joyous revel of the Holy One, when He ascended to heaven, unto His former dwelling. At that holy time the angel-band grew merry with joy and gladness. They saw the King of glory, the Chief of princes, come unto His father-land, unto the bright mansions. That exploit of the Prince was an eternal happiness to the blessed, the dwellers in the City.

Thus, while here on earth, the eternal Son of God leaped boldly over the hills and lofty mountains. So must we mortals, in the thoughts of our hearts, leap from strength to strength and strive after glory, so that we may rise by our holy works to the highest summit, where are hope and joy, a glorious band of liegemen. We have great need to follow after salvation with our hearts, to that place where we earnestly believe in our souls that the Saviour-son, the living God, hath ascended with our human body.

—Cynewulf, *Christ* (Charles Huntington Whitman)

Anselm. . . . It is opposed to the wisdom and justice of God that He should compel man to suffer death without any fault, since He created him righteous for the purpose of enjoying eternal blessedness. It follows, therefore, that if he had never sinned, he would never have died. . . . And from this a future resurrection of the dead at some time is clearly proved. For if man is to be perfectly restored, he ought to be restored to such a state as he would have been in if he had not sinned.

Boso. It cannot be otherwise.

Anselm. Since, therefore, if man had not sinned, he would have been changed to a state of incorruption with the same body which he had, it is necessary that when he is restored he should be restored with his own body in which he is living in this life.

Boso. What shall we answer if anyone says that this ought to be so in those in whom the human race is to be restored, but that it is not necessary in the case of the reprobate?

Anselm. Nothing can be conceived more just or proper than that, just as if man had persevered in righteousness he would have been eternally blessed in his whole nature, *i.e.,* in body and soul; so if he persists in unrighteousness he should be altogether miserable for ever.

Boso. You have satisfied me on these points in a very short time.

Anselm. From these things it is easy to learn that in regard to human nature God will either complete what He began, or that He made in vain so sublime a nature, capable of so great good. But if it is acknowledged that God made nothing more precious than a rational nature, to rejoice in Himself, it is exceedingly unlike Him to permit any rational nature altogether to perish.

Boso. No rational mind can think otherwise.

Anselm. It is needful, therefore, that in regard to human nature God should perfect what He begins. But, as we have said, this cannot be done except by a complete satisfaction for sin, which no sinner can make.

Boso. I see now that it is necessary God should complete what He begins, lest He seem to fail in His design in a way that is not fitting.

—St. Anselm, *Cur Deus Homo?* (Edward S. Prout)

RESURRECTION TO NEW LIFE

Although men will rise as the same individuals, they will not have the same kind of life as before. Now their life is corruptible;

then it will be incorruptible. If nature aims at perpetual existence in the generation of man, much more so does God in the restoration of man. Nature's tendency toward never-ending existence comes from an impulse implanted by God. The perpetual existence of the species is not in question in the restoration of risen man, for this could be procured by repeated generation. Therefore, what is intended is the perpetual existence of the individual. Accordingly risen men will live forever.

Besides, if men once risen were to die, the souls separated from their bodies would not remain forever deprived of the body, for this would be against the nature of the soul . . . Therefore they would have to rise again; and the same thing would happen if they were to die again after the second resurrection. Thus death and life would revolve around each man in cycles of infinite succession; which seems futile. . . .

—St. Thomas Aquinas, *Compendium Theologiae, 155* (Cyril Vollert, S.J.)

RENOVATION OF MAN AND OF MATERIAL NATURE

It is manifest that all things existing for some definite end are disposed in an order required by the end. Therefore, if that to which other things are related as means can vary from perfect to imperfect, the means subordinated to it must be subject to parallel variation, so as to serve the end in either state. Food and clothing, for instance, are prepared otherwise for a child than for a grown man. We have already called attention to the fact that material creation is subordinated to rational nature as to its end. Consequently, when man is admitted to his final perfection after the resurrection, material creation must take on a new condition. This is why we are told that the world is to undergo renovation when man rises, as is taught in the Apocalypse 21:1: "I saw a new heaven

and a new earth," and in Isaias 65:17: "For behold, I create new
heavens and a new earth."

—St. Thomas Aquinas, *Compendium
Theologiae, 169* (Cyril Vollert)

AND DEATH SHALL HAVE NO DOMINION

And death shall have no dominion.
Dead men naked they shall be one
With the man in the wind and the west moon;
When their bones are picked clean and the clean bones gone,
They shall have stars at elbow and foot;
Though they go mad they shall be sane,
Though they sink through the sea they shall rise again;
Though lovers be lost love shall not;
And death shall have no dominion.

And death shall have no dominion.
Under the windings of the sea
They lying long shall not die windily;
Twisting on racks when sinews give way,
Strapped to a wheel, yet they shall not break;
Faith in their hands shall snap in two,
And the unicorn evils run them through;
Split all ends up they shan't crack;
And death shall have no dominion.

And death shall have no dominion.
No more may gulls cry at their ears
Or waves break loud on the seashores;
Where blew a flower may a flower no more
Lift its head to the blows of the rain;
Though they be mad and dead as nails,
Heads of the characters hammer through daisies;

Break in the sun till the sun breaks down,
And death shall have no dominion.

—D<small>YLAN</small> T<small>HOMAS</small>

THE GLORIFIED BODY

". . . When the glorious and sanctified flesh shall be put on us
again, our persons will be more pleasing through being all complete; wherefore whatever of gratuitous light the Supreme Good
gives us will be increased,—light which enables us to see him; so
that our vision needs must increase, our ardor increase which by
that is kindled, our radiance increase which comes from this. But
even as a coal which gives forth flame, and by a vivid glow sur-
passes it, so that it defends its own aspect, thus this effulgence,
which already encircles us, will be vanquished in appearance by
the flesh which all this while the earth covers. Nor will so great a
light be able to fatigue us, for the organs of the body will be strong
for everything which shall have power to delight us."

—Solomon to D<small>ANTE</small> in Canto XIV, *Paradiso*

(C. E. N<small>ORTON</small>)

QUALITIES OF
THE GLORIFIED BODY

. . . The soul is both the form and the motive force of the body.
In its function as form, the soul is the principle of the body, not
only as regards the body's substantial being, but also as regards its
proper accidents, which arise in the subject from the union of
form with matter. The more dominant the form is, the less can
any outside cause interfere with the impression made by the form
on the matter. We see this verified in the case of fire, whose form,

generally accounted the noblest of all elementary forms, confers on fire the power of not being easily diverted from its natural disposition by the influence emanating from any cause.

Since the blessed soul, owing to its union with the first principle of all things, will be raised to the pinnacle of nobility and power, it will communicate substantial existence in the most perfect degree to the body that has been joined to it by divine action. And thus, holding the body completely under its sway, the soul will render the body subtile and spiritual. The soul will also bestow on the body a most noble quality, namely, the radiant beauty of clarity. Further, because of the influence emanating from the soul, the body's stability will not be subject to alteration by any cause; which means that the body will be impassible. Lastly, since the body will be wholly submissive to the soul, as a tool is to him who plies it, it will be endowed with agility. Hence the properties of the bodies belonging to the blessed will be these four: subtility, clarity, impassibility, and agility.

This is the sense of the Apostle's words in I Corinthians 15:42ff.: In death the body "is sown in corruption, it shall rise in incorruption"; this refers to impassibility. "It is sown in dishonor, it shall rise in glory"; this refers to clarity. "It is sown in weakness, it shall rise in power," and hence will have agility. "It is sown a natural body, it shall rise a spiritual body"; in other words, it will be endowed with subtility.

—St. Thomas Aquinas, *Compendium
Theologiae, 168* (Cyril Vollert)

MEMENTO MORI

Beneath that stone, lies buried one,
    Confined in narrow room;
Whose vaster mind, no rest could find,
    Till laid within this tomb.

Whilst upon earth he was alive,
  All was but air and wind;
The world too narrow was to give
  Contentment to his mind.

Not all the treasures, nor the pleasures,
  Wherewith the earth is filled,
Can meat afford, fit for the board,
  Where souls are to be stilled.

Life is the shadow of a dream,
  Which he for sleep did rightly take,
Till death did jog him from the same,
  He never truly was awake.

But now mine eyes (above the skies)
  Are open; and I see
Things in the Light, not in the night,
  But clearly shown to me.

Yes, Lord! though here my body lies
  Confused with other earth;
At Thy command my crumbs shall rise,
  The same as at my birth.

—THOMAS TRAHERNE

Give me my scallop-shell of quiet,
  My staff of faith to walk upon,
My scrip of joy, immortal diet,
  My bottle of salvation,
My gown of glory, hope's true gage,
And thus I'll take my pilgrimage.

Blood must be my body's balmer;
  No other balm will there be given;

Whilst my soul, like quiet palmer,
   Travelleth towards the land of heaven;
Over the silver mountains,
Where spring the nectar fountains;
    Then will I kiss
    The bowl of bliss,
And drink mine everlasting fill
Upon every milken hill.
My soul will be a-dry before;
But, after, it will thirst no more.
          —SIR WALTER RALEIGH,
             The Passionate Man's
             Pilgrimage

Even such is Time, that takes in trust
Our youth, our joys, our all we have,
And pays us but with earth and dust;
Who in the dark and silent grave,
When we have wandered all our ways
Shuts up the story of our days;
But from this earth, this grave, this dust,
My God shall raise me up, I trust.
      —SIR WALTER RALEIGH, *The Author's Epitaph*

THAT NATURE IS A HERACLITEAN FIRE AND OF THE COMFORT OF THE RESURRECTION

Cloud-puffball, torn tufts, tossed pillows flaunt forth, then
   chevy on an air-
built thoroughfare: heaven-roysterers, in gay-gangs   they
   throng; they glitter in marches.

Down roughcast, down dazzling whitewash,   wherever an
   elm arches,
Shivelights and shadowtackle in long   lashes lace, lance, and
   pair.
Delightfully the bright wind boisterous   ropes, wrestles, beats
   earth bare
Of yestertempest's creases;   in pool and rut peel parches
Squandering ooze to squeezed   dough, crust, dust; stanches,
   starches
Squadroned masks and manmarks   treadmire toil there
Footfretted in it. Million-fuelèd,   nature's bonfire burns on.
But quench her bonniest, dearest   to her, her clearest-selvèd
   spark
Man, how fast his firedint,   his mark on mind, is gone!
Both are in an unfathomable, all is in an enormous dark
Drowned. O pity and indig   nation! Manshape, that shone
Sheer off, disseveral, a star,   death blots black out; nor mark
      Is any of him at all so stark
But vastness blurs and time   beats level. Enough! the Resur-
   rection,
A heart's-clarion! Away grief's gasping,   joyless days, de-
   jection.
      Across my foundering deck shone
A beacon, an eternal beam.   Flesh fade, and mortal trash
Fall to the residuary worm;   world's wildfire, leave but ash:
      In a flash, at a trumpet crash,
I am all at once what Christ is,   since he was what I am, and
This Jack, joke, poor potsherd,   patch, matchwood, immortal
   diamond,
      Is immortal diamond.
                                      —GERARD MANLEY HOPKINS

Look now also at the very examples of the divine power. Day
dies into night and is everywhere buried by darkness. The glory of

the universe is shrouded in gloom, everything is blackened. All things are bemeaned, silenced, paralysed, everywhere there is a stoppage of work. Thus is the loss of light mourned. And yet back it comes to life again for the whole world with its outfit, with its dowry, with the sun, being whole and unimpaired, putting to death its own slayer which is night, tearing open its own burial place which is darkness, appearing as heir to itself, until night also comes to life again, it being likewise accompanied by its own equipment. For the rays of the stars which the morning light had put out are re-ignited; the absent constellations, too, which a difference in season had removed, are brought back; the mirror-like moons also, which the progress of the month had worn away, are repaired. Winters and summers, springs and autumns come back again in their courses with their strength, characteristics and fruits. Nay more, even the earth gets its training from the sky: the clothing of the trees after they have been stript, the colouring of the flowers anew, the spreading again of the grass, the display of the identical seeds that have been wasted, and the fact that this does not happen till they have been wasted. A wondrous plan! it is first a cheat, then a preserver; it kills that it may give back; it destroys that it may keep; it corrupts that it may renew; it first breaks up that it may actually enlarge. Since it restores them in a more fertile and cultivated state than they were when they were destroyed, destruction may truly be said to have meant increase, harm profit, and loss gain. Let me say it once for all: Every creation is subject to recurrence. Everything you meet had a previous existence: whatever you have lost will come again. Everything comes a second time: all things return to a settled position when they have gone away, all things begin when they have ceased to be. They are brought to an end in order that they may come into being: nothing is lost except that it may be recovered. All this revolving order of things, therefore, is evidence of the resurrection of the dead. God ordained it in works before He commanded it in writing, He proclaimed it by strength before He proclaimed it in words. He first sent you nature as teacher, intending to send you prophecy also, in order that having learnt from nature, you may the more easily believe prophecy, in order that you may receive at once when you hear what you have already seen everywhere, and that you may not doubt God to be the resuscitator of flesh also, since you know Him to be the restorer of all things. And, to be sure, if all things rise again for man for whom they have been arranged, it follows that this cannot be for man unless for flesh also, and therefore it is absurd to conclude that the thing itself should perish entirely, on whose account and for whom nothing perishes.

—TERTULLIAN, *Concerning the Resurrection*
of the Flesh (A. SOUTER)

11. Hell

. . . the wicked shall not rise again in judgment: nor sinners in the council of the just. For the Lord knoweth the way of the just: and the way of the wicked shall perish.

—Psalm 1:5–6

. . . if you will forgive men their offences, your heavenly Father will forgive you also your offences. But if you will not forgive men, neither will your Father forgive you your offences.

—St. Matthew 6:14–15

And when the Son of man shall come in his majesty, and all the angels with him, then shall he sit upon the seat of his majesty: and all nations shall be gathered together before him, and he shall separate them one from another, as the shepherd separateth the sheep from the goats: and he shall set the sheep on his right hand, but the goats on his left. . . . Then he shall say to them also that shall be on his left hand: Depart from me, you cursed, into everlasting fire which was prepared for the devil and his angels. For I was hungry, and you gave me not to eat: I was thirsty, and you gave me not to drink. I was a stranger, and you took me not in; naked, and you covered me not, sick and in prison, and you did not visit me. Then they also shall answer him, saying: Lord, when did we see thee hungry, or thirsty, or a stranger, or naked, or sick, or in prison, and did not minister to thee? Then he shall answer them, saying: Amen I say to you, as long as you did it not to one of these least, neither did you do it to me. And these shall go into everlasting punishment: but the just, into life everlasting.

—St. Matthew 25:31–33; 41–46

. . . The amiable Dr. Adams suggested that God was infinitely good. JOHNSON: "That He is infinitely good, as far as the perfection of his nature will allow, I certainly believe; but it is necessary for good upon the whole, that individuals should be punished. As to an *individual,* therefore, He is not infinitely good; and as I cannot be *sure* that I have fulfilled the conditions on which salvation is granted, I am afraid I may be one of those who shall be damned." (Looking dismally.) DR. ADAMS: "What do you mean by damned?" JOHNSON (passionately and loudly): "Sent to hell, Sir, and punished everlastingly." DR. ADAMS: "I don't believe that doctrine." JOHNSON: "Hold, Sir; do you believe that some will be punished at all?" DR. ADAMS: "Being excluded from heaven will be a punishment; yet there may be no great positive suffering." JOHNSON: "Well, Sir, but if you admit any degree of punishment, there is an end of your argument. . . . BOSWELL: "But may not a man attain to such a degree of hope as not to be uneasy from the fear of death?" JOHNSON: "A man may have such a degree of hope as to keep him quiet. You see I am not quiet, from the vehemence with which I talk; but I do not despair." MRS. ADAMS: "You seem, Sir, to forget the merits of our Redeemer." JOHNSON: "Madam, I do not forget the merits of my Redeemer; but my Redeemer has said that he will set some on his right hand and some on his left."

—Boswell's *Life of Johnson*

To be, or not to be: that is the question:
Whether 'tis nobler in the mind to suffer
The slings and arrows of outrageous fortune,
Or to take arms against a sea of troubles,
And by opposing end them? To die: to sleep;
No more; and, by a sleep to say we end
The heart-ache and the thousand natural shocks
That flesh is heir to, 'tis a consummation
Devoutly to be wish'd. To die, to sleep;
To sleep: perchance to dream: ay, there 's the rub;
For in that sleep of death what dreams may come
When we have shuffled off this mortal coil,
Must give us pause. There 's the respect
That makes calamity of so long life;
For who would bear the whips and scorns of time,
The oppressor's wrong, the proud man's contumely,
The pangs of dispriz'd love, the law's delay,
The insolence of office, and the spurns
That patient merit of the unworthy takes,
When he himself might his quietus make
With a bare bodkin? who would fardels bear,
To grunt and sweat under a weary life,
But that the dread of something after death,
The undiscover'd country from whose bourn
No traveller returns, puzzles the will,
And makes us rather bear those ills we have
Than fly to others that we know not of?
                    —WILLIAM SHAKESPEARE, *Hamlet*, III, i

It is not impossible that one who is infinitely interested in his
eternal happiness may sometime come into possession of it. But
it is surely quite impossible for one who has lost a sensibility for

it (and this can scarcely be anything else than the infinite interest) ever to enjoy an eternal happiness. If the sense for it is once lost, it may be impossible to recover it. The foolish virgins had lost the infinite passion of expectation. And so their lamps were extinguished. Then came the cry: "The bridegroom cometh." Thereupon they run to the marketplace to buy new oil for themselves, hoping to begin all over again, letting bygones be bygones. And so it was, to be sure, everything was forgotten. The door was shut against them, and they were left outside; when they knocked for admittance, the bridegroom said: "I do not know you." This was no mere quip in which the bridegroom indulged, but the sober truth; for they had made themselves strangers, in the spiritual sense of the word, through having lost the infinite passion.

—Soren Kierkegaard, *Concluding Unscientific Postscript*
(D. F. and L. M. Swenson, and Walter Lowrie)

Oh my black Soul! now thou art summoned
By sickness, death's herald, and champion;
Thou art like a pilgrim, which abroad hath done
Treason, and durst not turn to whence he is fled,
Or like a thief, which till death's doom be read,
Wisheth himself delivered from prison;
But damn'd and hal'd to execution,
Wisheth that still he might be imprisoned.
Yet grace, if thou repent, thou canst not lack;
But who shall give thee that grace to begin?
Oh make thy self with holy mourning black,
And red with blushing, as thou art with sin;
Or wash thee in Christ's blood, which hath this might
That being red, it dyes red souls to white.

—John Donne

OF THE SWEETNESS OF THE COMMANDMENT WHICH GOD HAS GIVEN US OF LOVING HIM ABOVE ALL THINGS

Man is the perfection of the universe; the spirit is the perfection of man; love, that of the spirit; and charity, that of love. Wherefore the love of God is the end, the perfection and the excellence of the universe. In this, Theotimus, consists the greatness and the primacy of the commandment of divine love, which the Saviour calls *the first and greatest commandment.* This commandment is as a sun which gives lustre and dignity to all the sacred laws, to all the divine ordinances, and to all the Holy Scriptures. All is done for this heavenly love, and all has reference to it. From the sacred tree of this commandment grow all the counsels, exhortations, inspirations, and the other commandments, as its flowers, and eternal life as its fruit; and all that does not tend to eternal love tends to eternal death. . . .

God at the Day of Judgment will imprint in the souls of the damned the knowledge of their loss, in a wondrous manner: for the divine majesty will make them clearly see the sovereign beauty of his face, and the treasures of his goodness; and at the sight of this abyss of infinite delights, the will with an extreme effort will desire to cast itself upon him, to be united unto him and enjoy his love. But all in vain, for it shall be as a woman, who in the pangs of childbirth, after having endured violent pains, cruel convulsions, and intolerable pangs, dies in the end without being delivered. For as soon as the clear and fair knowledge of the divine beauty shall have penetrated the understandings of those unhappy spirits, the divine justice shall in such sort deprive the will of its strength that it will be in no wise able to love this object which the understanding purposes to it, and represents to be so amiable; and the sight which should beget in the will so great a love, instead thereof shall engender an infinite sadness. This shall be made eternal by the memory of the sovereign beauty they saw, which shall for ever live in these lost souls; a memory void of all good, yea full of trouble, pains, torments and undying despair, because at the same time there shall be found in the will an impossibility of loving, yea a frightful and everlasting aversion and repugnance to loving this excellence so desirable. Thus the miserable damned shall live for ever in despairing rage—to know so sovereignly amiable a perfection, without being able ever to have the enjoyment or the love of it, because while they might have loved it they would not: they shall burn with a thirst so much the more violent as the remembrance of this fountain of waters of eternal life shall more inflame their ardour: they shall die immortally, *as dogs,* of a famine as much more vehement, as their memory shall more sharpen its insatiable cruelty by the remembrance of the banquet of which they are deprived. *The wicked shall see, and shall be angry, he shall gnash with his teeth and pine away: the desire of the wicked shall perish.* I would not indeed affirm for certain, that the view of God's beauty which the damned shall have, like a flash of lightning, will be as bright as that of the Blessed; but still it will be clear enough to let them see *the Son of man in his majesty. They shall look on him whom they pierced;* and by the view of this glory shall learn the greatness of their loss. Ah! if God had forbidden man to love him, what a torment would that have been to generous hearts! What efforts would they not make to obtain permission to love him? David braved the hazard of a most severe combat to gain the King's daughter,—and what did not Jacob do to espouse Rachel, and the Prince of Sichem to have Dina in marriage? The damned would repute themselves blessed if they could entertain a hope of ever loving God: and the Blessed would esteem themselves damned, if they thought they could ever be deprived of this sacred love.

—St. Francis de Sales, *Treatise on the Love of God* (Henry Benedict Mackey)

HE FORGETS NOTHING

He gives men time, and He can afford to give them time, since He has eternity and is eternally unchangeable. He gives time, and that with premeditation. And then there comes an accounting in eternity, where nothing is forgotten, not even a single one of the improper words that were spoken; and He is eternally unchanged. And yet, it may be also an expression for His mercy that men are thus afforded time, time for conversion and betterment. But how fearful if the time is not used for this purpose! For in that case the folly and frivolity in us would rather have Him straightway ready with His punishment, instead of thus giving men time, seeming to take no cognizance of the wrong, and yet remaining eternally unchanged.

Ask one experienced in bringing up children—and in relation to God we are all more or less as children; ask one who has had to do with transgressors—and each one of us has at least once in his life gone astray, and goes astray for a longer or a shorter time, at longer or shorter intervals: you will find him ready to confirm the observation that for the frivolous it is a great help, or rather, that it is a preventive of frivolity (and who dares wholly acquit himself of frivolity!) when the punishment follows if possible instantly upon the transgression, so that the memory of the frivolous may acquire the habit of associating the punishment immediately with the guilt. Indeed, if transgression and punishment were so bound up with one another that, as in a double-barreled shooting weapon, the pressure on a spring caused the punishment to follow instantly upon the seizure of the forbidden fruit, or immediately upon the commitment of the transgression—then I think that frivolity might take heed. But the longer the interval between guilt and punishment (which when truly understood is an expression for the gravity of the case), the greater the temptation to frivolity; as if the whole might perhaps be forgotten, or as if justice itself might alter and acquire different ideas with the passage of time, or as if at least it would be so long since the wrong was committed that it will become impossible to make an unaltered presentation of it before the bar of justice. Thus frivolity changes, and by no means for the better. It comes to feel itself secure; and when it has become secure it becomes more daring; and so the years pass, punishment is withheld, forgetfulness intervenes, and again the punishment is withheld, but new transgressions do not fail, and the old evil becomes still more malignant. And then finally all is over; death rolls down the curtain—and to all this (it was only frivolity!) there was an eternally unchangeable witness: is this also frivolity? One eternally unchangeable, and it is with this witness that you must make your reckoning. In the instant that the minute-hand of time showed seventy years, and the man died, during all that time the clock of eternity has scarcely moved perceptibly; to such a degree is everything present for the eternal, and for Him who is unchangeable.

And therefore, whoever you may be, take time to consider what I say to myself, that for God there is nothing significant and nothing insignificant, that in a certain sense the significant is for Him insignificant, and in another sense even the least significant is for Him infinitely significant. If then your will is not in harmony with His will, consider that you will never be able to evade Him. Be grateful to Him if through the use of mildness or of severity He teaches you to bring your will into agreement with His—how fearful if He makes no move to arrest your course, how fearful if in the case of any human being it comes to pass that he almost defiantly relies either upon the notion that God does not exist, or upon His having been changed, or even upon His being too great to take note of what we call trifles! For the truth is that God both exists and is eternally unchangeable; and His infinite greatness consists precisely in seeing even the least thing, and remembering even the least thing. Aye, and if you do not will as He wills, that He remembers it unchanged for an eternity!

—Soren Kierkegaard, *The Unchangeableness of God* (D. F. Swenson)

As external death divides the flesh from the soul, so internal death severs the soul from God. Thus "the shadow of death" is the darkness of separation, in that every one of the damned, whilst he is consumed with everlasting fire, is in darkness to the internal light. . . . Accordingly, if the fire that torments the lost could have had light, he that is cast off would never be said to "be cast into darkness." Hence too the Psalmist hath it; "Fire hath fallen upon them, and they have not seen the sun." For "fire falls" upon the ungodly, but "the sun is not seen" on the fire falling; for as the flame of hell devours them, it blinds them to the vision of the true Light, that at the same time both the pain of consuming fire should torment them without, and the infliction of blindness darken them within, so that they, who have done wrong against their Maker both in body and in heart, may at once and the same time be punished in body and in heart, and that they may be made to feel pangs in both ways, who, whilst they lived here, ministered to their depraved gratifications in both.

—St. Gregory the Great, *Morals on the Book of Job*

OF HELL AND FIRE,
A MYSTIC REFLECTION

Fathers and teachers, I ponder "What is hell?" I maintain that it is the suffering of being unable to love. Once in infinite existence, immeasurable in time and space, a spiritual creature was given on his coming to earth, the power of saying, "I am and I love." Once, only once, there was given him a moment of active *living* love and for that was earthly life given him, and with it times and seasons. And that happy creature rejected the priceless gift, prized it and loved it not, scorned it and remained callous. Such a one, having left the earth, sees Abraham's bosom and talks with Abraham as we are told in the parable of the rich man and Lazarus, and beholds heaven and can go up to the Lord. But that is just his torment, to

rise up to the Lord without ever having loved, to be brought close
to those who have loved when he has despised their love. For he
sees clearly and says to himself, "Now I have understanding and
though I now thirst to love, there will be nothing great, no sacrifice
in my love, for my earthly life is over, and Abraham will not come
even with a drop of living water (that is the gift of earthly, active
life) to cool the fiery thirst of spiritual love which burns in me now,
though I despised it on earth; there is no more life for me and will
be no more time! Even though I would gladly give my life for
others, it can never be, for that life is passed which can be sacrificed
for love, and now there is a gulf fixed between that life and this
existence."

They talk of hell fire in the material sense. I don't go into that
mystery and I shun it. But I think if there were fire in material
sense, they would be glad of it, for, I imagine, that in material
agony, their still greater spiritual agony would be forgotten for a
moment. Moreover, that spiritual agony cannot be taken from
them, for that suffering is not external but within them. And if it
could be taken from them, I think it would be bitterer still for the
unhappy creatures. For even if the righteous in Paradise forgave
them, beholding their torments, and called them up to heaven in
their infinite love, they would only multiply their torments, for
they would arouse in them still more keenly a flaming thirst for
responsive, active and grateful love which is now impossible. In
the timidity of my heart I imagine, however, that the very recognition of this impossibility would serve at last to console them. For
accepting the love of the righteous together with the impossibility
of repaying it, by this submissiveness and the effect of this humility,
they will attain at last, as it were, to a certain semblance of that
active love which they scorned in life, to something like its outward expression. . . . I am sorry, friends and brothers, that I cannot express this clearly. But woe to those who have slain themselves
on earth, woe to the suicides! I believe that there can be none more
miserable than they. They tell us that it is a sin to pray for them
and outwardly the Church, as it were, renounces them, but in my

secret heart I believe that we may pray even for them. Love can never be an offence to Christ. For such as those I have prayed inwardly all my life, I confess it, fathers and teachers, and even now I pray for them every day.

Oh, there are some who remain proud and fierce even in hell, in spite of their certain knowledge and contemplation of the absolute truth; there are some fearful ones who have given themselves over to Satan and his proud spirit entirely. For such, hell is voluntary and ever consuming; they are tortured by their own choice. For they have cursed themselves, cursing God and life. They live upon their vindictive pride like a starving man in the desert sucking blood out of his own body. But they are never satisfied, and they refuse forgiveness, they curse God Who calls them. They cannot behold the living God without hatred, and they cry out that the God of life should be annihilated, that God should destroy Himself and His own creation. And they will burn in the fire of their own wrath for ever and yearn for death and annihilation. But they will not attain to death. . . .

—FYODOR DOSTOYEVSKY, *The Brothers Karamazov*
(CONSTANCE GARNETT)

A POISON TREE

I was angry with my friend:
I told my wrath, my wrath did end.
I was angry with my foe:
I told it not, my wrath did grow.

And I water'd it in fears,
Night & morning with my tears;
And I sunned it with smiles,
And with soft deceitful wiles.

And it grew both day and night,
Till it bore an apple bright;
And my foe beheld it shine,
And he knew that it was mine,

And into my garden stole
When the night had veil'd the pole:
In the morning glad I see
My foe outstretch'd beneath the tree.

—WILLIAM BLAKE

SATAN'S SPEECH OF STATE

"Thrones, Dominations, Princedoms, Virtues, Powers!—
For in possession such, not only of right,
I call ye, and declare ye now, returned,
Successful beyond hope, to lead ye forth
Triumphant out of this infernal pit
Abominable, accursed, the house of woe,
And dungeon of our tyrant! Now possess,
As lords, a spacious World, to our native Heaven
Little inferior, by my adventure hard
With peril great achieved. Long were to tell
What I have done, what suffered, with what pain
Voyaged th' unreal, vast, unbounded Deep
Of horrible confusion—over which
By Sin and Death a broad way now is paved,
To expedite your glorious march; but I
Toiled out my uncouth passage, forced to ride
Th' untractable Abyss, plunged in the womb
Of unoriginal Night and Chaos wild,
That, jealous of their secrets, fiercely opposed
My journey strange, with clamorous uproar

Protesting Fate supreme; thence how I found
The new-created World, which fame in Heaven
Long had foretold, a fabric wonderful,
Of absolute perfection; therein Man
Placed in a paradise, by our exile
Made happy. Him by fraud I have seduced
From his Creator, and, the more to increase
Your wonder, with an apple! He, thereat
Offended—worth your laughter!—hath given up
Both his beloved Man and all his World
To Sin and Death a prey, and so to us,
Without our hazard, labour, or alarm,
To range in, and to dwell, and over Man
To rule, as over all he should have ruled.
True is, me also he hath judged; or rather
Me not, but the brute Serpent, in whose shape
Man I deceived. That which to me belongs
Is enmity, which he will put between
Me and Mankind: I am to bruise his heel;
His seed—when is not set—shall bruise my head:
A world who would not purchase with a bruise,
Or much more grievous pain? Ye have th' account
Of my performance; what remains, ye Gods,
But up and enter now into full bliss?"

—JOHN MILTON, *Paradise Lost*, Book X

TO LOSE ONE'S SOUL

The pleasures of the world no man can have for a hundred years,
and no man hath pleasure a hundred days together, but he hath
some trouble intervening: or at least a weariness and a loathing of
the pleasure; and therefore to endure insufferable calamities (suppose it be) for a hundred years, without any interruption, without

so much comfort as the light of a small candle, or a drop of water amounts to in a fever, is a bargain to be made by no man that loves himself, or is not in love with infinite affliction.

If a man were condemned but to lie still, or to lie abed in one posture without turning, for seven years together, would he not buy it off with the loss of all his estate? If a man were to be put upon the rack, for every day, three months together, (suppose him able to live so long) what would he do to be quit of his torture? Would any man curse the King to his face, if he were sure to have both his hands burnt off, and to be tormented with torments three years together? Would any man in his wits accept of a hundred pound a year for forty years, if he were sure to be tormented in the fire for the next hundred years together without intermission? Think then what a thousand years signify: Ten ages, the age of two Empires; but this account I must tell you is infinitely short, though I thus discourse to you, how great fools wicked men are, though this opinion should be true: A goodly comfort surely! that for two or three years' sottish pleasure, a man shall be infinitely tormented but for *a thousand years*. But then when we cast up the minutes, and years, and ages of eternity, the consideration it self is a great hell to those persons who by their evil lives are consigned to such sad and miserable portions.

A thousand years is a long while to be in torment; we find a fever of 21 days to be like an age in length: but when the duration of an intolerable misery is for ever in the height, and for ever beginning, and ten thousand years hath spent no part of its term, but it makes a perpetual efflux, and is like the centre of a circle, which ever transmits lines to the circumference; this is a consideration so sad that the horror of it and the reflexion upon its abode and duration, make a great part of the hell; for hell could not be hell without the despair of accursed souls; for any hope were a refreshment, and a drop of water, which would help to allay those flames, which as they burn intolerably, so they must burn for ever.

And I desire you to consider that although the Scripture uses the word [fire] to express the torments of accursed souls, yet fire can no more equal the pangs of hell than it can torment a material substance; the pains of perishing souls being as much more afflictive than the smart of fire, as the smart of fire is troublesome beyond the softness of Persian carpets, or the sensuality of the Asian Luxury: for the pains of hell; and the perishing or losing of the soul is to suffer the wrath of God, "our God is a consuming fire": that is the fire of hell, when God takes away all comfort from us, nothing to support our spirit is left us, when sorrow is our food and tears our drink; when it is eternal night without Sun or star, or lamp, or sleep; when we burn with fire without light, that is, are loaden with sadness, without remedy or hope or ease, and that this wrath is to be expressed, and to fall upon us, in spiritual, immaterial, but most accursed, most pungent and dolorous emanations, then we feel what it is to lose a soul.

—JEREMY TAYLOR, *XXVIII Sermons*

THE GATES OF HELL

"Through me is the way into the woeful city; through me is the way into eternal woe; through me is the way among the lost people. Justice moved my high creator: the divine Power, the supreme Wisdom and the primal Love made me. Before me were no things created, unless eternal, and I eternal last. Abandon all hope, ye who enter!"

These words of color obscure I saw written at the top of a gate; whereat I, "Master, their meaning is dire to me."

And he to me, like one who knew, "Here it behoves to leave every fear; it behoves that all cowardice should here be dead. We have come to the place where I have told thee that thou shalt see the woeful people, who have lost the good of the understanding."

And when he had put his hand on mine, with a glad countenance, wherefrom I took courage, he brought me within the secret things. Here sighs, laments, and deep wailings were resounding through the starless air; wherefore at first I wept thereat. Strange tongues, horrible cries, words of woe, accents of anger, voices high and hoarse, and sounds of hands with them, were making a tumult which whirls forever in that air dark without change, like the sand when the whirlwind breathes.

—Dante, *Inferno,* Canto III (C. E. Norton)

O Christians, it is time to defend your King and to stand by Him in His great loneliness. For very few of His liegemen have remained faithful to Him, whereas following Lucifer there is a great multitude. And what is worse, they declare themselves His friends in public, yet secretly betray Him: there is scarcely one whom He can trust. O true Friend, how ill art Thou recompensed by him who betrays Thee! O true Christians! Stand by your God as He weeps, for those tears of compassion were not shed for Lazarus only but for others who would never rise from the dead, even though His Majesty were to cry to them in a loud voice. O my Good, all the faults I have committed against Thee were then before Thine eyes. May there be no more of them, Lord, may there be no more either of them or of the faults of others. Raise up these dead souls; and may Thy voice, Lord, be so powerful as to give them life even though they ask it not of Thee, and then, my God, they will come forth, even from the depths of their pleasures.

Lazarus did not ask Thee to raise him from the dead. Thou didst it for a woman who was a sinner. Behold her here, my God, behold a far greater sinner; let Thy mercy shine forth upon her. Miserable creature though I am, I pray to Thee on behalf of those who will not pray to Thee themselves. Well knowest Thou, my King, how tormented I am to see them so forgetful of the great and endless torments which they will have to suffer if they turn not to Thee. Oh, you who are accustomed to delights and pleasures and comforts and to following your own will, take pity upon yourselves! Remember that, for ever and for ever, you will be subject to the unending furies of hell. Behold, behold, the Judge Who will pass sentence upon you is now entreating you. Not for a single moment are you sure of life: why, then, have you no desire to live for ever? O hardness of human hearts! May Thy boundless compassion soften them, my God.

—St. Teresa of Avila, *Exclamations of the Soul to God*
(E. Allison Peers)

To have blessings and to prize them is to be in Heaven; to have them and not to prize them is to be in Hell, I would say, upon earth: to prize them and not to have them is to be in Hell. Which is evident by the effects. To prize blessings while we have them is to enjoy them, and the effect thereof is contentment, pleasure, thanksgiving, happiness. To prize them when they are gone produces envy, covetousness, repining, ingratitude, vexation, misery. But it was no great mistake to say that to have blessings and not to prize them is to be in Hell. For it makes them ineffectual, as if they were absent. Yes, in some respects it is worse than to be in Hell. It is more vicious, and more irrational.

*   *   *

They are deep instructions that are taken out of Hell, and heavenly documents that are taken from above. Upon earth we learn nothing but vanity. Where people dream, and loiter and wander, and disquiet themselves in vain, to make a vain show; but do not profit because they prize not the blessings they have received. To prize what we have is a deep and heavenly instruction. It will make us righteous and serious, wise and holy, divine and blessed. It will make us escape Hell and attain Heaven. For it will make us careful to please Him from whom we have received all, that we may live in Heaven.

—Thomas Traherne, *The First Century*

12. Purgatory

Then they all blessed the just judgment of the Lord, who had discovered the things that were hidden. And so betaking themselves to prayers, they besought him, that the sin which had been committed might be forgotten. But the most valiant Judas exhorted the people to keep themselves from sin, forasmuch as they saw before their eyes what had happened, because of the sins of those that were slain. And making a gathering, he sent twelve thousand drachmas of silver to Jerusalem for sacrifice to be offered for the sins of the dead, thinking well and religiously concerning the resurrection. (For if he had not hoped that they that were slain should rise again, it would have seemed superfluous and vain to pray for the dead,) And because he considered that they who had fallen asleep with godliness, had great grace laid up for them. It is therefore a holy and wholesome thought to pray for the dead, that they may be loosed from sins.

—II Machabees 12:41–45

I desire therefore, first of all, that supplications, prayers, intercessions, and thanksgivings be made for all men: For kings, and for all that are in high stations: that we may lead a quiet and a peaceable life in all piety and chastity. For this is good and accept-

able in the sight of God our Saviour, Who will have all men to be
saved, and to come to the knowledge of the truth.

—St. Paul I Timothy 2:1–4

ON PURGATORY

I proceeded: "What do you think, Sir, of Purgatory, as believed
by the Roman Catholicks?" JOHNSON: "Why, Sir, it is a very
harmless doctrine. They are of opinion that the generality of mankind are neither so obstinately wicked as to deserve everlasting
punishment, nor so good as to merit being admitted into the
society of blessed spirits; and therefore that God is graciously
pleased to allow of a middle state, where they may be purified by
certain degrees of suffering. You see, Sir, there is nothing unreasonable in this." BOSWELL: "But then, Sir, their masses for the
dead?" JOHNSON: "Why, Sir, if it be once established that there
are souls in purgatory, it is as proper to pray for *them,* as for our
brethren of mankind who are yet in this life."

—BOSWELL's *Life of Johnson*

Why, here is a man who has lost all the labour of a whole life:
not one day has he lived for himself, but to luxury, to debauchery,
to covetousness, to sin, to the devil. Then, say, shall we not bewail
this man? shall we not try to snatch him from his perils? For it is,
yes, it is possible, if we will, to mitigate his punishment, if we
make continual prayers for him, if for him we give alms. However
unworthy he may be, God will yield to our importunity. For if
Paul shewed mercy on one (who had no claims on his mercy), and
for the sake of others spared one (whom he would not have spared),
much more is it right for us to do this. By means of his substance,

by means of thine own, by what means thou wilt, aid him: pour in oil, nay rather, water. Has he no almsdeeds of his own to exhibit? Let him have at least those of his kindred. Has he none done by himself? At least let him have those which are done for him, that his wife may with confidence beg him off in that day, having paid down the ransom for him. The more sins he has to answer for, the greater need has he of alms, not only for this reason, but because the alms has not the same virtue now, but far less: for it is not all one to have done it himself, and to have another do it for him; therefore, the virtue being less, let us by quantity make it the greatest. Let us not busy ourselves about monuments, not about memorials. This is the greatest memorial: set widows to stand around him. Tell them his name: bid them all make for him their prayers, their supplications: this will overcome God: though it have not been done by the man himself, yet because of him another is the author of the almsgiving. Even this pertains to the mercy of God: "widows standing around and weeping" know how to rescue, not indeed from the present death, but from that which is to come. Many have profited even by the alms done by others on their behalf: for even if they have not got perfect (deliverance), at least they have found some comfort thence. If it be not so, how are children saved? And yet there, the children themselves contribute nothing, but their parents do all: and often have women had their children given them, though the children themselves contributed nothing. Many are the ways God gives us to be saved, only let us not be negligent.

How then if one be poor? say you. Again I say, the greatness of the alms is not estimated by the quantity given, but by the purpose. Only give not less than thine ability, and thou hast paid all. . . . Knowing these things, let us devise what consolations we can for the departed, instead of tears, instead of laments, instead of tombs, our alms, our prayers, our oblations, that both they and we may attain unto the promised blessings, by the grace and loving-kindness of His only-begotten Son our Lord Jesus Christ, with Whom to the Father and the Holy Ghost together be glory, dominion, honour, now and ever, world without end. Amen.

—St. John Chrysostom, *Homily XXI, On the*
Acts of the Apostles

. . . a single prayer by a devout pauper may avail more with God than a thousand Masses endowed by a millionaire for the repose of his soul or for the souls of his relations. The priest at the altar is not a magician; he is an ambassador.

—Arnold Lunn, *Within That City*

. . . what belongs to God must by all means and at any cost be preserved for Him. If, then, on the one hand, the soul is un-encumbered with superfluities and no trouble connected with the body presses it down, its advance towards Him Who draws it to Himself is sweet and congenial. But suppose, on the other hand, that it has been transfixed with the nails of propension so as to be held down to a habit connected with material things,—a case like that of those in the ruins caused by earthquakes, whose bodies are crushed by the mounds of rubbish; and let us imagine by way of illustration that these are not only pressed down by the weight of the ruins, but have been pierced as well with some spikes and splinters discovered with them in the rubbish. What, then, would naturally be the plight of those bodies, when they were being dragged by relatives from the ruins to receive the holy rites of burial, mangled and torn entirely, disfigured in the most direful manner conceivable, with the nails beneath the heap harrowing them by the very violence necessary to pull them out?—Such I think is the plight of the soul as well, when the Divine force, for God's very love of man, drags that which belongs to Him from the ruins of the irrational and material. Not in hatred or revenge for a wicked life, to my thinking, does God bring upon sinners those painful dispensations; He is only claiming and drawing to Himself whatever, to please Him, came into existence. But while He for a noble end is attracting the soul to Himself, the Fountain of all Blessedness, it is the occasion necessarily to the being so attracted of a state of torture. Just as those who refine gold from the dross which it contains not only get this base alloy to melt in the fire, but are obliged to melt the pure gold along with the alloy, and then while this last is being consumed the gold remains, so, while evil is being consumed in the purgatorial fire, the soul that is welded to this evil must inevitably be in the fire, too, until the spurious material alloy is consumed and annihilated by this fire. If a clay of the more tenacious kind is deeply plastered round a rope, and then the end of the rope is put through a narrow hole, and then some one on the further side violently pulls it by that end, the result must be that, while the rope itself obeys the force exerted, the clay that has been plastered upon it is scraped off it with this violent pulling and is left outside the hole, and, moreover, is the cause why the rope does not run easily through the passage, but has to undergo a violent tension at the hands of the puller. In such a manner, I think, we may figure to ourselves the agonized struggle of that soul which has wrapped itself up in earthly material passions, when God is drawing it, His own one, to Himself, and the foreign matter, which has somehow grown into its substance, has to be scraped from it by main force, and so occasions it that keen intolerable anguish.

—St. Gregory of Nyssa, *On the Soul and the Resurrection* (William Moore and Henry Austin Wilson)

"The soul . . . seeing" (its own imperfection) and, "that it cannot, because of the impediment" (of this imperfection) "attain (*acostarsi*) to its end, which is God; and that the impediment cannot be removed (*levato*) from it, except by means of Purgatory, swiftly and of its own accord (*volontieri*) casts itself into it." . . . the soul is here absolutely impeded in that, now immensely swift, movement, and is brought to a dead stop, as though by something hard on the soul's own surface, which acts as a barrier between itself and God; it is offered the chance of escaping from this intolerable suffering into the lesser one of dissolving this hard obstacle in the ocean of the purifying fire: and straightway plunges into the latter.

"If the soul could find another Purgatory above the actual one, it would, so as more rapidly to remove from itself so important (*tanto*) an impediment, instantly cast itself into it, because of the impetuosity of that love which exists between God and the soul and tends to conform the soul to God. . . .

"I see the divine essence to be of such purity, that the soul which should have within it the least mote (*minimo chè*) of imperfection, would rather cast itself into a thousand hells, than find itself with that imperfection in the presence of God. . . .

"The soul which, when separated from the body, does not find itself in that cleanness (*nettezza*) in which it was created, seeing in itself the stain, and that this stain cannot be purged out except by means of Purgatory, swiftly and of its own accord casts itself in; and if it did not find this ordination apt to purge that stain, in that very moment there would be spontaneously generated (*si generebbe*) within itself a Hell worse than Purgatory."

—St. Catherine of Genoa, translated and glossed by
Friedrich von Hügel in *The Mystical Element
in Religion*

. . . and lo! the venerable old man crying, "What is this, ye laggard spirits? What negligence, what stay is this? Run to the mountain to strip off the slough that lets not God be manifest to you."

—Dante, *Purgatorio,* Canto II (C. E. Norton)

We have to do with the mystery of a grace that forgives and creates anew. When he is judged, the man sees himself entirely in the holy light of God, sees the circumstances, the causes, the accidental and the essential, sees the outside and the inside, sees to the very bottom, what was known to him or what was hidden from him because it lay too deep, or had been forgotten, suppressed, or slighted. And he sees it all without a shadow of protection. Pride, vanity, evasion, indifference are gone. He is exposed, sensitive, collected. He is on the side of truth in opposition to himself. He is prepared to face his own life with its undone duties, its loose ends, its muddle. In a mystery of suffering the heart adjusts itself to contrition and delivers itself up to the power of the holy Creator-Spirit. Opportunities misused are re-bestowed, wrong turns retraced and taken rightly. Evil, by being lived again, is made over into good. The improvement is not an external matter. The whole nature, plunged into re-creating grace, through the mystery of effectual repentance, comes out new-made.

This is what the Church calls Purgatory. Let no rightly disposed heart say it is no concern of his. Rather does not what is deepest in us respond thankfully to the assurance that it shall be thus? Does it not say, "I wish I had reached that goal"?

—ROMANO GUARDINI, *The Last Things*
(C. B. FORSYTH AND G. B. BRANHAM)

Ah! my Theotimus, the souls in Purgatory are there doubtless for their sins, and for sins which they have detested and do supremely detest, but as for the abjection and pain which remain from being detained in that place, and from being deprived for a space of the enjoyment of the blessed love which is in Paradise, they endure this lovingly, and they devoutly pronounce the canticle of the Divine justice: *Thou art just, O Lord, and thy judgment is right.*

—ST. FRANCIS DE SALES, *Treatise on the Love of God*
(HENRY BENEDICT MACKEY)

PARADISE

I bless thee, Lord, because I GROW
Among thy trees, which in a ROW
To thee both fruit and order OWE.

What open force, or hidden CHARM
Can blast my fruit, or bring me HARM,
While the enclosure is thine ARM?

Inclose me still for fear I START.
Be to me rather sharp and TART,
Than let me want thy hand and ART.

When thou dost greater judgements SPARE,
And with thy knife but prune and PARE,
Ev'n fruitful trees more fruitful ARE,

Such sharpness shows the sweetest FREND,
Such cuttings rather heal than REND,
And such beginnings touch their END.

—GEORGE HERBERT

THE DREAM OF GERONTIUS

ANGEL

Thy judgment now is near, for we are come
Into the veilèd presence of our God.

SOUL

I hear the voices that I left on earth.

ANGEL

It is the voice of friends around thy bed,
Who say the "Subvenite" with the priest.

Hither the echoes come; before the Throne
Stands the great Angel of the Agony,
The same who strengthen'd Him, what time He knelt
Lone in that garden shade, bedew'd with blood.
That Angel best can plead with Him for all
Tormented souls, the dying and the dead.

ANGEL OF THE AGONY

Jesu! by that shuddering dread which fell on Thee;
Jesu! by that cold dismay which sicken'd Thee;
Jesu! by that pang of heart which thrill'd in Thee;
Jesu! by that mount of sins which crippled Thee;
Jesu! by that sense of guilt which stifled Thee;
Jesu! by that innocence which girdled Thee;
Jesu! by that sanctity which reign'd in Thee;
Jesu! by that Godhead which was one with Thee;
Jesu! spare these souls which are so dear to Thee;
Souls, who in prison, calm and patient, wait for Thee;
Hasten, Lord, their hour, and bid them come to Thee,
To that glorious Home, where they shall ever gaze on Thee.

SOUL

I go before my Judge. Ah! . . . .

ANGEL

. . . . Praise to His Name!
The eager spirit has darted from my hold,
And, with the intemperate energy of love,
Flies to the dear feet of Emmanuel;
But, ere it reach them, the keen sanctity,
Which with its effluence, like a glory, clothes
And circles round the Crucified, has seized,
And scorch'd, and shrivell'd it; and now it lies
Passive and still before the awful Throne.
O happy, suffering soul! for it is safe,
Consumed, yet quicken'd, by the glance of God.

SOUL

Take me away, and in the lowest deep
    There let me be,
And there in hope the lone night-watches keep,
    Told out for me.
There, motionless and happy in my pain,
    Lone, nor forlorn,—
There will I sing my sad perpetual strain,
    Until the morn.
There will I sing, and soothe my stricken breast,
    Which ne'er can cease
To throb, and pine, and languish, till possest
    Of its Sole Peace.
There will I sing my absent Lord and Love:—
    Take me away,
That sooner I may rise, and go above,
And see Him in the truth of everlasting day.

ANGEL

Now let the golden prison ope its gates,
Making sweet music, as each fold revolves
Upon its ready hinge. And ye, great powers,
Angels of Purgatory, receive from me
My charge, a precious soul, until the day,
When, from all bond and forfeiture released,
I shall reclaim it for the courts of light.

SOULS IN PURGATORY

1. Lord, Thou hast been our refuge: in every generation;
2. Before the hills were born, and the world was: from age
    to age Thou art God.
3. Bring us not, Lord, very low: for Thou hast said, Come
    back again, ye sons of Adam.
4. A thousand years before Thine eyes are but as yesterday:
    and as a watch of the night which is come and gone.

5. The grass springs up in the morning: at evening tide it shrivels up and dies.

6. So we fail in Thine anger: and in Thy wrath are we troubled.

7. Thou hast set our sins in Thy sight: and our round of days in the light of Thy countenance.

8. Come back, O Lord! how long: and be entreated for Thy servants.

9. In Thy morning we shall be filled with Thy mercy: we shall rejoice and be in pleasure all our days.

10. We shall be glad according to the days of our humiliation: and the years in which we have seen evil.

11. Look, O Lord, upon Thy servants and on Thy work: and direct their children.

12. And let the beauty of the Lord our God be upon us: and the work of our hands, establish Thou it.

Glory be to the Father, and to the Son: and to the
Holy Ghost.

As it was in the beginning, is now, and ever shall
be: world without end. Amen.

ANGEL

Softly and gently, dearly-ransom'd soul,
In my most loving arms I now enfold thee,
And, o'er the penal waters, as they roll,
I poise thee, and I lower thee, and hold thee.

And carefully I dip thee in the lake,
And thou, without a sob or a resistance,
Dost through the flood thy rapid passage take,
Sinking deep, deeper, into the dim distance.

Angels, to whom the willing task is given,
Shall tend, and nurse, and lull thee, as thou liest;
And masses on the earth, and prayers in heaven,
Shall aid thee at the Throne of the Most Highest.

Farewell, but not for ever! brother dear,
 Be brave and patient on thy bed of sorrow;
Swiftly shall pass thy night of trial here,
 And I will come and wake thee on the morrow.

      —JOHN HENRY NEWMAN

13. Heaven

The Lord is sweet to all: and his tender mercies are over all his works. Let all thy works, O Lord, praise thee: and let thy saints bless thee. They shall speak of the glory of thy kingdom: and shall tell of thy power: To make thy might known to the sons of men: and the glory of the magnificence of thy kingdom. Thy kingdom is a kingdom of all ages: and thy dominion endureth throughout all generations.

—Psalm 144:8–13

. . . we speak the wisdom of God in a mystery, a wisdom which is hidden, which God ordained before the world, unto our glory: Which none of the princes of this world knew; for if they had known it, they would never have crucified the Lord of glory. But, as it is written: *That eye hath not seen nor ear heard, neither hath it entered into the heart of man, what things God hath prepared for them that love him.*

—St. Paul I Corinthians 2:7–9

And I saw a new heaven and a new earth. For the first heaven and the first earth was gone, and the sea is now no more. And I John saw the holy city, the new Jerusalem, coming down out of heaven from God, prepared as a bride adorned for her husband. And I heard a great voice from the throne, saying: Behold the tabernacle of God with men, and he will dwell with them. And they shall be his people; and God himself with them shall be their God. And God shall wipe away all tears from their eyes: and death shall be no more, nor mourning, nor crying, nor sorrow shall be any more, for the former things are passed away. And he that sat on the throne, said: Behold, I make all things new.

—Apocalypse 21:1–5

It is a sad perverseness of man to prefer war to peace, cares to rest, grief to joy, and the vanities of this narrow stage to the true and solid comforts in heaven.

—Henry Vaughan, *Man in Darkness, or,*
A Discourse of Death

. . . it is God's will that we have true liking with him in our salvation. And therein he will, that we be mightily comforted and strengthened. And thus will he merrily, with his grace, that our soul be occupied; for we be his bliss, for in us he liketh without end, and so shall we in him with his grace.

—Juliana of Norwich, *Revelations of Divine Love*

If anyone were able rightly to weigh time and eternity, he ought rather to desire to lie in a fiery furnace for a hundred years than to be deprived in eternity of the smallest reward for the smallest suffering; for this has an end, but the other is without end.

—Blessed Henry Suso, *Eternal Wisdom*

ETERNITY

He who bends to himself a joy
Does the winged life destroy;
But he who kisses the joy as it flies
Lives in eternity's sun rise.

—WILLIAM BLAKE

CONTEMPLATION OF HEAVEN

We attribute but one privilege and advantage to Man's body, above other moving creatures, that he is not as others, groveling, but of an erect, of an upright form, naturally built and disposed to the contemplation of Heaven. Indeed it is a thankful form, and recompenses that soul, which gives it, with carrying that soul so many feet higher, towards heaven. Other creatures look to the earth; and even that is no unfit object, no unfit contemplation for Man; for thither he must come; but because Man is not to stay there, as other creatures are, Man in his natural form is carried to the contemplation of that place which is his home, Heaven. This is Man's prerogative; but what state hath he in this dignity? A fever can fillip him down, a fever can depose him; a fever can bring that head, which yesterday carried a crown of gold, five feet towards a crown of glory, as low as his own feet today. When God came to breathe into Man the breath of life, He found him flat upon the ground; when He comes to withdraw that breath from him again, He prepares him to it, by laying him flat upon his bed. Scarce any prison so close, that affords not the prisoner two or three steps. The anchorites that barqued themselves up in hollow trees, and immured themselves in hollow walls; that perverse man that barrelled himself in a tub, all could stand, or sit, and enjoy some change of posture. A sick bed is a grave; and all that the patient says there is but a varying of his own Epitaph. Every night's bed is a type of the grave: at night we tell our servants at what hour we will rise; here we cannot tell ourselves, at what day, what week, what month. Here the head lies as low as the foot; the head of the people as low as they whom those feet trod upon; and that hand that signed pardons is too weak to beg his own, if he might have it for lifting up that hand: strange fetters to the feet, strange manacles to the hands, when the feet and hands are bound so much the faster by how much the cords are slacker; so much the less able to do their offices, by how much more the sinews and ligaments are the looser. In the grave I may speak through the stones, in the voice of my friends, and in the accents of those words which their love may afford my memory; here I am mine own Ghost, and rather affright my beholders than instruct them; they conceive the worst of me now, and yet fear worse; they give me for dead now, and yet wonder how I do, when they wake at midnight, and ask how I do tomorrow. Miserable and (though common to all) inhuman posture, where I must practice my lying in the grave, by lying still, and not practice my Resurrection, by rising any more.

—JOHN DONNE, *Devotions on Emergent Occasions*

. . . in that place there is no want, nor any deficiency, nor concupiscence, nor generation, nor ending, nor failure, nor death, nor termination, nor old age. There is neither hatred, nor wrath, nor envy, nor weariness, nor toil, nor darkness, nor night, nor falsehood. There is not in that place any want at all; but it is full of light, and life, and grace, and fulness, and satisfaction, and renewal, and love, and all the good promises that are written but not yet sealed. For there is there *that which eye hath not seen and ear hath not heard, and which hath not come up into the heart of man,* that which is unspeakable and which a man cannot utter. And the Apostle said:—*That which God hath prepared from them that love Him.* (Gal. iii, 28)

—Aphrahat, *Select Demonstrations: Of Death and the Latter Times*

He that asks me what heaven is, means not to hear me, but to silence me; he knows I cannot tell him: when I meet him there, I shall be able to tell him, and then he will be as able to tell me; yet then we shall be but able to tell one another, this, this that we enjoy is heaven, but the tongues of angels, the tongues of glorified saints, shall not be able to express what that heaven is; for even in heaven our faculties shall be finite. Heaven is not a place that was created; for all place that was created shall be dissolved. God did not plant a Paradise for himself, and remove to that, as he planted a Paradise for Adam, and removed him to that; but God is still where he was before the world was made. And in that place, where there are more suns than there are stars in the firmament, (for all the saints are suns) and more light in another Sun, The S[o]n of righteousness, the Son of Glory, the Son of God, than in all them, in that illustration, that emanation, that effusion of beams of glory, which began not to shine 6000 years ago, but 6000 millions of millions ago, had been 6000 millions of millions before that, in those eternal, in those uncreated heavens, shall we see God.

—John Donne, *Sermon XXIII*

PEACE

My soul, there is a country
Far beyond the stars,
Where stands a winged sentry
All skilfull in the wars,

There above noise, and danger
   Sweet Peace sits crown'd with smiles,
And one born in a manger
   Commands the beauteous files,
He is thy gracious friend,
   And (O my soul awake!)
Did in pure love descend
   To die here for thy sake,
If thou canst get but thither,
   There grows the flower of Peace,
The Rose that cannot wither,
   Thy fortress, and thy ease;
Leave then thy foolish ranges;
   For none can thee secure,
But one, who never changes,
   Thy God, thy life, thy cure.
           —Henry Vaughan, *Silex Scintillans*

THE NEW JERUSALEM

Hierusalem, my happy home,
   When shall I come to thee?
When shall my sorrows have an end,
   Thy joys when shall I see?

O happy harbour of the Saints!
   O sweet and pleasant soil!
In thee no sorrow may be found,
   No grief, no care, no toil.

There lust and lucre cannot dwell,
   There envy bears no sway;
There is no hunger, heat, nor cold,
   But pleasure every way.

Thy walls are made of precious stones,
   Thy bulwarks diamonds square;
Thy gates are of right orient pearl,
   Exceeding rich and rare.

Thy turrets and thy pinnacles
   With carbuncles do shine;
Thy very streets are paved with gold,
   Surpassing clear and fine.

Ah, my sweet home, Hierusalem,
   Would God I were in thee!
Would God my woes were at an end,
   Thy joys that I might see!

                —ANONYMOUS (1601)

In Sion lodge me (Lord) for pity,
Sion, David's kingly City.

Built by him that's only good,
Whose gates are of the cross's wood.

Whose keys are Christ's undoubted word,
Whose dwellers fear none but the Lord.

Whose walls are stone, strong, quick and bright,
Whose keeper is the Lord of light.

Here the light doth never cease
Endless spring and endless peace.

Here is music, heaven filling,
Sweetness evermore distilling.

Here is neither spot nor taint,
No defect, nor no complaint.

No man crookèd, great nor small,
But to Christ conformèd all.
                    —HILDEBERT OF LAVARDIN, *Prayer to the*
                        Holy Trinity (WILLIAM CRASHAW)

CHRIST'S KINGDOM

Christ's Kingdom being in order to the Kingdom of his Father, which shall be manifest at the day of Judgment, must therefore be spiritual, because then it is that all things must become spiritual, not only by way of eminency, but by entire constitution and perfect change of natures. Men shall be like Angels, and Angels shall be comprehended in the lap of spiritual and eternal felicities; the soul shall not understand by material phantasms, neither be served by the provisions of the body, but the body it self shall become spiritual, and the eye shall see intellectual objects, and the mouth shall feed upon hymns and glorifications of God; the belly shall be then satisfied by the fullness of righteousness, and the tongue shall speak nothing but praises, and the propositions of a celestial wisdom; the motion shall be the swiftness of an Angel; and it shall be clothed with white as with a garment: holiness is the Sun, and righteousness is the Moon in that region; our society shall be choirs of singers, and our conversation wonder; contemplation shall be our food, and love shall be the wine of elect souls; and as to every natural appetite there is now proportion'd an object, crass, material, unsatisfying, and allayed with sorrow and uneasiness: so there be new capacities and equal objects, the desires shall be fruition, and the appetite shall not suppose want, but a faculty of delight, and an unmeasureable complacency: the will and the understanding, love and wonder, joys every day and the same forever; this shall be their state who shall be accounted worthy of the resurrection to this life; where the body shall be a partner, but no servant; where it shall have no work of its own, but it shall rejoice with the soul; where the soul shall rule without resistance, or an enemy, and we shall be fitted to enjoy God who is the Lord and Father of spirits. In this world we see it is quite contrary: we long for perishing meat, and fill our stomachs with corruption; we look after white and red, and the weaker beauties of the night; we are passionate after rings and seals, and enraged at the breaking of a crystal; we delight in the society of fools and weak persons; we laugh at sin, and contrive mischiefs; and the body rebels against the soul, and carries the cause against all its just pretences; and our soul it self is above half of it earth, and stone in its affections, and distempers; our hearts are hard, and inflexible to the softer whispers of mercy and compassion, having no loves for any thing but strange flesh, and heaps of money, and popular noises, for misery and folly; and therefore we are a huge way off from the Kingdom of God, whose excellencies, whose designs, whose ends, whose constitution is spiritual and holy, and separate, and sublime, and perfect.

—JEREMY TAYLOR, *XXV Sermons*

Let the soul, then, be not too eager, while it is still on earth among the "women" to search out heavenly things, lest glory overwhelm it. "The vision you demand, O Bride, in asking where I feed My flock, where I repose at noon," the Bridegroom says, "is too sublime for you. While you are in the body, you have not strength to look upon the marvellous noon-day light wherein I dwell. You must wait till the very last for that, when I shall have made you glorious before Me, without spot or wrinkle or any such thing. And then, when I shall have appeared, you will be wholly fair, as I am wholly fair; you will be altogether like Me, for you will see Me as I am. And you will hear Me say, 'Thou art all fair, My love, and there is no spot in thee.' "

—ST. BERNARD, *On the Song of Songs*
(A Religious of C.S.M.V.)

That the high and the next way to heaven is run by desires, and not by paces of feet.

. . . thee thinkest that thou hast every evidence that heaven is upwards; for Christ ascended the air bodily upwards, and sent the Holy Ghost as He promised coming from above bodily, seen of all His disciples; and this is our belief. And therefore thee thinkest, since thou hast thus very evidence, why shalt thou not direct thy mind upward in the time of thy prayer?

And to this will I answer thee so feebly as I can, and say: since it so was, that Christ should ascend bodily and thereafter send the Holy Ghost bodily, then it was more seemly that it was upwards and from above than either downwards and from beneath, behind, or before, on one side or on the other. But else than for this seemliness, Him needed never the more to have went upwards than downwards; I mean for nearness of the way. For heaven ghostly is as nigh down as up, and up as down: behind as before, before as behind, on one side as other. Insomuch, that whoso had a true desire for to be at heaven, then that same time he were in heaven ghostly. For the high and the next way thither is run by desires, and not by paces of feet. And therefore saith Saint Paul of himself and many other thus; although our bodies be presently here in earth, nevertheless yet our living is in heaven. He meant their love and their desire, the which is ghostly their life. And surely as verily is a soul there where it loveth, as in the body that liveth by it and to the which it giveth life. And therefore if we will go to heaven ghostly, it needeth not to strain our spirit neither up nor down, nor on one side nor on other.

—*The Cloud of Unknowing*, 60
(Ed. EVELYN UNDERHILL)

NOW AND THEN

. . . If individual goods are delectable, strive to imagine how delectable is that good which contains the enjoyment of all goods, not such as we have experienced in created objects, but as different as the Creator from the creature. If the created life is good, how good is the creative life? If the salvation granted is delightful, how delightful is the salvation which has given all salvation? If wisdom in the knowledge of the created world is sweet, how sweet is the wisdom which has created all things from nothing? Lastly, if there are many great delights in pleasurable things, how fine and how great is the delight in Him who has made these delightful things?

Who shall enjoy this good? What shall belong to him and what shall not belong to him? Whatever he shall want shall be his and whatever he shall not want shall not be his. The goods of body and soul will be such as eye hath not seen and ear heard, neither has the heart of man conceived.

Why do you wander abroad, little man, in search of the goods of soul and body? Love the one good in which are all goods, and it is enough. Seek the simple good which is all good, and it is enough. What do you love, my flesh? What do you seek, my soul? There is whatever you love, whatever you seek.

If beauty delights them, there "shall the just shine as the sun." If swiftness or endurance or freedom of body, which nothing can withstand, delight them, they shall be as angels of God—because though "it is sown a natural body, it shall rise a spiritual body"— in power certainly, though not in nature. If it is a long and sound life that pleases them, there is a healthy eternity and an eternal health because the righteous shall live forever and "the salvation of the just is from the Lord." If it is satisfaction of hunger, they shall be satisfied when the glory of the Lord has appeared. If it is quenching of thirst, they shall be abundantly satisfied with the plenty of God's house. If it is melody, there the choir of angels sings forever before God. If it is anything not impure, but pure pleasure, Thou shalt make them drink of the river of Thy pleasure, O God.

If it is wisdom that delights them, the very wisdom of God will reveal itself to them. If friendship, they shall love God more than themselves, and one another as themselves. God shall love them more than they themselves, for they love Him and themselves and one another through Him, and He loves Himself and them through Himself. If they seek agreement, they shall all have a single will because they will have no will but God's will.

If they seek power, they shall have all power to fulfill their will, as God has to fulfill His. As God has power to do what He wills, through Himself, so they will have power, through Him, to do what they will. Since they will not will anything except what He wills, He shall will whatever they will, and what He shall will cannot fail to be. If honor and riches are their delight, God shall make His good and faithful servants rulers over many things. They shall be called the children of God and gods. Where His Son shall be, there also shall be "the heirs indeed of God and joint heirs with Christ."

If true security delights them, undoubtedly they will be as sure that these goods, or rather that good, will never fail them, as they will be sure that they will not lose it of their own accord. That God, who loves them, will not take it away against the will of those who love Him. Nothing more powerful than God will separate Him from them against His will and theirs.

But what a joy and how great it is, where is there a good of such a kind or so great? Heart of man, needy heart, heart acquainted with sorrows, overwhelmed with sorrows, how greatly would you rejoice if you abounded in all these things? Ask your inner self whether it could contain its joy over so great a blessedness for itself.

Yet, if anyone else whom you love as much as yourself possessed the same blessedness, your joy would be doubled because you would rejoice as much for him as for yourself. If two or many more have the same joy, you would rejoice as much for each one as for yourself, if you love each as yourself. Thus in that perfect love of innumerable blessed angels and sainted men where none will love another less than himself, everyone will rejoice for each of the others as for himself.

If the heart of man will scarcely contain his joy over his own great good, how will it contain so many great joys? Because everyone rejoices as much in another's good as he loves the other, it follows that, as in perfect happiness each one undoubtedly will love God beyond comparison and more than himself and all the others with himself, so he will rejoice beyond measure in the happiness of God, more than in his own and that of all the others with him.

If they will so love God with all their heart and all their mind and all their soul, still all their heart and all their mind and all their soul will not suffice for the worthiness of this love. Surely they will so rejoice with all their heart and all their mind and all their soul that all their heart and all their mind and all their soul will not suffice for the fullness of their joy.

Not yet, then, have I told or conceived, O Lord, how greatly Your blessed shall rejoice. They will rejoice according as they will love, and they will love according as they will know. How far will they know You, Lord, and how much will they love You? Truly eye has not seen nor ear heard, nor has it entered into the heart of man in this life how much they will know You and love You in that life.

I pray, O God, to know You, to love You, that I may rejoice in You. If I cannot attain full joy in this life, may I at least advance from day to day until that joy becomes full. May the knowledge of You advance in me here, and there be made full. May love of You increase here, and there be full that here my joy may be great in hope and there full in fact. Lord, through Your Son You command, You counsel us to ask, and You promise that we shall receive that our joy may be full. I ask, true Lord, that I may be granted that my joy be full. I ask, O Lord, as You counsel through the wonderful Counsellor, that I receive what You promise by virtue of Your truth, that my joy may be full. Meanwhile, let my mind meditate upon it, let my tongue speak of it, let my heart love it, let my mouth talk of it, let my soul hunger for it, let my flesh thirst for it, let my whole being desire it until I enter into the joy of my

Lord who is the Three and the One God, "who is blessed forever. Amen."

—St. Anselm, *Proslogion* (E. E. Nemmers)

THE VISION OF GOD
IN HIS ESSENCE

The created intellect will see God in His essence, and not in any mere likeness. In the latter kind of vision, the object understood may be at a distance from the present intellect; for example, a stone is present to the eye by its likeness, but is absent in substance. But . . . God's very essence is in some mysterious way united to the created intellect, so that God may be seen just as He is. Thus, when we arrive at our last end, what was formerly believed about God will be seen, and what was hoped for as absent will be closely embraced.

—St. Thomas Aquinas, *Compendium
Theologiae, 164* (Cyril Vollert)

SUPREME PERFECTION AND
HAPPINESS IN
THE VISION OF GOD

We should further understand that delight is engendered by the apprehension of a suitable good. Thus sight rejoices in beautiful colors, and taste in sweet savors. But this delight of the senses can be prevented if the organ is indisposed; the same light that is charming to healthy eyes is annoying to sore eyes. However, since the intellect does not understand by employing a bodily organ, as we showed above, no sorrow mars the delight that consists in the contemplation of truth. Of course, sadness can indirectly attend the mind's contemplation, when the object of truth is apprehended as harmful. Thus knowledge of truth may cause pleasure in the intellect, while at the same time the object known may engender sorrow in the will, not precisely because the object is known, but because its action is pernicious. God, however, by the very fact that He exists, is truth. Therefore the intellect that sees God cannot but rejoice in the vision of Him.

Besides, God is goodness itself, and goodness is the cause of love. Hence God's goodness must necessarily be loved by all who apprehend it. Although an object that is good may fail to call forth love, or may even be hated, the reason is not that it is apprehended as good, but that it is apprehended as harmful. Consequently in the vision of God, who is goodness and truth itself, there must be love or joyous fruition, no less than comprehension. This accords with Isaias 66:14: "You shall see and your heart shall rejoice."

—St. Thomas Aquinas, *Compendium Theologiae, 165* (Cyril Vollert)

THE FLESH AND THE SPIRIT

The City where I hope to dwell,
There's none on Earth can parallel:
The stately walls both high and strong,
Are made of precious jasper stone;
The gates of pearl, both rich and clear,
And angels are for porters there;
The streets thereof transparent gold,
Such as no eye did e're behold;
A chrystal river there doth run,
Which doth proceed from the Lamb's throne.
Of life there are the waters sure,
Which shall remain for ever pure;

Nor sun, nor moon, they have no need,
For glory doth from God proceed;
No candle there, nor yet torch light,
For there shall be no darksome night.
From sickness and infirmity
For evermore they shall be free,
Nor withering age shall e're come there,
But beauty shall be bright and clear. . . .
If I of Heaven may have my fill,
Take thou the world, and all that will.

—ANNE BRADSTREET

THE ULTIMATE END OF MAN

Man's consummation consists in the attainment of his last end, which is perfect beatitude of happiness, and this consists in the vision of God, as was demonstrated above. The beatific vision entails immutability in the intellect and will. As regards the intellect, its questing ceases when at last it comes to the first cause, in which all truth can be known. The will's variability ceases, too; for, when it reaches its last end, in which is contained the fullness of all goodness, it finds nothing further to be desired. The will is subject to change because it craves what it does not possess. Clearly, therefore, the final consummation of man consists in perfect repose or unchangeableness as regards both intellect and will.

—ST. THOMAS AQUINAS, *Compendium
Theologiae, 149* (CYRIL VOLLERT)

. . . Musing, I asked, "What basis I could find
To fix my trust?" An inward voice replied,
"Trust to the Almighty: He thy steps shall guide;

He never fails to hear the faithful prayer,
But worldly hope must end in dark despair."
Now, what I am, and what I was, I know;
I see the seasons in procession go
With still increasing speed; while things to come,
Unknown, unthought, amid the growing gloom
Of long futurity, perplex my soul,
While life is posting to its final goal.
Mine is the crime, who ought with clearer light
To watch the winged years' incessant flight;
And not to slumber on in dull delay
Till circling seasons bring the doomful day.
But grace is never slow in that, I trust,
To wake the mind, before I sink to dust,
With those strong energies that lift the soul
To scenes unhoped, unthought, above the pole.
While thus I pondered, soon my working thought
Once more that ever-changing picture brought
Of sublunary things before my view,
And thus I questioned with myself anew:—
"What is the end of this incessant flight
Of life and death, alternate day and night?
When will the motion on these orbs impressed
Sink on the bosom of eternal rest?"
At once, as if obsequious to my will,
Another prospect shone, unmoved and still;
Eternal as the heavens that glowed above,
A wide resplendent scene of light and love.
The wheels of Phoebus from the zodiac turned;
No more the nightly constellations burned;
Green earth and undulating ocean rolled
Away, by some resistless power controlled;
Immensity conceived, and brought to birth
A grander firmament, and more luxuriant earth.
What wonder seized my soul when first I viewed

How motionless the restless racer stood,
Whose flying feet, with winged speed before,
Still marked with sad mutation sea and shore.
No more he swayed the future and the past,
But on the moveless present fixed at last;
As at a goal reposing from his toils,
Like earth unclothed of all its vernal foils.
Unvaried scene! where neither change nor fate,
Nor care, nor sorrow, can our joys abate;
Nor finds the light of thought resistance here,
More than the sunbeams in a crystal sphere.
But no material things can match their flight,
In speed excelling far the race of light.
Oh! what a glorious lot shall then be mine
If Heaven to me these nameless joys assign!

       —FRANCIS PETRARCH, *The Triumph of Eternity,*

                (HUGH BOYD)

What wonder that Jesus stressed that to works of mercy for our humble, suffering, disinherited brethren shall be accorded the merit of love towards Himself? The path to heaven starts with love and ends in love; love makes us know reality, and knowledge of love increases love. To give loving help to those who suffer leads us to know and love our brethren more, and to see in them the image of God, and all this leads us to God. Human brotherhood is a stair to brotherhood with Jesus Christ, Man and God, and by Him and in Him to the state of adoptive children which God has granted us by His grace. There is no other way. "He who loves not remains in death," says St. John. Love and love only is life, and the want of love is pride, envy, anger, sloth, avarice, greed, lechery—it is the egoism that separates us from others and from God, and condemns us to remoteness from any fellowship with good.

The True Life is love—natural and supernatural, human and divine, on earth and in heaven, in an ineffable fusion in which though we are absorbed in God, our own personality will not be lost, but changed. God will make us partakers of His Godhead, so that without our losing the consciousness of being men He will make us feel that we are His children, sharers in His nature, beatified by His vision. Then "God will wipe away every tear from their eyes. And death shall be no more; neither shall there be mourning, nor crying, nor pain any more, for the former things have passed away" (Apoc. 21:4). There will be neither before nor after. The past with its sins, tears of repentance, heaviness of heart, all will be changed into love, taken away from our consciousness, in a "renewal of youth." And the future will not be unknown to us nor distress us by its shadow. All will be present, in an infinite act in which we shall partake, the divine act itself; while time will flow on at our feet in the new heavens and new earth which, with their countless rhythms, will join in the song of the blessed: "Glory to God in the highest."

" 'I am the Alpha and the Omega, the first and the last, the beginning and the end. . . . I, Jesus, have sent My angel to testify to you. . . . I am the Root and Offspring of David, the bright Morning Star. And the Spirit and the bride say "Come!" And let him who hears say "Come!" And let him who thirsts come; and he who wishes, let him receive the water of life freely. . . . It is true, I come quickly!' Amen! Come, Lord Jesus! The grace of our Lord Jesus Christ be with all. Amen" (Apoc. 22:13–21).

—Don Luigi Sturzo, *The True Life*

And after this our Lord said, '*I thank thee of thy service, and of thy travel of thy youth.*' And in this my understanding was lifted up into heaven, where I saw our Lord God as a lord in his own house, which lord hath called all his dear worthy friends to a solemn feast. Then I saw the Lord taking no place in his own house; but I saw him royally reign in his house, and all fulfilleth it with joy and mirth, endlessly to glad and solace his dear worthy friends, full homely and full courteously with marvelous melody in endless love, in his own fair blessedful cheer: which glorious cheer of the Godhead fulfilleth all heaven of joy and bliss. God showed *three degrees* of bliss that each soul shall have in heaven, that willingfully hath served God in any degree in earth. The *first* is, the worship and thanks that he shall receive of our Lord God when he is delivered of pain: this thanks is so high and so worshipful, that him thinketh that it filleth him, though there were no more; for methought all the pain and travel that might be suffered of all living men, might not have deserved the worshipful thank that one man shall have that wilfully hath served God. For the *second*, that all the blessed creatures that be in heaven, shall see the worshipful thanking: and he maketh his service known to all that be in heaven. And in this time this example was showed: A king, if he thank his subjects, it is a great worship to them, and if he make it known to all the realm, then their worship is much encreased. And for the *third*, that as new, and as liking as it is undertaken that time, right so shall it last without end. And I saw that homely and sweetly was this showed, that the age of every man shall be known in heaven, and be rewarded for his wilful service, and for his time; and namely the age of them that wilfully and freely offer their youth to God, passingly is rewarded, and wonderfully thanked; for I saw that when or what time that a man or woman be truly turned to God, for one day's service, and for his endless will, he shall have all these three degrees of bliss. And the more that the loving soul seeth this courtesy of God, the readier she is to serve him all her life.

—Juliana of Norwich, *Revelations of Divine Love*

"In love, the Blessed rejoice in My eternal vision, participating in that good that I have in Myself, every one according to his measure, that is that, with that measure of love, with which they have come to Me, is it measured to them. Because they have lived in love of Me and of the neighbour, united together with the general love, and the particular, which, moreover both proceed from the same love. And they rejoice and exult, participating in each other's good with the affection of love, besides the universal good that they enjoy altogether. And they rejoice and exult with the angels with whom they are placed, according to their diverse and various virtues in the world, being all bound in the bonds of love. And they have a special participation with those whom they closely loved with particular affection in the world, with which affection they grew in grace, increasing virtue, and the one was the occasion to the other of manifesting the glory and praise of My name, in themselves and in their neighbour; and, in the life everlasting, they have not lost their love, but have it still, participating closely, with more abundance, the one with the other, their love being added to the universal good, and I would not that thou shouldest think that they have this particular good, of which I have told thee, for themselves alone, for it is not so, but it is shared by all the proved citizens, My beloved sons, and all the angels—for, when the soul arrives at eternal life, all participate in the good of that soul, and the soul in their good. . . . And their desires for ever cry out to Me, for the salvation of the whole world. And because their life ended in the love of the neighbour, they have not left it behind, but, with it, they will pass through the Door, My only-begotten Son, in the way that I will relate to thee. So thou seest that in those bonds of love in which they finished their life, they go on and remain eternally. . . . The desire of the blessed is to see My honour in you wayfarers, who are pilgrims, for ever running on towards the term of death. In their desire for My honour, they desire your salvation, and always pray to Me for you. . . ."

—St. Catherine of Siena,
A Treatise of Discretion

THE BEATIFIC VISION

O Supreme Light, that so high upliftest Thyself from mortal conceptions, re-lend a little to my mind of what Thou didst appear, and make my tongue so powerful that it may be able to leave one single spark of Thy glory for the future people; for, by returning somewhat to my memory and by sounding a little in these verses, more of Thy victory shall be conceived.

*   *   *

Within the profound and clear subsistence of the lofty Light appeared to me three circles of three colors and of one dimension; and one appeared reflected by the other, as Iris by Iris, and the third appeared fire which from the one and from the other is equally breathed forth.

O how short is the telling, and how feeble toward my conception! and this toward what I saw is such that it suffices not to call it little.

O Light Eternal, that sole dwellest in Thyself, sole understandest Thyself, and, by Thyself understood and understanding, lovest and smilest on Thyself! That circle, which, thus conceived, appeared in Thee as a reflected light, being somewhile regarded by my eyes, seemed to me depicted within itself, of its own very color, by our effigy, wherefore my sight was wholly set upon it. As is the geometer who wholly applies himself to measure the circle, and finds not by thinking that principle of which he is in need, such was I at that new sight. I wished to see how the image accorded with the circle, and how it has its place therein; but my own wings were not for this, had it not been that my mind was smitten by a flash in which its wish came.

To my high fantasy here power failed; but now my desire and my will, like a wheel which evenly is moved, the Love was turning which moves the Sun and the other stars.

—Dante, *Paradiso*, Canto XXXIII (C. E. Norton)

14. Prayers

My children, behold the generations of men: and know ye that no one hath hoped in the Lord, and hath been confounded. For who hath continued in his commandment, and hath been forsaken? or who hath called upon him, and he despised him? For God is compassionate and merciful. . . . He will not despise the prayers of the fatherless; nor the widow. . . . The prayer of him that humbleth himself, shall pierce the clouds. . . . The mercy of God is beautiful in the time of affliction, as a cloud of rain in the time of drought.

—Ecclesiasticus 2:11–13; 35:17, 21, 26

Ask, and it shall be given you: seek, and you shall find: knock, and it shall be opened to you. For every one that asketh, receiveth: and he that seeketh, findeth: and to him that knocketh, it shall be opened. For what man is there among you, of whom if his son shall ask bread, will he reach him a stone? Or if he shall ask him a fish, will he reach him a serpent? If you then being evil, know how to give good gifts to your children: how much more will your Father who is in heaven give good things to them that ask him?

—St. Matthew 7:7–11

Amen I say to you, that whosoever shall say to this mountain, Be thou removed and be cast into the sea, and shall not stagger in his heart, but believe, that whatsoever he saith shall be done; it shall be done unto him. Therefore I say unto you, all things whatsoever you ask when ye pray, believe that you shall receive; and they shall come unto you.

—St. Mark 11:23–24

Be nothing solicitous; but in every thing, by prayer and supplication, with thanksgiving, let your petitions be made known to God. And the peace of God, which surpasseth all understanding, keep your hearts and minds in Christ Jesus.

—St. Paul Philippians 4:6–7

PRAYER

Prayer is the lifting up of the mind and heart to God, the contemplation of God, the daring converse of the creature with the Creator, the soul reverently standing before Him, as before the King and the Life Itself, giving life to all; the oblivion of everything that surrounds us, the food of the soul; its air and light, its lifegiving warmth, its cleansing from sin; the easy yoke of Christ, His light burden. Prayer is the constant feeling (the recognition) of our infirmity or spiritual poverty, the sanctification of the soul, the foretaste of future blessedness, angelic bliss, the heavenly rain, refreshing, watering, and fertilising the ground of the soul, the power and strength of the soul and body, the purifying and freshening of the mental air, the enlightenment of the countenance, the joy of the spirit, the golden link, uniting the creature to the Creator, courage and valour in all the afflictions and temptations of life, the lamp of life, success in all undertakings, dignity equal with the angels, the strengthening of faith, hope and love. Prayer is intercourse with the holy angels and saints, who pleased God since the beginning of the world. Prayer is the amendment of life, the mother of heartfelt contrition and tears; a powerful motive for works of mercy; security of life; the destruction of the fear of death; the disdain of earthly treasures; the desire for heavenly blessings; the expectation of the universal Judge, of the common resurrection and of the life of the world to come; a strenuous effort to save ourselves from eternal torments; unceasing seeking for mercy (forgiveness) of the Sovereign; walking before God; the blissful vanishing of self before the all-creating and all-filling Creator; the living water of the soul. Prayer is holding all men in our hearts through love; the descent of heaven into the soul; the abiding of the most Holy Trinity in the soul, in accordance with that which has been said: "We will come to him and will make Our abode with him."

—JOHN SERGIEFF, *My Life in Christ*
(E. E. GOULAEFF)

... Let every man by the labour of his mind and help of prayer, enforce himself in all tribulation and affliction, labour, pain and travail, without spot of pride or ascribing any praise to himself, to conceive a delight and pleasure in such spiritual exercise, and thereby to rise in the love of our Lord, with an hope of heaven, contempt of the world, and longing to be with God.

—ST. THOMAS MORE, *The Four Last Things*

A COLLOQUY WITH GOD

Howe'er I rest, great God, let me
Awake again at last with thee;
And thus assur'd, behold I lie
Securely, or to awake or die.

—SIR THOMAS BROWNE

Great art Thou, O Lord, and greatly to be praised; great is Thy power, and Thy wisdom infinite. And Thee would man praise; man, but a particle of Thy creation; man, that bears about him his mortality, the witness of his sin, the witness, that *Thou resistest the proud:* yet would man praise Thee; he, but a particle of Thy creation. Thou awakest us to delight in Thy praise; for Thou madest us for Thyself, and our heart is restless, until it repose in Thee. . . .

* * *

Oh! that I might repose on Thee! Oh! that Thou wouldest enter into my heart, and inebriate it, that I may forget my ills, and embrace Thee, my sole good? What art Thou to me? In Thy pity, teach me to utter it. Or what am I to Thee that Thou demandest my love, and, if I give it not, are wroth with me, and threatenest me with grievous woes? Is it then a slight woe to love Thee not? Oh! for Thy mercies' sake, tell me, O Lord my God, what Thou art unto me. *Say unto my soul, I am thy salvation.* So speak, that I may hear. Behold, Lord, my heart is before Thee; open Thou the ears thereof, and *say unto my soul, I am thy salvation.* After this voice let me haste, and take hold on Thee. Hide not Thy face from me. Let me die—lest I die—only let me see Thy face.

—St. Augustine, *Confessions,* Book I (E. B. Pusey)

O my God! I give Thee thanks for allowing me time to amend, now that it is time of mercy and not of punishment. I would rather lose all things than forfeit Thy grace.

—St. Alphonsus de Liguori, *The Way of Salvation*

God be in my head
And in my understanding;
God be in my eyes

And in my looking;
God be in my mouth;
And in my speaking;
God be in my heart
And in my thinking:
God be at my end
And at my departing.

—ANONYMOUS, *fifteenth century*

Bestow on me, O Lord God, understanding to know Thee, diligence to seek Thee, wisdom to find Thee, a perseverance in waiting patiently for Thee, and a hope which may embrace Thee at the last.

—From a prayer of ST. CATHERINE OF SIENA

Give me, good Lord, a longing to be with Thee, not for the avoiding of the calamities of this wretched world, nor so much for the avoiding of the pains of purgatory, nor of the pains of hell neither, nor so much for the attaining of the joys of heaven in respect of mine own commodity, as even for a very love to Thee.

—ST. THOMAS MORE (Composed in the Tower)

PRAYER FOR
THE FAITHFUL DEPARTED

O Gracious Lord, we beseech Thee, remember not against them the sins of their youth and their ignorances; but according to Thy great mercy, be mindful of them in Thy heavenly glory. May the heavens be opened to them, and the Angels rejoice with them.

May the Archangel St. Michael conduct them to Thee. May Thy holy Angels come forth to meet them, and carry them to the city of the heavenly Jerusalem. May St. Peter, to whom Thou gavest the keys of the kingdom of heaven, receive them. May St. Paul, the vessel of election, stand by them. May St. John, the beloved disciple, who had the revelation of the secrets of heaven, intercede for them. May all the Holy Apostles, who received from Thee the power of binding and loosing, pray for them. May all the Saints and elect of God, who in this world suffered torments for Thy Name, befriend them; that, being freed from the prison beneath, they may be admitted into the glories of that kingdom, where with the Father and the Holy Ghost Thou livest and reignest one God, world without end.

Come to their assistance, all ye Saints of God; gain for them deliverance from their place of punishment; meet them, all ye Angels; receive these holy souls, and present them before the Lord. Eternal rest give to them, O Lord. And may perpetual light shine on them.

May they rest in peace. Amen.

—JOHN HENRY NEWMAN, *Meditations and Devotions*

A HYMN TO GOD THE FATHER

I

Wilt thou forgive that sin where I begun,
  Which is my sin, though it were done before?
Wilt thou forgive those sins, through which I run,
  And do run still: though still I do deplore?
    When thou hast done, thou hast not done,
      For, I have more.

II

Wilt thou forgive that sin by which I have won
  Others to sin? and, made my sin their door?

Wilt thou forgive that sin which I did shun
   A year, or two: but wallowed in, a score?
     When thou hast done, thou hast not done,
      For, I have more.

III

I have a sin of fear, that when I have spun
   My last thread, I shall perish on the shore;
Swear by thy self, that at my death thy son
   Shall shine as he shines now, and heretofore;
     And, having done that, Thou hast done,
      I fear no more.

                  —JOHN DONNE

FOR THE DEAD
(*A Hymn*)

Help, Lord, the souls which Thou hast made,
   The souls to Thee so dear,
In prison for the debt unpaid
   Of sins committed here.

Those holy souls, they suffer on,
   Resign'd in heart and will,
Until Thy high behest is done,
   And justice has its fill.
For daily falls, for pardon'd crime,
   They joy to undergo
The shadow of Thy cross sublime,
   The remnant of Thy woe.

Help, Lord, the souls which Thou hast made,
   The souls to Thee so dear,

In prison for the debt unpaid
    Of sins committed here.

Oh, by their patience of delay,
    Their hope amid their pain,
Their sacred zeal to burn away
    Disfigurement and stain;
Oh, by their fire of love, not less
    In keenness than the flame,
Oh, by their very helplessness,
    Oh, by Thy own great Name,
Good Jesu, help! sweet Jesu, aid
    The souls to Thee most dear,
In prison for the debt unpaid
    Of sins committed here.

—JOHN HENRY NEWMAN

A PRAYER FOR AID

Oh, make me see Thee, Lord, where'er I go!
    If mortal beauty sets my soul on fire,
    That flame when near to Thine must needs expire,
    And I with love of only Thee shall glow.
Dear Lord, Thy help I seek against this woe,
    These torments that my spirit vex and tire;
    Thou only with new strength canst re-inspire
    My will, my sense, my courage faint and low.
Thou gavest me on earth this soul divine;
    And Thou within this body weak and frail
    Didst prison it—how sadly there to live!
How can I make its lot less vile than mine?
    Without Thee, Lord, all goodness seems to fail.
    To alter fate is God's prerogative.

MICHELANGELO (JOHN ADDINGTON SYMONDS)

A PRAYER

Clother of the lily, Feeder of the sparrow,
    Father of the fatherless, dear Lord,
Tho' Thou set me as a mark against Thine arrow,
    As a prey unto Thy sword,
As a plough'd-up field beneath Thy harrow,
    As a captive in Thy cord,
Let that cord be love; and some day make my narrow
    Hallow'd bed according to Thy Word. Amen.

—CHRISTINA ROSSETTI

Grant, I Thee pray, such heat into mine heart
That to this love of Thine may be equal;
Grant me from Satan's service to astart,
With whom me rueth so long to have be thrall;
Grant me, good Lord and Creator of all,
The flame to quench of all sinful desire
And in Thy love set all mine heart afire;

That when the journey of this deadly life
My silly ghost hath finishèd, and thence
Departen must without his fleshly wife,
Alone into his Lordès high presence,
He may Thee find, O well of indulgence,
In Thy lordship not as a lord, but rather
As a very tender loving father.

Amen.

—PICO DELLA MIRANDOLA (ST. THOMAS MORE)

Lord Jesus, how few souls there are who want to follow Thee!
Everyone wants to reach Thee in the end, because they know that

"at Thy right Hand are pleasures for evermore." They want to have the happiness that Thou canst give, but not to imitate Thee; they want to reign with Thee, but not to suffer. Even the carnal-minded would like a holy death, although they cannot stand a holy life! But it was otherwise with those to whom Thou saidst, "Ye are they who have continued with Me in My Temptations." Blesséd were they to whom Thou spakest thus! They followed after Thee in truth, with their feet *and* their hearts. Thou madest known to them the ways of life, in calling them to follow Thee Who art both Life and Way. And it is thus that Thy Belovéd, having left all for Thee, desires always to go after Thee, knowing that Thy ways are ways of pleasantness, and all Thy paths are peace.

—St. Bernard, *On the Song of Songs*
(A Religious of C. S. M. V.)

At the round earth's imagin'd corners, blow
Your trumpets, Angels, and arise, arise
From death, you numberless infinities
Of souls, and to your scattered bodies go,
All whom the flood did, and fire shall o'erthrow,
All whom war, dearth, age, agues, tyrannies,
Despair, law, chance, hath slain, and you whose eyes,
Shall behold God, and never taste death's woe,
But let them sleep, Lord, and me mourn a space,
For, if above all these, my sins abound,
'Tis late to ask abundance of thy grace,
When we are there; here on this lowly ground,
Teach me how to repent; for that's as good
As if thou hadst seal'd my pardon, with thy blood.

—John Donne

Jesu Christ, have mercy on me,
As thou art king of majesty,

And forgive me my sins all
That I have done, both great and small.

And bring me, if it be thy will,
Till heaven, to live aye with thee still.   Amen.
—RICHARD ROLLE

Remember not, Lord, my sins,
nor the sins of my forefathers;
neither take vengeance for our sins, theirs, nor mine.
Spare us, Lord, them and me,
spare Thy people,
and, among Thy people, Thy servant,
who is redeemed with Thy precious blood;
and be not angry with us for ever.
Be merciful, be merciful; spare us, Lord,
and be not angry with us for ever.
Be merciful, be merciful; have pity on us, Lord,
and be not angry with us to the full.
Deal not, O Lord,
deal not with me after mine iniquities,
neither recompense me according to my sins;
but after Thy great pity,
deal with me,
and according to the multitude of Thy mercies,
recompense me
after that so great pity,
and that multitude of mercies,
as Thou didst to our fathers

in the times of old;—
by all that is dear unto Thee.
        —LANCELOT ANDREWES, *Private Devotions*
                (JOHN HENRY NEWMAN)

Hear us, O hear us Lord; to thee
A sinner is more music, when he prays,
    Than spheres, or Angels' praises be,
In Panegyric Allelujas;
            Hear us, for till thou hear us, Lord
            We know not what to say;
Thine ear to our sighs, tears, thoughts gives voice
            and word.
O Thou who Satan heard'st in Job's sick day,
Hear thy self now, for thou in us dost pray.

            .   .   .   .

    Son of God hear us, and since thou
By taking our blood, owest it us again,
    Gain to thy self, or us allow;
And let not both us and thy self be slain;
            O Lamb of God, which took'st our sin
            Which could not stick to thee,
O let it not return to us again,
But Patient and Physician being free,
As sin is nothing, let it no where be.
                    —JOHN DONNE, *The Litanie*

SIGHS AND GROANS

        Do not use me
After my sins! look not on my desert,
But on thy glory! then thou wilt reform,

And not refuse me: for thou only art
The mighty God, but I a silly worm:
   O do not bruise me;

   O do not urge me!
For what account can thy ill steward make?
I have abus'd thy flock, destroy'd thy woods,
Sucked all thy magazines: my head did ache,
Till it found out how to consume thy goods:
   O do not scourge me!

   O do not blind me!
I have deserv'd that an Egyptian night
Should thicken all my powers; because my lust
Hath still sow'd fig-leaves to exclude thy light:
But I am frailty, and already dust:
   O do not grind me!

   O do not fill me
With the turn'd vial of thy bitter wrath!
For thou hast other vessels full of blood,
A part whereof my Saviour emptied hath,
Ev'n unto death: since he died for my good,
   O do not kill me!

   But O reprieve me!
For thou hast life and death at thy command;
Thou art both Judge and Saviour, feast and rod,
Cordial and Corrosive: put not thy hand
Into the bitter box; but O my God,
   My God, relieve me!
       —GEORGE HERBERT

What have I left, that I should stay and grone?
  The most of me to heav'n is fled:

My thoughts and joys are all packed up and gone,
   And for their old acquaintance plead.
      O show thy self to me,
      Or take me up to thee!
          —GEORGE HERBERT, *Home*

HYMN TO GOD MY GOD, IN MY SICKNESS

Since I am coming to that holy room,
   Where, with Thy choir of Saints for evermore,
I shall be made Thy music; as I come
   I tune the instrument here at the door,
   And what I must do then, think here before.

Whilst my physicians by their love are grown
   Cosmographers, and I their map, who lie
Flat on this bed, that by them may be shown
   That this is my southwest discovery
   Per fretum febris, by these straits to die,

I joy, that in these straits, I see my west;
   For, though their currents yield return to none,
What shall my west hurt me? As west and east
   In all flat maps (and I am one) are none,
   So death doth touch the Resurrection.

Is the Pacific Sea my home? Or are
   The Eastern riches? Is Jerusalem?
Anyan, and Magellan, and Gibraltar,
   All straits, and none but straits are ways to them,
   Whether where Japhet dwelt, or Cham, or Sem.

We think that Paradise and Calvary,
   Christ's Cross, and Adam's tree, stood in one place;

Look Lord, and find both Adams met in me;
    As the first Adam's sweat surrounds my face,
    May the last Adam's blood my soul embrace.

So, in His purple wrapp'd receive me Lord,
    By these His thorns give me His other crown;
And as to others' souls I preach'd Thy word,
    Be this my text, my sermon to mine own,
    Therefore that He may raise the Lord throws down.
                      —JOHN DONNE

PRAYER FOR A HAPPY DEATH

Oh, my Lord and Saviour, support me in that hour in the strong arms of Thy Sacraments, and by the fresh fragrance of Thy consolations. Let the absolving words be said over me, and the holy oil sign and seal me, and Thy own Body be my food, and Thy Blood my sprinkling; and let my sweet Mother, Mary, breathe on me, and my Angel whisper peace to me, and my glorious Saints . . . smile upon me: that in them all, and through them all, I may receive the gift of perseverance, and die, as I desire to live, in Thy faith, in Thy Church, in Thy service, and in Thy love. Amen.
    —JOHN HENRY NEWMAN, *Meditations and Devotions*

A PRAYER IN
THE HOUR OF DEATH

O my most blessed and glorious Creator that hast fed me all my life long, and redeemed me from all evil, seeing it is Thy merciful pleasure to take me out of this frail body, and to wipe away all tears from mine eyes, and all sorrows from my heart, I do with all humility and willingness consent and submit myself wholly unto Thy sacred will. I desire to be dissolved and to be with my Saviour. I bless and praise Thy holy name for all Thy great mercies conferred upon me, from the first day of my life unto this present hour. I give Thee all possible thanks for this gracious and kind visitation, in which Thou art mercifully pleased to order this last act of Thy poor creature to Thy glory, and the fruition of those heavenly comforts which have already swallowed up my whole spirit. O let all that come after me speak of Thy wondrous mercies, and the generations which are yet unborn give praise unto Thy name.

Lord Jesus Christ my most loving Redeemer, into Thy saving and everlasting arms I commend my spirit, I am ready my dear Lord, and earnestly expect and long for Thy good pleasure; come quickly, and receive the soul of Thy servant which trusteth in Thee.

Blessing, and honour, and glory and power be unto Him that sitteth upon the throne, and unto the Lamb and to the Holy Ghost for ever and ever Amen.
Glory be to God on high, and on earth peace, good will towards men!

> *Blessed be God alone!*
> *Thrice blessed three in one!*
> —HENRY VAUGHAN, *Man in Darkness, or,*
> *A Discourse of Death*

TO THE GOOD ANGEL

O angel dear, where ever I go,
    Who am committed to thine award,
Save, defend, and govern also,
    That in heaven with thee be my reward.

Cleanse my soul from sin that I have do,
   And virtuously me wiss to Godward;
Shield me from the fiend evermo,
   And from the painës of hell so hard.

O thou comely angel, so good and clear;
   That ever art abiding with me,
Though I can neither thee see nor hear,
   Yet devoutly, with trust, I pray to thee.

My body and soul thou keep in fear,
   With sudden death parted not they be;
For that is thine office, both far and near,
   In every place wherever I be.

O blessed angel, to me so dear,
   Thou messenger of God Almight;
Govern my deeds and thought in fear,
   To the pleasance of God both day and night!

                         —ANONYMOUS

PRAYER OF THE OLD WOMAN, VILLON'S MOTHER

Mother of God that's Lady of the Heavens, take myself, the poor sinner, the way I'll be along with them that's chosen.

Let you say to your own Son that He'd have a right to forgive my share of sins, when it's the like He's done, many's the day, with big and famous sinners. I'm a poor aged woman was never at school, and is no scholar with letters, but I've seen pictures in the chapel with Paradise on one side, and harps and pipes in it, and the place on the other side, where sinners do be boiled in torment; the one gave me great joy, the other a great fright and scaring; let me have the good place, Mother of God, and it's in your faith I'll live always.

It's yourself that bore Jesus, that has no end or death, and He the Lord Almighty, that took our weakness and gave Himself to sorrows, a young and gentle man. It's Himself is Our Lord surely, and it's in that faith I'll live always.

—François Villon (John Millington Synge)

THE QUEEN OF HEAVEN

"Virgin Mother, daughter of thine own Son, humble and exalted more than any creature, fixed term of the eternal counsel, thou art she who didst so ennoble human nature that its own Maker disdained not to become His own making. Within thy womb was rekindled the Love through whose warmth this flower has thus blossomed in the eternal peace. Here thou art to us the noonday torch of charity, and below, among mortals, thou art the living fount of hope. Lady, thou art so great, and so availest, that whoso wishes grace, and has not recourse to thee, wishes his desire to fly without wings. Thy benignity not only succors him who asks, but oftentimes freely foreruns the asking. In thee mercy, in thee pity, in thee magnificence, in thee whatever of goodness is in any creature, are united. Now doth this man, who, from the lowest abyss of the universe, far even as here, has seen one by one the lives of spirits, supplicate thee, through grace, for virtue such that he may be able with his eyes to uplift himself higher toward the Ultimate Salvation. And I, who never for my own vision burned more than I do for his, proffer to thee all my prayers, and pray that they be not scant, that with thy prayers thou wouldest dissipate for him every cloud of his mortality, so that the Supreme Pleasure may be displayed to him. Further I pray thee, Queen, who canst whatso thou wilt, that, after so great a vision, thou wouldest preserve his affections sound. May thy guardianship vanquish human impulses."

—St. Bernard to the Blessed Virgin Mary, Canto
XXXIII, Dante's *Paradiso* (C. E. Norton)

O martyr! O virgin!—that Virgin's guardian,—who did earth's
    chief Glory bear!
From Whom is, in Whom is,—through Whom is everything,—
    may He through thee hear our prayer!

    O thou, beloved above the rest!
    Ask Christ, Who loved thee far the best,
        To Him pressing
        Prayers addressing,
    For His reconciling grace.
    River! lead us to the fountain;
    Hill! conduct us to the mountain;
        Who endurest
        Virgin purest!
    Let us see the Bridegroom's face.
    —Adam of St. Victor (Digby S. Wrangham)

AVE VERUM CORPUS

    Hail to Thee! true Body, sprung
      From the Virgin Mary's womb!
    The same that on the Cross was hung,
      And bore for man the bitter doom!

Thou, whose side was pierc'd and flow'd
Both with water and with blood;
Suffer us to taste of Thee,
In our life's last agony.

O kind, O loving One!
O sweet Jesu, Mary's Son.

—POPE INNOCENT VI

ANIMA CHRISTI

Soul of Christ, be my sanctification;
Body of Christ, be my salvation;
Blood of Christ, fill all my veins;
Water of Christ's side, wash out my stains;
Passion of Christ, my comfort be;
O good Jesu, listen to me;
In thy wounds I fain would hide,
Ne'er to be parted from Thy side;
Guard me, should the foe assail me;
Call me when my life shall fail me;
Bid me come to Thee above,
With Thy saints to sing Thy love,
    World without end. Amen.

—ST. IGNATIUS LOYOLA (JOHN HENRY NEWMAN)

THE GOOD SHEPHERD

Shepherd! who with thine amorous, sylvan song
Hast broken the slumber that encompassed me,
Who mad'st Thy crook from the accursèd tree

On which Thy powerful arms were stretched so long!
Lead me to mercy's ever-flowing fountains;
For Thou my shepherd, guard, and guide shalt be;
I will obey Thy voice, and wait to see
Thy feet all beautiful upon the mountains.
Hear, Shepherd, Thou who for Thy flock art dying,
Oh, wash away these scarlet sins, for Thou
Rejoicest at the contrite sinner's vow!
Oh, wait! to Thee my weary soul is crying,
Wait for me: Yet why ask it, when I see,
With feet nailed to the cross, Thou'rt waiting still for me!

—LOPE DE VEGA (HENRY WADSWORTH LONGFELLOW)

In the merits and mediation of thy Son, our Saviour Christ Jesus, be merciful unto us. Suffer not, O Lord, so great a waste, as the effusion of his blood, without any return to thee, suffer not the expence of so rich a treasure, as the spending of his life, without any purchase to thee; but as thou didst empty and evacuate his glory here upon earth, glorify us with that glory which his humiliation purchased for us in the kingdom of Heaven. And as thou didst empty that Kingdom of thine, in a great part, by the banishment of those Angels, whose pride threw them into everlasting ruin, be pleased to repair that Kingdom, which their fall did so far depopulate, by assuming us into their places, and making us rich with their confiscations. And to that purpose, O Lord, make us capable of that succession to thine Angels there; begin in us here in this life an angelical purity, an angelical chastity, an angelical integrity to thy service, an angelical acknowledgment that we always stand in thy presence, and should direct all our actions to thy glory.

—JOHN DONNE, *Essays in Divinity*

LITANY TO THE HOLY SPIRIT

In the hour of my distress,
When temptations me oppress,
And when I my sins confess,
      Sweet Spirit comfort me!

When I lie within my bed,
Sick in heart, and sick in head,
And with doubts discomforted,
      Sweet Spirit comfort me!

When the house doth sigh and weep,
And the world is drown'd in sleep,
Yet mine eyes the watch do keep;
      Sweet Spirit comfort me!

When the artless doctor sees
No one hope, but of his fees,
And his skill runs on the lees;
      Sweet Spirit comfort me!

When his potion and his pill,
Has, or none, or little skill,
Meet for nothing, but to kill;
      Sweet Spirit comfort me!

When the passing-bell doth toll,
And the Furies in a shoal
Come to fright a parting soul;
      Sweet Spirit comfort me!

When the tapers now burn blue,
And the comforters are few,
And that number more than true;
      Sweet Spirit comfort me!

When the Priest his last hath pray'd,
And I nod to what is said,
'Cause my speech is now decay'd;
    Sweet Spirit comfort me!

When (God knows) I'm tossed about,
Either with despair, or doubt;
Yet before the glass be out,
    Sweet Spirit comfort me!

When the Tempter me pursu'th
With the sins of all my youth,
And half damns me with untruth;
    Sweet Spirit comfort me!

When the flames and hellish cries
Fright mine ears, and fright mine eyes,
And all terrors me surprise;
    Sweet Spirit comfort me!

When the Judgment is reveal'd,
And that open'd which was seal'd,
When to Thee I have appeal'd;
    Sweet Spirit comfort me!

—ROBERT HERRICK

LITANY OF THANKSGIVING

For all Thou hast given
    Deo Gratias.
For all Thou hast withheld
    Deo Gratias.
For all Thou hast withdrawn
    Deo Gratias.

For all Thou hast permitted
> Deo Gratias.

For all Thou hast prevented
> Deo Gratias.

For all Thou hast forgiven me
> Deo Gratias.

For all Thou hast prepared for me
> Deo Gratias.

For the death Thou hast chosen for me
> Deo Gratias.

For the place Thou art keeping for me in heaven
> Deo Gratias.

For having created me to love Thee for eternity
> Deo Gratias.
> Deo Gratias.
> Deo Gratias.

—Recited by the Religious of the Cenacle of St. Regis

INVOCATION

Maker of earth and sky, from age to age
Who rul'st the world by reason; at whose word
Time issues from Eternity's abyss:
To all that moves the source of movement, fixed
Thyself and moveless. Thee no cause impelled
Extrinsic this proportioned frame to shape
From shapeless matter; but, deep-set within
Thy inmost being, the form of perfect good,
From envy free; and Thou didst mould the whole
To that supernal pattern. Beauteous
The world in Thee thus imaged, being Thyself
Most beautiful. So Thou the work didst fashion

In that fair likeness, bidding it put on
Perfection through the exquisite perfectness
Of every part's contrivance.
                              Thou dost bind
The elements in balanced harmony,
So that the hot and cold, the moist and dry,
Contend not; nor the pure fire leaping up
Escape, or weight of waters whelm the earth.
  Thou joinest and diffusest through the whole,
Linking accordantly its several parts,
A soul of threefold nature, moving all.
This, cleft in twain, and in two circles gathered,
Speeds in a path that on itself returns,
Encompassing mind's limits, and conforms
The heavens to her true semblance. Lesser souls
And lesser lives by a like ordinance
Thou sendest forth, each to its starry car
Affixing, and dost strew them far and wide
O'er earth and heaven. These by a law benign
Thou biddest turn again, and render back
To thee their fires.
                     Oh, grant, almighty Father,
Grant us on reason's wing to soar aloft
To heaven's exalted height; grant us to see
The fount of good; grant us, the true light found,
To fix our steadfast eyes in vision clear
On Thee. Disperse the heavy mists of earth,
And shine in Thine own splendour. For Thou art
The true serenity and perfect rest
Of every pious soul—to see Thy face,
The end and the beginning—One the guide,
  The traveller, the pathway, and the goal.
        —BOETHIUS, *The Consolation of Philosophy*, III, 9
                                        (H. R. JAMES)

The Lord bless us, and keep us,
and shew the light of His countenance upon us,
And be merciful unto us,
The Lord lift up His countenance upon us,
And give us peace!
I commend to Thee, O Lord,
my soul, and my body,
my mind, and my thoughts,
my prayers, and my vows,
my senses, and my limbs,
my words, and my works,
my life, and my death;
my brothers, and my sisters,
and their children;
my friends, my benefactors, my well wishers,
those who have a claim on me;
my kindred, and my neighbours,
my country, and all Christendom.
I commend to Thee, Lord,
my impulses, and my startings,
my intentions, and my attempts,
my going out, and my coming in,
my sitting down, and my rising up.

—LANCELOT ANDREWES, *Private Devotions*
(JOHN HENRY NEWMAN)

O Lord Almighty, Thou art truly the infinitely loving and amiable guest of the virtuous soul, which, after having served Thee faithfully and generously during the long exile, the painful journey, the hard bondage of this life, returns to Thee, the Father, the King and the Judge of the living and the dead. Oh how lovingly and kindly, with what readiness and fatherly goodness dost Thou receive the souls who, notwithstanding temptations, trials and persecutions, have always served Thee faithfully and have persevered to the end in Thy service! Then Thou pourest into their bosom the measure of which the Gospel speaks, "good measure and pressed down and shaken together and running over." (Lk. 6:38) They have esteemed and loved Thee above all things; and in return Thou givest them Thyself, Thou revealest Thyself clearly, Thou showest to them Thy great beauty and all the riches of Thy glory; Thou bringest them to Thy Heart, and castest them into the centre thereof, into the bosom of Thy love, into the unfathomable depth of Thy mercy. There, in Thy Heart, Thou makest known clearly how tenderly Thou hast loved them from all eternity, and how great has been Thy mercy in choosing them to enjoy unspeakable blessedness, in having predestined them to see, to praise, and to love Thee for ever.

—DENYS THE CARTHUSIAN, *The Eternal Reward of the Friends of the Heart of Jesus*

O Thou who hast redeemed me to be a son of God, and called me from vanity to inherit all things, I praise Thee, that having loved me, and given Thyself for me, Thou commandest us saying, As I have loved you, so do ye also love one another. Wherein Thou hast commanded all men, so to love me as to lay down their lives for my peace and welfare. Since love is the end for which Heaven and earth was made, enable me to see and discern the sweetness of so great a treasure. And since Thou hast advanced me into the throne of God, in the bosom of all angels and men, commanding them by this precept to give me a union and communion with Thee in their dearest affection, in their highest esteem, and in the most near and inward room and seat in their hearts, give me the grace which St. Paul prayed for, that I may be acceptable to the saints; fill me with Thy Holy Spirit, and make my soul and life beautiful, make me all wisdom, goodness and love, that I may be worthy to be esteemed and accepted by them, that being delighted also with their felicity, I may be crowned with Thine, and with their Glory.

* * *

O Jesus, who having prepared all the joys in Heaven and earth for me, and redeemed me to inherit Thy Father's treasures, hast prepared for me the most glorious companions, in whose presence and society I may enjoy them: I bless Thee for the communion of saints, and for Thy adorning the same with all manner of beauties, excellences, perfections and delights. O what a glorious assembly is the Church of the first born, how blessed and divine! What perfect lovers! How great and honorable! How wise! How sweet and delightful! Every one being the end, every one the king of heaven; every one the son of God in greatness and glory; every one the entire and perfect friend of all the rest; every one the joy of each other's soul; every one the light and ornament of Thy Kingdom; every one Thy particular friend, yet loving every one as Thy particular friend; and rejoicing in the pleasures and delights of every one! O my God, make me one of that happy assembly. And let me love every one for whom Christ died, with a love as great and lively as His. That I may dwell in Him, and He in me, and that we all may be made perfect in one, even as Thou, O Jesus, art in the Father and the Father is in Thee: that Thy love may be in us, and Thou in me for evermore.

—Thomas Traherne, *The First Century*

Give me Thy grace to amend my life and to have an eye to mine and without grudge of death, which to them that die in Thee, good Lord, is the gate of a wealthy life.

—St. Thomas More (Composed in the Tower)

Lord, receive the soul of this Thy servant: enter not into judgment with Thy servant: spare him whom Thou hast redeemed with Thy most precious blood: deliver him from all evil, for whose sake Thou didst suffer all evil and mischief; from the crafts and assaults of the devil, from the fear of death, and from everlasting death, good Lord deliver him. Amen.

* * *

O Almighty and eternal God, there is no number of Thy days or of Thy mercies: Thou hast sent us into this world to serve Thee, and to live according to Thy laws; but we by our sins have provoked Thee to wrath, and we have planted thorns and sorrows round about our dwellings: and our life is but a span long, and yet very tedious, because of the calamities that enclose us in on every side; the days of our pilgrimage are few and evil; we have frail and sickly bodies, violent and distempered passions, long designs and but a short stay, weak understandings and strong enemies, abused fancies, perverse wills. O dear God, look upon us in mercy and pity: let not our weaknesses make us to sin against Thee, nor our fear cause us to betray our duty, nor our former follies provoke Thy eternal anger, nor the calamities of this world vex us into tediousness of spirit and impatience: but let Thy holy spirit lead us through this valley of misery with safety and peace, with holiness and religion, with spiritual comforts and joy in the Holy Ghost: that when we have served Thee in our generations, we may be gathered unto our fathers, having the testimony of a holy conscience, in the communion of the catholic church, in the confidence of a certain faith, and the comforts of a reasonable, religious, and holy hope, and perfect charity with Thee our God and all the world; that neither death, nor life, nor angels, nor principalities, nor powers, nor things present, nor things to come, nor height, nor depth, nor any other creature, may be able to separate us from the love of God, which is in Christ Jesus our Lord. Amen.

—JEREMY TAYLOR, *Holy Dying*

"WHETHER WE LIVE OR WHETHER WE DIE, WE ARE THE LORD'S"

Oh my God! what is death or life to me? Life is nothing, it is even a snare if it be too dear to me. Death can only destroy this house of clay; it delivers the soul from the contamination of the body, and from its own pride. It frees it from the acts of the tempter, and introduces it forever into the kingdom of truth.

I ask not, then, oh my father, for health or for life. I make an offering to thee of all my days. Thou hast counted them. I would know nothing more. All I ask is to die rather than live as I have lived, and if it be thy will that I depart, let me die in patience and love. Almighty God, who holdest the keys of the tomb in thy hand, to open and close it at thy will, give me not life if I shall love it too well. Living or dying, I would be thine.

—ARCHBISHOP FÉNELON

AN EVENING PRAYER

Awaken thoroughly in us a serious sense of these things, that so today, while it is called today, we may see and know the things that belong to our peace, before they be hid from our eyes, before that long night cometh when no man can work. O that every night may so effectually put us in mind of our last, that we may every day take care so to live, as we shall then wish we had lived when we come to die: that so when that night shall come, we may as willingly put off these bodies, as we now put off our clothes, and may rejoice to rest from our labours, and that our war with the world, the devil, and our own corrupt nature, is at an end. . . . We beseech thee to take us, and ours, and all that belongs to us, into thy fatherly care this night. Let thy holy angels be our guard,

while we are not in a condition to defend ourselves, that we may
not be under the power of devils, or wicked men; and preserve us,
also, O Lord, from every evil accident, that, after a comfortable
and refreshing sleep, we may find ourselves, and all that belongs
to us, in peace and safety. . . .

—JONATHAN SWIFT

May He support us all the day long, till the shades lengthen and
the evening comes, and the busy world is hushed and the fever of
life is over and our work is done. Then in His mercy may He give
us a safe lodging and a holy rest and peace at the last.

—JOHN HENRY NEWMAN

. . . Thou, Lord, ever workest, and art ever at rest. Nor dost
Thou see in time, nor art moved in time, nor restest in a time; and
yet Thou makest things seen in time, yea the times themselves, and
the rest which results from time.

We therefore see these things which Thou madest, because they
are: but they are, because Thou seest them. And we see without,
that they are, and within, that they are good, but Thou sawest
them there, when made, where Thou sawest them, yet to be made.
And we were at a later time moved to do well, after our hearts had
conceived of Thy Spirit; but in the former time we were moved
to do evil, forsaking Thee; but Thou, the One, the Good God,
didst never cease doing good. And we also have some *good works*,
of Thy gift, but not eternal; *after them* we trust to *rest* in Thy
great *hallowing*. But Thou, being the Good which needeth no
good, art ever at rest, because Thy rest is Thou Thyself. And what
man can teach man to understand this? or what Angel, an Angel?
or what Angel, a man? Let it be *asked* of Thee, *sought* in Thee,

knocked for at Thee; so, so shall it be *received,* so shall it be *found,* so shall it be *opened.* Amen.

—St. Augustine, *Confessions,* Book XII (E. B. Pusey)

ORDER OF MASS FOR THE DEAD

Introit

Lord, grant them eternal rest, and let perpetual light shine upon them. O God, thou shalt have praise in Sion; to thee let the vow be paid in Jerusalem. Heed my prayer; all mankind must come before thy judgement-seat. Lord, grant them eternal rest, and let perpetual light shine upon them.

Gradual

Lord, grant them eternal rest, and let perpetual light shine upon them. Men will remember the just man for ever; no fear shall he have of evil tidings.

Tract

Lord, release the souls of all the faithful departed from every bond of sin. By the help of thy grace enable them to escape avenging judgement. And to enjoy bliss in everlasting light.

Offertory

Lord Jesus Christ, king of glory, deliver the souls of all the faithful departed from the pains of hell and from the bottomless pit. Save them from the lion's jaws; let them not be engulfed in hell nor swallowed up in darkness. Let Saint Michael the standard-bearer bring them into that holy light which thou of old didst promise to Abraham and his posterity. Lord, in praise of thee we offer sacrifice and prayer; accept them for the good of those souls whom we call to mind this day. Lord, make them pass from death to life, which thou of old didst promise to Abraham and his posterity.

Preface

Right indeed it is and just, proper and for our welfare, that we should always and everywhere give thanks to thee, holy Lord, almighty Father, eternal God, through Christ our Lord. In him there has dawned for us the hope of a blessed resurrection, heartening with a promise of immortality to come those of us who are saddened by the certainty of dying. The life of those who are faithful to thee, Lord, is but changed, not ended; and when their earthly dwelling-place decays, an everlasting mansion stands prepared for them in heaven. Therefore it is that with Angels and Archangels, Thrones and Dominations, and all the warriors of the heavenly array, we chant an endless hymn in praise of thee, singing:

Agnus Dei

Lamb of God, who takest away the sins of the world, grant them rest.

Lamb of God, who takest away the sins of the world, grant them rest.

Lamb of God, who takest away the sins of the world, grant them eternal rest.

FOR THE GIFT OF TEARS

Collect

Almighty and most gentle God, who when thy people thirsted drewest running water out of a rock, draw tears of compunction from our stony hearts, giving us grace to bewail our sins and fitting us to receive thy merciful forgiveness: through our Lord.

Secret

Lord God, we pray thee look favourably upon this offering which we make to thy majesty in atonement for our sins. Draw from our eyes a flood of tears to quench the burning flames of that punishment which is our due: through our Lord.

Postcommunion

In thy mercy, Lord God, pour into our hearts the grace of the Holy Spirit, enabling us by sighs and tears to wash away the stain of our sins, and to win from thy bounty the pardon we desire: through our Lord . . . in the unity of the same Holy Spirit.

FEAST OF ALL SOULS

Collect

Lord God of mercies, grant to the souls of all thy servants a place of cool repose, the blessedness of quiet, the brightness of light: through our Lord.

FOR THE GRACE OF A HAPPY DEATH

Collect

Almighty and merciful God, who hast bestowed on mankind saving remedies and the gifts of everlasting life, look graciously upon us thy servants, and comfort the souls thou hast created, so that they may be found worthy at the hour of death to be presented by the holy angels, free from all stain of sin, to thee their maker: through our Lord.

Secret

Accept, we pray thee, Lord, the sacrificial gift we offer thee for the hour of our death, and grant that by it all our offences may be purged, so that we who in this life, under thy providence, are afflicted by thy scourges, may in the next have everlasting rest: through our Lord.

FOR THE LIVING AND THE DEAD

Collect

Almighty and eternal God, who hast dominion alike over the living and the dead, and art merciful to all who thou foreknowest will be thine by faith and good works: we humbly beseech thee that those for whom we are minded to offer up our prayers, whether this world still holds them in the flesh, or the next has already received them divested of the body, may, by the intercession of all thy saints, and through thy gracious pity, obtain pardon for all their sins: through our Lord.

Secret

God, who alone knowest how many souls are destined to enjoy the happiness of heaven, grant, we pray thee, that by the intercession of all thy saints, the names of each and every person who has been commended to our prayers, with those of all other faithful souls, may be found written in the book of blessed predestination: through our Lord.

. . . God first! To God the glory and let Him reward! God is no summer tourist. We're more than scenery to Him. He has a farmer's eye for ergot and tares. Oh delight higher than Everest and deeper than the Challenger Gulf! His commodores come into His council and His lieutenants know His love. Lord, I confess! I confess! I am all too weak and utterly unworthy. There is no other want. All actions and diversions of the people, their greyhound races, their football competitions, their clumsy acts of love, what are they but the pitiful, maimed expression of that entire passion, the positive tropism of the soul to God?

Oh Father, I am praising Thee, I have always praised Thee, I shall always praise Thee! Listen to the wooden sabots of Thy eager child running to Thy arms! Admit him to the fairs of that

blessed country where Thy saints move happily about their neat, clean houses under the blue sky! O windmills, O cocks, O clouds and ponds! Mother is waving from the tiny door! The quilt is turned down in my beautiful blue and gold room! Father, I thank Thee in advance! Everything has been grand! I am coming home!
—W. H. AUDEN, *Depravity: A Sermon*

ADORO TE DEVOTE

Godhead here in hiding, whom I do adore
Masked by these bare shadows, shape and nothing more,
See, Lord, at thy service low lies here a heart
Lost, all lost in wonder at the God thou art.

Seeing, touching, tasting are in thee deceived;
How says trusty hearing? that shall be believed;
What God's Son has told me, take for true I do;
Truth himself speaks truly or there's nothing true.

On the cross thy godhead made no sign to men;
Here thy very manhood steals from human ken:
Both are my confession, both are my belief,
And I pray the prayer of the dying thief.

I am not like Thomas, wounds I cannot see,
But can plainly call thee God and Lord as he:
This faith each day deeper be my holding of,
Daily make me harder hope and dearer love.

O thou our reminder of Christ crucified,
Living Bread the life of us for whom he died,
Lend this life to me then: feed and feast my mind,
There be thou the sweetness man was meant to find.

Bring the tender tale true of the Pelican;
Bathe me, Jesu Lord, in what thy bosom ran—
Blood that but one drop of has the world to win
All the world forgiveness of its world of sin.

Jesu, whom I look at shrouded here below,
I beseech thee send me what I thirst for so,
Some day to gaze on thee face to face in light,
And be blest for ever with thy glory's sight.

—St. Thomas Aquinas (Gerard Manley Hopkins)

Notes on Writers and Books

ADAM OF ST. VICTOR. Prolific writer of Latin hymns and sequences. Canon Regular of St. Victor in Paris. 1110–1172.

ST. ALPHONSUS DE LIGUORI. Moral theologian and psychologist of asceticism. Founder of the Redemptorists, Doctor of the Church. 1696–1787.

LANCELOT ANDREWES. Anglican bishop; leader of High Church group opposed to Puritanism, among those who produced the version of the Bible authorized by James I. 1555–1626.

ST. ANSELM. Theologian and philosopher. Abbot of Bec in Normandy, Archbishop of Canterbury, Doctor of the Church. 1033–1109.

ST. APHRAHAT. Writer of homilies. Bishop of the Syrian Church. Often referred to by the Greek form of his name, Aphraates. Fourth century A.D.

W. H. AUDEN. English poet and critic. Born 1907.

ST. AUGUSTINE. Rhetorician, theologian, philosopher. Bishop of Hippo, Doctor of the Church. 354–430.

FRANCIS BACON. Philosopher, essayist, statesman. 1561–1626.

ST. BASIL THE GREAT. Expositor of Christian doctrine, one of the principal Greek Fathers, Doctor of the Church. About 330–379.

CHARLES BAUDELAIRE. French poet. 1821–1867.

ST. BEDE. Historian, exegete, Doctor of the Church. Best known as the Venerable Bede, a title of affection and respect bestowed on the Benedictine monk long after he was honored as a saint. About 673–735.

St. Bernard. Theologian of the spiritual life; the "mellifluous Doctor." Second founder of the Cistercian Order. 1091–1153.

John Betjeman. English poet and celebrator of the recent past, especially as it is evoked in architecture and railroads. Born 1906.

William Blake. English poet and engraver. 1757–1827.

(Anicius Manlius Severinus) Boethius. Roman philosopher and statesman. Honored as martyr and saint in Pavia. About 475–525.

Jacques Bénigne Bossuet. French theologian, preacher, and polemicist. Bishop of Meaux. 1627–1704.

Anne Bradstreet. Poet, wife of a colonial governor of Massachusetts; first American woman to write verse in English. About 1612–1672.

Sir Thomas Browne. English meditative writer and physician. 1605–1682.

Samuel Butler. English novelist. 1835–1902.

St. Catherine of Genoa. Widow. Famous for her understanding and exposition of the doctrine of purgatory. Her life and thought are examined in detail in Baron Friedrich von Hügel's *The Mystical Element of Religion As Studied in Saint Catherine of Genoa and Her Friends* (1908). 1447–1510.

St. Catherine of Siena. Dominican nun and mystic who persuaded Gregory XI to leave Avignon and thus to end the "Babylonian Captivity" of the papacy. 1347–1380.

Dom John Chapman. Scripture scholar and patrologist. Abbot of Downside. 1865–1933.

John Clare. English poet. 1793–1864.

The Cloud of Unknowing. A classic of the life of the spirit written by an English mystic of the fourteenth century who chose to remain unknown.

Samuel Taylor Coleridge. English poet, critic, and philosopher. 1772–1834.

CYNEWULF. Old English poet whose signature is found in runes in four poems of the late eighth or early ninth century.

ST. CYPRIAN. Rhetorician and philosopher, Father of the Church. Bishop of Carthage. He was beheaded in 258.

ST. CYRIL OF JERUSALEM. Expositor of doctrine, Doctor of the Church. Bishop of Jerusalem. 315–386.

DANTE (ALIGHIERI). Italian poet. 1265–1321.

SIR JOHN DAVIES. English poet. 1569–1626.

C. DAY LEWIS. English poet and detective-story writer (under the name of Nicholas Blake). Born 1904.

DENYS THE CARTHUSIAN. Ascetical writer of the fifteenth century whose *Mirror of the Conversion of a Sinner* was probably the first book printed in Belgium (1473).

JOHN DONNE. Poet and Anglican divine. 1572–1631.

FYODOR DOSTOYEVSKY. Russian novelist. 1821–1881.

JOHN DRYDEN. English poet, dramatist, and critic. 1631–1700.

EMILE DURKHEIM. French sociologist. 1858–1917.

SIR ARTHUR STANLEY EDDINGTON. English astronomer and physicist. 1882–1944.

T. S. ELIOT. English poet and critic. Born 1888.

(DESIDERIUS) ERASMUS. Dutch priest and humanist. About 1469–1536.

DIEGO DE ESTELLA. Spanish monk, mystic, and ascetical writer. 1524–1578.

FRANÇOIS DE SALIGNAC DE LA MOTHE FÉNELON. French theologian and rhetorician. Archbishop of Cambrai. 1651–1715.

ST. FRANCIS DE SALES. Theologian of the spiritual life. Founder of the Order of the Visitation, Bishop of Geneva, and Doctor of the Church. 1567–1622.

ST. GREGORY OF NYSSA. Expositor of doctrine and Greek Father. Brother of St. Basil the Great. About 330–390.

ST. GREGORY THE GREAT. Pope and exegete. Doctor of the Church. About 540–604

ELIZABETH GRYMESTON. English aphorist and poet. About 1563–1604.

ROMANO GUARDINI. German theologian and philosopher. Born 1885.

GIOVANNI BATTISTA GUARINI. Italian poet and dramatist. 1537–1612.

GUIDO GUINICELLI. Italian poet, precursor of Dante. About 1230–1276.

THEODOR HAECKER. German philosopher and critic. His *Journal in the Night* was written as a meditative refuge against the double nightmare of Hitler and the war. 1879–1945.

JOHN HARRINGTON. Under-treasurer to Henry VIII and husband of one of the king's daughters; father of the satirist and translator of Ariosto, Sir John Harrington, with whom he is sometimes confused. Imprisoned in the cause of Queen Elizabeth. Sixteenth century.

BLESSED HENRY SUSO. German Dominican spiritual writer. Died 1365.

GEORGE HERBERT. English poet and clergyman. 1593–1633.

ROBERT HERRICK. English poet and clergyman. 1591–1674.

ST. HILARY OF POITIERS. Rhetorician and theologian. He wrote his famous treatise on the Trinity in the course of a life-long combat against the Arian heresy. Doctor of the Church. Died 368.

HILDEBERT OF LAVARDIN. French theologian and poet. Archbishop of Tours. Died about 1134.

RICHARD HOOKER. Anglican theologian. About 1554–1600.

GERARD MANLEY HOPKINS. English poet and Jesuit priest. 1844–1889.

HSÜNTZE. Chinese philosopher of the Confucian school; a vigorous and highly practical moralist. About 298–238 B.C.

ST. IGNATIUS LOYOLA. Mystic. Founder of the Jesuits. 1491–1556.

INNOCENT VI. STEPHEN AUBERT, Cardinal-Bishop of Ostia, Pope from 1352 to 1362.

BEDE JARRETT. English Dominican preacher, essayist, and historian. 1881–1934.

KARL JASPERS. German philosopher of existence with a background in psychiatry (he holds a medical degree). Born 1883.

ELIZABETH JENNINGS. English poet. Born 1926.

ST. JOHN CHRYSOSTOM. Theologian, exegete, liturgist, preacher. Patriarch of Constantinople, Doctor of the Church. Born about 347, he died in exile in 407.

BLESSED JOHN OF AVILA. Preacher and mentor in the contemplative life of St. Teresa, St. John of God, St. Francis Borgia and others. About 1500–1569.

ST. JOHN OF THE CROSS. Theologian of the mystical life. Founder of the Discalced Carmelites. 1542–1591.

SAMUEL JOHNSON. Satirist, lexicographer, writer of literary biography, whose own biographer, JAMES BOSWELL, recorded almost every possible aspect of his life, thought, and conversations. 1709–1784.

JULIANA OF NORWICH. English mystical writer of great ardor. Fourteenth and fifteenth centuries.

IMMANUEL KANT. German philosopher. 1724–1804.

SOREN KIERKEGAARD. Danish philosopher, minister, and polemicist. 1813–1855.

HENRY KINGSLEY. English novelist and essayist. 1830–1876.

LACTANTIUS. Rhetorician and apologist. About 260–340.

W. S. LANDOR. English poet and writer of dialogues (*Imaginary Conversations*). 1775–1864.

PAUL-LOUIS LANDSBERG. German philosopher. 1901–1944.

LAO-TSE. Chinese philosopher, founder of Taoism. Sixth century B.C.

GIACOMO LEOPARDI. Italian poet. 1798–1837.

(FELIX) LOPE DE VEGA. Spanish dramatic poet. 1562–1635.

HENRI DE LUBAC, S.J. French theologian. Born 1896.

SIR ARNOLD LUNN. English skier, mountaineer, and apologist. Born 1888.

LOUIS MACNEICE. English poet. Born 1907.

GABRIEL MARCEL. French philosopher, playwright, and critic. Born 1889.

JACQUES MARITAIN. French philosopher. Born 1882.

MICHELANGELO (BUONARROTI). Italian sculptor, painter, architect, and poet. 1475–1564.

JOHN MILTON. English poet. 1608–1674.

MICHEL EYQUEM DE MONTAIGNE. French philosopher. 1533–1592.

EMMANUEL MOUNIER. French philosopher, founder of Personalist movement. 1905–1950.

EDWIN MUIR. Scottish poet, critic, and translator. 1887–1959.

THOMAS NASHE. English novelist, pamphleteer, and poet. 1567–1601.

JOHN HENRY NEWMAN. English theologian, philosopher, and poet. Cardinal-priest. 1801–1890.

BLAISE PASCAL. French philosopher, mathematician, and scientist. 1623–1662.

CHARLES PÉGUY. French poet and polemicist. 1873–1914.

FRANCIS PETRARCH. Italian poet and humanistic philosopher. 1304–1374.

(GIOVANNI) PICO DELLA MIRANDOLA. Italian humanistic philosopher. 1463–1494.

RUTH PITTER. English poet. Born 1897.

PRUDENTIUS. Spanish writer of Latin hymns. 348 to about 405.

SIR WALTER RALEIGH. English statesman, voyager, and man of letters. Born about 1552; executed for treason in 1618.

RICHARD ROLLE OF HAMPOLE. English hermit; mystical writer of great charm and vitality. About 1300–1349.

EUGEN ROSENSTOCK-HUESSY. German-American philosopher of history. Born 1888.

FRANZ ROSENZWEIG. German Jewish philosopher of existence. 1886–1929.

CHRISTINA ROSSETTI. English poet. 1830–1894.

JOHN RUSKIN. English art critic and social philosopher. 1819–1900.

JAN VAN RUYSBROEK. Dutch mystical writer. Augustinian monk. 1293–1381.

ERWIN SCHRÖDINGER. Austrian physicist and philosopher of science. Born 1887.

JOHN SERGIEFF. Russian priest and writer on the life of the spirit. 1829–1908.

WILLIAM SHAKESPEARE. English poet and dramatist. 1564–1616.

SIR PHILIP SIDNEY. English poet, literary theorist, soldier, statesman. 1554–1586.

DAME EDITH SITWELL. English poet and critic. Born 1887.

ALEXANDER SMITH. Scottish essayist and poet. 1830–1867.

VLADIMIR SOLOVYEV. Russian philosopher and poet. 1853–1900.

DON LUIGI STURZO. Italian statesman and social philosopher. 1871–1959.

JONATHAN SWIFT. English satirist, poet, and clergyman. 1667–1745.

The Talmud. The oral law of the Jews (as distinguished from the written laws or Scriptures) and rabbinical commentaries upon it. There are two sets of commentaries on the basic text (or *Mishna*), named after their countries of origin: the Palestinian Talmud (which dates from the fifth century A.D.) and the Babylonian (the end of the fifth). But later commentaries are included in all printings since the first complete edition issued in Venice in the sixteenth century.

TORQUATO TASSO. Italian epic and pastoral poet. 1544–1595.

JEREMY TAYLOR. Anglican bishop; chaplain to Archbishop Laud and Charles I. Preacher and devotional writer. 1613–1667.

St. Teresa of Avila. Spanish Carmelite nun. Mystic and mystical theologian. 1515–1582.

Tertullian. Roman theologian and rhetorician. About 150 to about 230.

St. Thérèse of Lisieux. French Carmelite nun. Master of the spirituality that consecrates the ordinary life and its most trivial tasks. 1873–1897.

Thomas a Kempis. German monk to whom is usually attributed the compilation or actual writing of *The Imitation of Christ*. About 1380–1471.

St. Thomas Aquinas. Dominican theologian and philosopher; the "Angelic Doctor." 1225–1274.

St. Thomas More. English humanist, statesman, and martyr. 1478–1535.

Dylan Thomas. English poet (born in Wales). 1914–1953.

James Thomson. English poet (born in Scotland). 1700–1748.

Thomas Traherne. English poet, writer of meditations, and clergyman. About 1637–1674.

Ivan Turgenev. Russian novelist. 1818–1883.

Henry Vaughan. English poet (born in Wales). 1621–1695.

François Villon. French poet. Many times imprisoned on charges of murder and robbery. His last known sentence—to death—was commuted to ten years' exile in 1463. Born in 1431; death date unknown.

Juan Luis Vives. Spanish humanistic philosopher. 1492–1540.

Walt Whitman. American poet. 1819–1892.

William Wordsworth. English poet. 1770–1850.

Wilhelmine Gerber Wright. American skier and mountaineer whose poems were collected after her death in 1931.

Eugenio Zolli. Scripture scholar and sometime Chief Rabbi of Rome. 1879–1956.

Index